The Castles and Mansions of Ayrshire

The Castles and Mansions of Ayrshire

Illustrated in Seventy Views

with

Historical and Descriptive Accounts

by

A. H. Millar, F. S. A. Scot.

1885

The Grimsay Press

2004

The Grimsay Press
an imprint of
Zeticula
57 St Vincent Crescent
Glasgow
G3 8NQ

http://www.thegrimsaypress.co.uk
admin@thegrimsaypress.co.uk

Transferred to digital printing in 2004

Copyright © Zeticula 2004

First published in Great Britain, in a Limited Edition of 200 copies, in 1885 by William Paterson, Edinburgh

ISBN 1 84530 019 x

All rights reserved. No part of this publication may be reproduced, stored in a retrieval system, or transmitted in any form or by any means, electronic, mechanical, photocopying, recording or otherwise, without the prior permission of the publishers.

Preface to the Original Edition

THIS volume has been issued, for the purpose of presenting, in an accessible and attractive form, views of the numerous beautiful inhabited Castles and Mansions which adorn Ayrshire.

The Plates have been prepared specially for the Work by Messrs ANNAN, Glasgow, and the Publisher believes that their artistic quality will at least fulfil expectation. The Letterpress has been drawn up under the editorial care of A. H. MILLAR, F.S.A.Scot., and embraces much interesting historical information. In most instances the descriptions have been revised by the Owners of the Mansions, and a few of them have been entirely written by them.

The Impression has been limited to Two Hundred Copies, of which this is No. ...,

EDINBURGH, October 1884.

Note to the Reprint

The original edition was printed in a large format. The photographs were mounted on the right-hand pages, inter-leaved with a page or two pages of text.
Some changes have been made in this edition.
The overall page size is now considerably smaller.
The complete text has been re-set. In the original, the text was sometimes spread over two pages. In this edition, the print has been reduced in size, where necessary, to allow all the text to be read without turning the page, on the left-hand page, facing the photograph.
The photographs are reproduced in the original size. In the original, the photographs were arranged to view at right-angles to the page. In this edition, the photographs are turned to a normal position. Two photographs were used for Woodside. Both are included in this edition.

Contents

5	Preface to the Original Edition		
5	Note to the Reprint		
8	ANNICK LODGE.	78	FAIRLIE HOUSE.
10	ARDEER.	80	FULLERTON HOUSE.
12	ARDMILLAN.	82	GARRALLAN HOUSE.
14	THE OLD HOUSE OF AUCHANS.	84	GIFFEN HOUSE.
16	THE NEW HOUSE OF AUCHANS.	86	GIRGENTI.
18	AUCHENCRUIVE.	88	GLENAPP HOUSE.
20	AUCHENDRANE.	90	HILLHOUSE.
22	OLD AUCHENDRANE.	92	HOLMS.
24	AUCHINLECK.	94	HUNTERSTON.
26	BALLOCHMYLE.	96	KELBURNE CASTLE.
28	BARGANY.	98	KILKERRAN.
30	BEACH HOUSE.	100	KILLOCHAN CASTLE.
32	BELLEISLE.	102	KIRKHILL.
34	BERBETH.	104	KNOCK CASTLE.
36	BLAIR HOUSE.	106	KNOCKDOLIAN CASTLE.
38	BLAIRQUHAN.	108	LAINSHAW.
40	BRISBANE.	110	LANFINE HOUSE.
42	CAMBUSDOON.	112	LOUDOUN CASTLE.
44	CAPRINGTON CASTLE.	114	MOUNT CHARLES.
46	CASSILLIS HOUSE.	116	NEWARK CASTLE.
48	CESSNOCK.	118	NEWFIELD.
50	CLONCAIRD CASTLE.	120	PENKILL.
52	COILSFIELD.	122	PERCETON.
54	COODHAM.	124	PINMORE.
56	CORWAR.	126	ROSEMOUNT.
58	CRAIGIE HOUSE.	128	ROWALLAN.
60	CRAUFURDLAND CASTLE.	130	SEAFIELD.
62	CROSBIE CASTLE.	132	SHEWALTON HOUSE.
64	CULZEAN CASTLE.	134	SKELMORLIE CASTLE.
66	DALJARROCK.	136	SORN CASTLE.
68	DALQUHARRAN.	138	SUNDRUM.
70	DUMFRIES HOUSE.	140	SWINDRIDGEMUIR.
72	DUNLOP HOUSE.	142	TREESBANK HOUSE.
74	EGLINTON CASTLE.	144	WELLWOOD.
76	ENTERKINE.	146	WOODSIDE.

ANNICK LODGE.

THE estate at present known as Annick Lodge has been formed gradually by the purchase of several contiguous estates, some of which can be traced back to a very ancient date. The mansion-house occupies the site of the old manorial dwelling of Pearston-hall, the house of the Lairds of Over-Pearston in the fifteenth century. The lands of Pewston were aequired by the Blairs of Adamton through the marriage of one of that family with the heiress of Sir William Douglas of Pearston, and remained in their possession till the beginning of last century. The name of James Montgomerie appears as Laird of Over-Pearston in 1717; and though the lands passed out of the possession of that family for some time, they were again acquired in 1790 by Alexander Montgomerie, second son of Alexander Montgomerie of Coilsfield, a brother of Hugh, twelfth Earl of Eglinton, who named the place Annick Lodge. The manor-house is described by Pont as "a proper bulding, veill planted, the inheritance of Blaire, Laird of Adamtoune;" and it is probable that the erection to which he alludes was in the very spot upon which the modern mansion stands, as some traces of an old foundation were discovered while the present house was under repair a few years ago: Lieut.-Colonel William Eglinton Montgomerie, the second Laird of Annick Lodge, succeeded his father in 1802, and died in 1852, leaving five sons and three daughters. The eldest son, Alexander, was formerly Captain, 10th Regiment; whilst the second is Rear-Admiral John Eglinton Montgomerie, C.B. The third son, Roger Montgomerie, born 1828, was Advocate-Depute under several Conservative administrations, and was M.P. for North Ayrshire from 1874 until his death in 1880. Thomas George, the fourth son, who was Lieut.- Colonel of the Royal Engineers, an F.R.S., and Gold Medallist of the Royal Geographical Society, died in 1878; and Archibald William, late Lieutenant, Royal Artillery, died in 1877. The present proprietrix is the widow of Lieut.-Colonel William Eglinton Montgomerie, who succeeded to the estate on his father's death in 1802.

The mansion-house, which was erected at the close of last century, is a commodious and unpretending structure, architecturally decorated with a porch supported upon elegant Corinthian pillars, and surmounted by a facade bearing sculptured urns at its three angles. The tympanum is filled in with a heraldic shield and scroll-work in high relief. The river Annick, which gives its name to this residence, takes its rise in Renfrewshire, flowing south-westward by Stewarton, and falls into Irvine Water at a short distance above the town of Irvine.

ARDEER.

ETYMOLOGISTS have derived the name of Ardeer from the Gaelic Ard-dyir, which signifies "the barren promontory", and so far as the outward appearance of the locality is concerned, the descriptive cognomen seems appropriate. The shore for miles around is composed almost entirely of sand-hills, which alter their conformation with every hurricane. The land for a great distance inland is bare of forest-trees, and the stunted shrubs which eke out a sickly existence in that quarter intensify the feeling of desolation which oppresses the visitor in his journey from the sea-coast. The wealth of the district, however, lies underground; and one of the most valuable sandstone quarries in Scotland is upon the estate of Ardeer. Coal has been wrought in the neighbourhood since 1675, and though the industry of the place was only developed some thirty years ago (1851), the mining interest has been most remunerative. The recent establishment of works for the manufacture of Nobels' Explosives (dynamite) on the sand-dunes of Ardeer has directed special attention to the district. Traces of very early fortifications may be found on the trap-rock mound still called Castlehill, which lies near the main road between Stevenston and Kilwinning, though it may be doubted whether this post was other than a beacon-fire to signal the advent of an invading force on the Scottish shore. In ancient times the estate of Ardeer belonged to the Cuninghames of Auchenhervie, but it was purchased from them in 1708 by the Rev. Patrick Warner, and remains in the family of his descendants. The daughter of the first Warner of Ardeer was married to the Rev. Robert Wodrow (1679-1734), the eminent historian of the Church of Scotland, and she survived her husband for twenty-five years.

The mansion of Ardeer does not occupy the position of the original manor-house, but seems to have been built near the old house of Ducat-hall, the property so named having been purchased by the Rev. Patrick Warner in 1708, when he became proprietor of Ardeer. An avenue and carriage-drive lead to the door of a regularly built dwelling, over the entrance to which a balconied porch has been erected, supported on four Ionic pillars and pilasters. The style of the triangle facade and heavily corniced windows places the date of the structure towards the close of last century.

ARDMILLAN.

THE mansion-house of Ardmillan is pleasantly situated near the coast: a few miles southwards from the town of Girvan. It consists of two portions erected at different dates, the earlier part following the Scottish Baronial style of architecture, with crenelled battlements, turrets, and crow-step gables, while the later is in the domestic style of last century. The front elevation is of ashlar, relieved by two pilasters surmounted by elegant vases. The close porch, which gives access to the mansion, reproduces the outline of the front of the building in miniature. The name of Ardmillan is inseparably associated with that of the late James Craufurd, who occupied an honourable place on the Scottish Bench as Lord Ardmillan for over twenty years. He was the son of Archibald C. B. Craufurd, Esq. of Ardmillan, and was born at Havant, Hants, in 1805. His education was begun at Ayr Academy, and completed at the Universities of Glasgow and Edinburgh. Having chosen Law as his profession, he was called to the Bar in 1829, while Jeffrey was Lord-Advocate and Cockburn was Solicitor-General. He was appointed Advocate-Depute along with Lord Deas in 1840, under the Melbourne Government; became Sheriff of Perthshire in 1849, and Solicitor-General in 1853 when the Aberdeen Ministry came into power. On the death of Lord Robertson in 1855, he was raised to the Bench, taking the title of Lord Ardmillan from his patrimonial estate; and he retained this honourable position until his death in 1876. He was the first Scottish Judge before whom the celebrated Yelverton Case was brought up, and the decision which he gave against the claimant, Theresa Longworth, was sustained by the highest Law-Courts in the kingdom. The mother of the late Lord Ardmillan was known throughout Ayrshire for the many benevolent bequests which she made. Amongst other benefactions, she laid aside £1000, the interest of which was to be paid to the parochial schoolmaster of Girvan, on condition of his teaching forty poor children *gratis*, and a special fund was provided for the instruction of ten of these forty children in the practice of music. The coal-measures in the neighbourhood of Ardmillan are not extensive, but copper-ore of superior quality has been found on the estate, and is supposed to exist in great profusion.

Ardmillan is found to have been in the possession of the Kennedys of Bargany so early as 1476, and the estate continued in a younger branch of this family - designated "Kennedy of Ardmillane " - for nearly two hundred years. It came at last into the hands of James Craufurd of Baidland in 1658 through his marriage with Marion Kennedy; and the frequent intermarriages between these two families served to keep the estate amongst them. The name of Craufurd was thus associated with the estate of Ardmillan for over two centuries. The present representative of the family is Thomas MacMicken Craufurd, Esq. of Grange House, Ayrshire.

THE OLD HOUSE OF AUCHANS.

No far from the ruins of the ancient Castle of Dundonald stands the deserted House of Auchans, a ruin of a much later date, yet haunted by many interesting memories of other times. The old Castle of Dundonald, in which King Robert II died, had fallen so seriously into decay before some parts of Auchans House were built, that the stones of the ancient stronghold of the Stewarts were freely used in the newer erection, if tradition may be believed. Auchans itself has fallen upon evil days, having been utilised for cottars' houses lately; but there still remain sufficient traces of its former grandeur to indicate the important position which it once held in the district.

The architectural peculiarities of the building have attracted much notice; and R. W. Billings thus refers to them in his *Antiquities of Scotland:* "The square balustraded tower is in direct opposition to the cone-covered staircase, which breaks the monotony of the main wall-face of the mansion in its centre. But the picturesque is more particularly evinced in the arrangement of the crow-stepped gables, and especially of the one surmounting the round tower to the right. The flank wall of this gable continues the line of the house, instead of being corbelled upon the tower, which is finished by being simply sloped off to the wall, leaving as a questionable feature what has evidently been a change from the original design." The building is not all of the same period, but the date 1644, which is to be found on one of the newer portions, leads us to discover the principal builder.

The earliest name associated with Auchans is that of Wallace of Dundonald, a branch of the Wallaces of Riccarton, who came into the estate in 1527; although it is probable that the lands were included in the grant of the Castle of Dundonald made to Lord Cathcart by James III in 1482. Auchans remained in the Wallace family even after they had parted with the greater portion of the Dundonald property; and the last of the family of whom any trace can be found was Colonel James Wallace of Auchans, who led the unfortunate Covenanters' raid, known in history as the "Pentland Rising," in November 1666, and died in exile at Rotterdam in 1678. The lands of Dundonald were purchased from the Wallace family in 1638 by Sir William Cochrane of Coldoun, and to him may we ascribe the erection of that portion of Auchans House which bears the date of 1644. Having remained faithful to the Stewart line during the Commonwealth, and suffered pecuniarily at the hands of Cromwell, Sir William was rewarded, after the Restoration, with the title of Earl of Dundonald, and from him the earldom has descended in almost unbroken line. The House of Auchans afterwards came into the possession of the Earls of Eglintoun, and became the jointure-house of Susanna Kennedy of Culzean, who was married to the ninth Earl of Eglintoun in 1707. This lady was celebrated as one of the most beautiful and accomplished ladies of her time; and as she was an especial patroness of the literary stars whom she encountered during an exceptionally long life, her virtues and graces have found their way into the foremost poetic literature of the period. Allan Ramsay and William Hamilton of Bangour have vied with each other in her praise; and traditions as to her elegant personal appearance, winning manner, and intellectual ability still linger in the society of Edinburgh. After the murder, by Mungo Campbell, of her son Alexander, tenth Earl of Eglintoun, in 1769, she retired from the position which she held in society; and when her second son Archibald was married in 1772, she took up her residence permanently at Auchans. Whilst there, she received a memorable visit from Dr Samuel Johnson and his companion, James Boswell of Auchinleck, her High-Churchism and Jacobite fervour having won the heart of the Doctor. The right of the Stewart Kings to reign she maintained most steadfastly; and it is said that for many years she kept the portrait of the unhappy Prince Charles Edward hung up in her bedroom, so that her glance might first light upon it when awaking. She died at Auchans in 1780, having attained the advanced age of ninety-one years.

Since that time the House of Auchans has been allowed to fall into disrepair through neglect, though the exterior portion is still almost complete. Some valuable documents connected with the Eglintoun family were recently discovered in one of the apartments, and it is not improbable that further disclosures would result from a diligent search of the venerable ruin. In the orchard at Auchans - part of which may still be traced - the famous pear-tree once stood, from which the Auchans pears were first obtained. It is averred that it was brought originally from France, and remained in good condition until a violent storm destroyed it about a hundred years ago.

THE NEW HOUSE OF AUCHANS.

The modern mansion of Auchans is an erection of recent date, built in the style of an Italian villa, with projecting glazed porch, giving access to the hall and main staircase. The land around the house is richly wooded, and its sylvan character has been carefully preserved, so that from whatever side the dwelling is approached it is brought into relief against a background of umbrageous foliage. The carriage-drive is bordered for a considerable distance with a symmetrical parterre of flowers, and an extensive conservatory forms an exterior wing to the mansion-house. The ground-plan and arrangement of the interior have been carefully studied. No space is lost by the display of architectural eccentricities; and the principal decoration of the main front wall consists of the ivy and other trained shrubs, which are rapidly covering the stonework with their leafy shade. The proprietor is the Earl of Eglinton, and his Lordship's Commissioner, the Hon. Greville Richard Vernon, resides there.

AUCHENCRUIVE.

THE stately mansion of Auchencruive is situated in the parish of St Quivox, not far from one of the winding links of the Water of Ayr. It dates probably from the latter half of the last century, and has been built with a thorough regard to comfort and accommodation. The exterior is devoid of all attempts at meretricious ornamentation; and the structure has grown to its present extent through the independent additions made by succeeding Lairds, as their requirements and rent-rolls increased. No trace of an earlier dwelling has been found, though the records of the estate carry its history back to the beginning of the thirteenth century. Richard Wallace of Hackencrow appears in a charter dated 1208, and though there is no clear proof of his identity, it has been surmised, with some show of probability, that he belonged to the family of the Wallaces of Riccartoun. The lands of Auchencruive gave the principal territorial title to this branch of the Wallaces, until Sir Duncan Wallace acquired the heritage of Sundrum, and assumed the latter in preference to the former designation. This well-known knight, who was married to Eleanor de Brus, Countess of Carrick, died without male issue about 1380, and the property of Auchencruive fell to his sister's son, Alan de Kathkert, ancestor of the present Earl Cathcart. With the exception of a short period during the sixteenth century, when the house and lands of Auchencruive were in the possession of the Craufurds of Drongane, they remained in the hands of the Cathcart family until they were acquired by Richard Oswald, the ancestor of the present proprietor, about 1760.

Of this remarkable man, the first of the Oswalds of Auchencruive, no adequate biography has been written, although he figured largely in the political history of his time, and his career was a most romantic one. According to the late Right Hon. Sir John Sinclair of Ulbster, who was probably acquainted with him personally, he derived his origin from Thurso, one of his ancestors having been a bailie in that burgh during the seventeenth century. Regarding Richard Oswald, Sir John relates that "he was, in his younger days, an unsuccessful candidate, upon a comparative trial, for the office of master of the parochial school of Thurso, whereof the salary was £100 Scots, and took his disappointment so much to heart that he left the country in disgust, and never more returned to it. But for that circumstance, it is probable, he would have lived and died in obscurity." Removing to London, Richard Oswald embarked at once upon the career of a merchant, and had risen to fortune and reputation as an Army-contractor before 1763. With the wealth thus won, he purchased the estate of Auchencruive about this period, though he continued to reside in London, and to take part in politics, leaving it under the care of his brother, the Rev. Dr James Oswald. His capacity for business was so great that it attracted the notice of the leading politicians, and he became an object of suspicion to the followers of Fox, and of hope to that statesman's opponents. When the rebellion of George Washington had been crowned with success, and the British Government found it impossible to ignore a Republic which had accredited ambassadors at the principal European Courts, they resolved to make terms of peace with the revolted states; and on 25th July 1782, a Commission was granted to Richard Oswald of Auchencruive to proceed to Paris and confer with Benjamin Franklin and the other representatives of "certain colonies in North America," as to the conditions of a pacific agreement. The voluminous correspondence betwixt the plenipotentiary and Lord Shelburne is still in preservation amongst the documents of the Marquess of Lansdowne; and the story of the long conflict which he had to secure reasonable terms may be learned from his private letters to Sir Henry Strachey, which are among the family papers at Sutton Court. The Provisional Articles for a pacification were signed by the Commissioners on 30th November 1782, by which the independence of the thirteen United States was formally acknowledged. The materials for a life of this eminent politician may be found in Lord Edmund Fitzmaurice's *Life of Lord Shelburne*, *Bancroft's History of the United States*, and amongst the manuscripts in possession of the Duke of Manchester.

Dr James Oswald, who was *de facto* Laird of Auchencruive during his brother's absence, died in 1819, and was succeeded by his son, George Oswald of Scotstoun and Auchencruive. The eldest son of the latter was Richard Alexander Oswald of Auchencruive, who was Member of Parliament for Ayrshire from 1833 till 1835, and closed his long career of usefulness and public spirit in 1841. As his only son had predeceased him, he was succeeded by his cousin, James Oswald-Oswald of Shield-hall, a merchant in Glasgow, and Member for that burgh from the meeting of the first reformed Parliament of 1833 almost continuously till 1847. He died unmarried in 1855, and a statue to his memory has been erected by his fellow-citizens in George Square, Glasgow. The estate went to his nephew, Alexander Haldane Oswald, who sat as Member for Ayrshire from 1843 till 1852, and died in 1868. He was succeeded by his brother, George Oswald, the father and immediate predecessor of the present proprietor, Richard Alexander Oswald of Auchencruive, who came into the estate in 1871.

AUCHENDRANE.

Some confusion is apt to arise from the fact that two separate houses on the banks of Doon are called alike by the name of Auchendrane, although the difficulty is capable of a simple explanation. The property now in the possession of Miss Cathcart, the mansion-house of which stands close by the river side, about four miles from Ayr, is upon that portion of the old estate of Middle Auchendrane, for some time called Blairstoun; and the proprietor of this place was formerly known as the Laird of Blairstoun, to distinguish him from the Laird of Auchendrane proper, after Mure of the Barony of Auchendrane, to which it was attached, had sold this part of the estate to one of the family of Blair of Blair. Hew Blair of Blairstoun appears as proprietor in 1645, having been accused by the Presbytery of Ayr of complicity with the great Marquis of Montrose in his Royalist rising. James Blair of Blairstoun obtained permission to bury his family within the precincts of Alloway Kirk about the year 1694. The property was bought back by John Mure in 1698. He was a scion of the ancient family of the Mures of Auchendrane, and was uncle and guardian of the then young Laird of the Barony lands. John Mure was Provost of Ayr in 1687-1697, and did much to preserve the liberties of his fellow-citizens. He represented the burgh of Ayr in the Convention from 1689 till 1702. There are still some fine old silver fir trees at Auchendrane which were planted by this John Mure. The Cathcart family came into possession of it through the marriage of David Cathcart, Lord Alloway, with Mary Mure, daughter of Robert Mure of Blairstoun. Of the first Cathcart of Blairstoun some notice is due.

David Cathcart was the son of Elias Cathcart, who was grandson of Cathcart of Carbiston, a successful wine merchant in Ayr. He was at one time Provost of that burgh, and latterly purchased the estate of Greenfield - now Cambusdoon - from the Magistrates of Ayr, and spent the closing years of his life there. Having obtained the elements of his education at Ayr, the place of his nativity, David Cathcart proceeded to Edinburgh, to prosecute his studies for the legal profession, and soon won distinction at the Bar. In 1793, when he was twenty-nine years of age, he married Mary Mure of Blairstoun, whose estate adjoined that of Greenfield, and thus became Laird of Middle Auchendrane. He took much delight in the improvement of these two properties; and to him must be attributed the principal work of reconstructing the ancient mansion-house. When raised to the Bench he took the title of Lord Alloway, from the locality with which his earliest and most pleasant recollections were associated; and when he died at Blairstoun in 1829, his remains were deposited within the ruined Kirk of Alloway, in accordance with the territorial right obtained more than a hundred and twenty years before. Lord Cockburn records his estimate of him as "an excellent and most useful man; kind in private life, and honest in the discharge of his public duties; without learning or talent, and awkward in expressing himself either orally or in writing, he was a good practical lawyer, and remarkably knowing in the management of the common business of life; and having more sense and modesty than to aim at objects he could not reach, experience and industry gave him no competitor within this not very high but most useful range." A classical monument, copied by permission of the late Earl of Elgin from a sarcophagus and Broomhall, has been erected at the Kirk as a memorial of Lord Alloway.

He was succeeded by his son, Elias Cathcart, who also followed the profession of law, was admitted as an advocate in 1817, and had the degree of LL.D. conferred upon him. His translation of Charles von Savigny's *History of Roman Law*, which appeared in 1830, received the commendation alike of the original author and of the critics, and is now the accepted version of this oft-quoted work. He changed the name of his residence to the ancient local title of Auchendrane, under which it is now known, having bought back the Barony lands from the late Sir Charles Fergusson, and completed the building which his father, Lord Alloway, had begun. He afterwards sold in 1841 that portion of the land on which stood the ruins of the Old Castle of Auchendrane to Mr Fergusson of Monkwood, and on this site the mansion of Sir Peter Coats is now erected. (See *Old Auchendrane.*)

The mansion-house is situated in a romantic spot near the brink of the river Doon, and is well sheltered by the fine old trees which surround it. The style is an adaptation of the Scottish Baronial architecture to the requirements of modern life, and the effect is very pleasing.

OLD AUCHENDRANE.

UNTIL a few years ago, the ancient mansion-house of Auchendrane, which was associated with one of the darkest crimes in Scottlsh history, was a bare and roofless ruin, occupying a most picturesque situation by one of the crooks of the river Doon. It had been the residence of the family of the Mures of Auchendrane for many generations, but after the decay of that race in the eighteenth century, it had been allowed to sink into a dilapidated and ruinous condition. In 1868 that portion of the estate on which it stood was acquired by Sir Peter Coats, the successful and philanthropic merchant of Paisley; and in 1881 he built the present mansion on the site of the older erection. The different portions of the structure are grouped in a most effective manner, and the quaint turrets and Flemish gables make the place especially attractive.

The name of Mure has been associated with that of the estate of Auchendrane from a very early period; but they were linked in an especially sinister manner during the sixteenth century by the criminal actions of John Mure and his son, the perpetrators of what is known in history as "the Ayrshire Tragedy." The details of this strangely complicated crime may be found in Pitcairn's Criminal Trials, and reference is made to it in the preface to Sir Walter Scott's play of Auchendrane founded upon this incident; but the story may be thus briefly related.

For a long period both before and after the Reformation the control of West Ayrshire was entirely in the hands of the Kennedys - the Earl of Cassillis and the Lairds of Culzean and Bargany dividing the power amongst them. The death of the fourth Earl in 1576 left his successor a minor, and Sir Thomas of Culzean obtained the position of tutor by very questionable means. Bargany was thus forced to occupy an inferior place, and Mure of Auchendrane, who had married his daughter, determined to advance the interests of his father-in-law at all hazards. In those rude days the simplest method of checkmating an adversary was to murder him; and Mure and some companions accordingly lay in wait for Sir Thomas one night as he was returning from a supper-party, and sought to take his life by firing upon him with pistols. The attempt was unsuccessful, and Mure was about to be prosecuted for his lawless treachery, when he succeeded in obtaining the pardon and good-will of his intended victim, who crowned his forgiveness by bestowing the hand of his daughter upon Mure's eldest son. Auchendrane had no intention, however, of abandoning his wicked purpose against the life of the doomed knight, and an opportunity of gratifying his malice soon presented itself.

Sir Thomas Kennedy had occasion to go to Edinburgh early in the month of May 1602, and out of pure friendship he sent word to Auchendrane of his intention, offering to execute any business which the latter might have in the metropolis. He directed his servant to inquire for Auchendrane at Maybole, and should he fail to find him there, to send word by letter of the proposed journey. The servant missed Auchendrane, and, in compliance with his master's orders, he requested Mr Robert Mure, schoolmaster of Maybole, to write a note advising him of the matter, which note was sent to Auchendrane by the hands of William Dalrymple, "ane boy of his school " - not a "poor student," as stated by Sir Walter Scott. This messenger found Auchendrane at his own place along with his cousin, Walter Mure of Cloncaird, and these two companions in guilt devised a horrid plot for the assassination of the unfortunate Laird of Culzean. Having read the letter, Auchendrane returned it to the boy Dalrymple, telling him to take it back and say that he had been unable to find him; and he arranged that his cousin of Cloncaird, and their kinsman, Kennedy of Drumurchy, with four or five armed retainers, should lie in wait for Culzean at a point on the road which he should pass. Sir Thomas Hamilton, the King's Advocate, who conducted the legal proceedings that took place afterwards, relates that Sir Thomas Kennedy of Culzean "being in full security of his dangerless estate, riding upon ane pacing nag, and having with him ane servant only, they suddenly surprised him, and with their pistols and swords gave him ane number of deadly wounds; and not content to have so barbarously and traitorously bereft him of his life, spoiled him of ane thousand merks of gold, being in his purse, ane number of gold buttons upon his coat, and some rings and other jewels."

Cloncaird and Drumurchy were accused of the murder, but failed to appear, and were outlawed. Suspicion naturally pointed towards Auchendrane as the instigator of the deed, and he determined to brave out the accusation. The only witness who could connect him with the murderers was the boy Dalrymple; and to get him out of the way he kidnapped him and kept him in confinement in his own house for some time, and afterwards had him conveyed to the barren shores of the Isle of Arran, and placed in the charge of Graham of Skelmorlie. Confident that no certain evidence could thus be brought against him, he boldly presented himself before his accusers, challenging them to put him on trial; but as they knew the weakness of their proof, and were aware that if he once "tholed an assize" he could not again be tried for the crime, they did not proceed against him. Finding himself thus far secure, he ventured to bring Dalrymple back from exile to his house of Auchendrane, where he kept him under surveillance for some time, until he succeeded in drafting him as a soldier to the Low Countries, trusting that the fortune of war would rid him for ever of the presence of this inconvenient witness.

Five years afterwards the youth, having grown tired of soldiering, returned to the spot where his mother and sister resided at Maybole, and became once more a source of uneasiness to Auchendrane. The laird and his son took counsel together as to how they should get rid of him; and having beguiled him by professions of friendship to a lonely spot on the sands near Girvan, they put an end to his existence in a most cruel and treacherous manner. They had been assisted in the vile deed by James Bannatyne of Chapel-donan, and he aided them in their futile attempt to bury the body in the shifting sands. Finding they could not securely hide the traces of their crime in this fashion, they threw the body into the sea, expecting that it would be carried far from the shore; but five days afterwards the corpse of the murdered youth was cast upon the beach near the same place where the deed of blood had been committed, and was identified by Dalrymple's nearest relatives. The finger of suspicion was once more pointed towards the Mures, and after some delay, caused by their committal of another crime, they were seized and thrown into prison to await their trial on the charge of the double murder.

Bannatyne of Chapel-donan had now become the inconvenient witness; but when a relative of Mure's had succeeded in spiriting him away to Ireland, the two murderers confidently went forward to their trial. Their judicial examination seemed rather in their favour through lack of clear proof against them; though Lord Chancellor Seton, who presided, declares in a private letter addressed to King James, 2d December 1608, that the answers of father and son were quite irreconcilable with their previous declarations, and that their statements were so contradictory that, he avers, "we are all compelled to think in our consciences thaj war baithe guiltie."* Nevertheless, the accused maintained so bold a front even under the torture of the "buittis," to which they had been subjected on the recommendation of the Earl of Cassillis, that public feeling was turning in their favour, when the Earl of Abercorn succeeded in discovering the retreat of Bannatyne in Ireland, and produced him in time to procure their condemnation. As several attempts had been made upon Bannatyne's life, whilst he was in exile: at the instigation of the Mures, it may be imagined that he did not mitigate the evidence which he had to offer as to their guilt; and the result was that the Mures and himself were sentenced to be beheaded, though he obtained pardon for having brought them to justice by his voluntary confession. John Mure of Auchendrane, then eighty years of age, and his son James, the husband of Culzean's daughter, were both beheaded at the Cross of Edinburgh in July 1611; and thus was terminated one of the most remarkable stories of crime to be found, perhaps, in the annals of our race. Never was there a more evident confirmation of the time-worn adage that " murder will out."

*Seton's Memoir of Alexander Seton, Earl of Dunfermline, p. 89 (Edinburgh, Blackwood & Sons, 1882).

AUCHINLECK.

THE present mansion-house of Auchinleck is a handsome Grecian edifice, elaborately decorated, which was erected in 1780 by Alexander Boswell, Lord Auchinleck of Session. It occupies 'a pleasant site near the Lugar Water, and is approached by a long avenue partially shaded by trees. The place was in process of building when Dr Johnson visited the locality in company with his friend and biographer, James Boswell, the eldest son and successor of Lord Auchinleck; though the romantic mind of the Doctor, by his own account, "was less delighted with the elegance of the modern mansion than with the sullen dignity of the old castle" of Auchinleck, whose ruins are in the vicinity.

The original possessors of the estate now traceable were the Auchinlecks of that Ilk, who held the property from 1292 till the very close of the fifteenth century, when the Boswells became proprietors. The latter family had settled in Scotland whilst David I. occupied the throne (1124-1153), and their earliest location as landowners was at Balmuto, in Fifeshire, where the elder branch of the family is still represented. Sir John Boswell, or Boisivill, obtained the barony of Balmuto through his marriage with Mariota, daughter of Sir John Glen; and his grandson, David Boswell of Balmuto, was the father of the first of that name in Auchinleck. Thomas Boswell was a favourite at the court of James IV., and when the lands of Auchinleck were forfeited to the Crown, they were bestowed by the King upon this highly-valued companion. It was the misfortune of the latter to share the fate of his master at Flodden Field; but the family became connected with some of the foremost of the nobility of Scotland, through the marriage of his only son and successor, David Boswell of Auchinleck, with Lady Janet Hamilton, daughter of the first Earl of Arran, and great-grand-daughter of James II.

The first lawyer of eminence in the family was James Boswell, who married the Lady Elizabeth Bruce, daughter of the Earl of Kincardine, in 1704. The issue of this marriage could claim descent from the two regal houses of Bruce and Stewart; and his eldest son, Alexander, worthily sustained the dignity to which he had been born, gaining an eminent position in legal circles, and holding a prominent place for a long period amongst the Lords of Session as Lord Auchinleck. To him, as has been stated, belongs the credit due to the builder of the present mansion of Auchinleck. As the intimate associate of Lord Hailes and Lord Kames, he still survives in the memoirs of his period; and many strange anecdotes circulate in the society even of our own time, illustrating his quaint and pawky humour. It was his place to sit in judgment upon some of the most involved *causes célèbres* of his day - the Douglas Peerage amongst others - and his decisions were always marked with sound legal discretion.

To his son, James Boswell, however, the honour was reserved of raising the family name to a unique position in literature, and of attaining by the simplest means an honourable place amongst the British Classics. As the biographer of Dr Johnson he has won imperishable fame; and though his personal character was not estimable, nor his mental attainments great, his name will continue while English literature endures as "the prince of biographers." He was married to his cousin, Margaret Montgomerie of Lainshaw, and was succeeded in 1795 by his eldest son, Sir Alexander, the first baronet of Auchinleck.

Whilst the literary tastes of his father were reproduced increasedly in Sir Alexander, the petulance and acerbity which the latter showed was entirely awanting in the elder Boswell. He did much for literature by the establishment of the Auchinleck press, from which he issued reprints of rare documents; and his own poetical works - *Clan-Alpin's Vow, The East Neuk O' Fife*, and many well-known ballads - entitle him to an elevated position amongst the Scottish poets of his time. But it was his misfortune to have a caustic, satirical wit, which exasperated his enemies beyond endurance, and latterly proved the cause of his own untimely end. A bitterly personal squib which he published in an obscure paper called forth the remonstrance of the party attacked - Mr James Stuart of Dunearn - and as Sir Alexander refused to apologise, the duel in which he fell was the consequence. He died at Balmuto House, the seat of his friend and relative, Claud Boswell, Lord Balmuto of Session, on 26th March 1822. His body was brought to Auchinleck, followed by a train of sincere mourners, and laid in the family vault, hewn out of the solid stone, in which the ashes rest of his father, grandfather, and other kindred.* He was succeeded by his only son, Sir James Boswell, second baronet, who was born in 1806, and died in 1857, having married his cousin, Jessie Jane, daughter of Sir James Montgomery Cuninghame, Bart., in 1830. By her death, in March 1884, the direct line of the Boswells of Auchinleck became extinct.

* For an interesting account of this duel, and unpublished documents connected with the case, see *Records of Notable Scottish Trials* (Dundee: John Leng & Co., 1884).

BALLOCHMYLE.

The name of Ballochmyle is familiar to every admirer of Burns's poetry, as circumstances connected with the estate gave occasion for the production of two of his finest lyrics - *The Braes O' Ballochmyle* and *The Lass of Ballochmyle*. One of the retired walks by the river Ayr formed a favourite retreat for the poet whilst he lived in the locality; and many of his most memorable poems were composed within its sequestered shade. Etymologists differ as to the origin of the name, some asserting that the termination refers to an extinct mill (*myln*) which may have been near the river, and others, with more reason, deriving it from the descriptive Gaelic compound *Bealach maol*, "the bare or rocky pass." The name is not inappropriate when applied to the romantic ravines and bosky dells through which the river takes its way in the vicinity. The earliest name associated with Ballochmyle, of which any sure trace can be found, is that of Reid, which appears in 1613. The laird at that time was probably a scion of the Reids of Barskimming, and the estate remained in this family until about the middle of last century. It was acquired by the Whitefoords shortly before 1760; but Sir John Whitefoord, the friend and patron of Burns, was compelled, through financial misfortune, to part with the estate in 1786. The latter circumstance suggested the song of *The Braes O' Ballochmyle*, in which the poet represents Maria, the eldest daughter of Sir John - afterwards Mrs Cranston - as lamenting the fate which separated her from the scenes of her infancy:

> "*Low in your wintry beds, ye flowers,*
> *Again ye'll flourish fresh and fair;*
> *Ye birdies dumb, in withering bowers,*
> *Again ye 'll charm the vocal air.*
> *But here, alas! for me nae mair*
> *Shall birdie charm or floweret smile:*
> *Fareweel the bonny banks of Ayr,*
> *Fareweel, fareweel! sweet Ballochmyle!*"

The new proprietor was Claud Alexander, the first of that name in Ballochmyle, and the progenitor of the present occupant. He was the third son of Claud Alexander of Newton, Renfrewshire, and was born in 1756. In early life he and his younger brother, Boyd Alexander, entered the Civil Service of the Honourable East India Company, and proceeded to India, where they both amassed considerable fortunes, the elder rising to the position of Auditor-General of Army Accounts, and Paymaster-General. They returned to Scotland together in 1786; and whilst Boyd purchased the estates of Southbar and Boghall in Renfrewshire, and became Member for that shire - 1796-1806 - Claud took possession of Ballochmyle, which had been acquired for him during his absence. The latter died in 1809, and was succeeded by his eldest son Claud, at whose demise in 1846 the estate devolved first on one of his brothers, William Maxwell Alexander, and then on the other, Boyd Alexander of Southbar, who died in 1861. The present proprietor is Lieut.-Colonel Claud Alexander, son of Boyd, last named, and Sophia Elizabeth Hobhouse, half-sister of the late Lord Broughton (Sir John Cam Hobhouse). He holds a commission in the Grenadier Guards, won several decorations during the Crimean War, and has been Member of Parliament for South Ayrshire since 1874.

BARGANY.

The first Laird of Bargany who comes within the range of credible history is Thomas Kennedy, second son of that Sir Gilbert Kennedy of Dunure, who was one of the hostages delivered to the English in 1357 to procure the liberty of King David II. His elder brother Gilbert was slain it the battle of Bauge, and his younger half-brother having married Mary Stewart, daughter of Robert III, became the ancestor of the present Marquis of Ailsa. The Kennedys of Bargany are now represented by Rowland Fergussone Kennedy, Esq. of Bennane and Finnarts; and the families of Dunure and Knocknalling are amongst their lineal descendants.

On the death of his uncle, Sir Hew Kennedy of Ardstinchar, the first Laird of Bargany succeeded to that estate. By a charter dated 1450 he obtained confirmation of the Barony of Bargany, and was succeeded by his son Gilbert. The latter granted a precept, dated 17th October 1476, infefting his "weil belovyt Brother Johne" in the lands of Knocknalling and Knockreoch, which his descendants hold to this day. Margaret, daughter of Alexander Kennedy of Bargany, vas married to Gilbert, third Earl of Cassillis, who died at Dieppe in 1558; and from this marriage sprang the minor branch of the Kennedys of Culzean, who ultimately succeeded to the earldom. Alexander Kennedy of Bargany, who sat as a Minor Baron in the Convention of 1597, was a man of considerable influence in his day, and took a leading part with the Reforming nobles in the west of Scotland. Hewas married to a daughter of Sir John Gordon of Lochinvar, and died 7th November 1597. The eulogium upon him which appears in the *Historie of the Kennedies* not only shows the esteem in which he was held, but gives us also a glimpse of the style of living at Bargany at that period. "It pleased God to tak the Laird of Bergeny in His mercy; wha was the nobillest man that ever was in that country in his time. He was endued with mony guid virtues. First he rearit God, and was fra the beginning on the right side of religion. He was wise and courteous, and therewith stout and passing kind; and sic ane noble spender in outings with the best-halden house at hame that ever was in the land. He was never behind with na party, and keepit himself ever to the fore with his living. He had ever in his household twenty-four gallant gentlemen, double-horsit, and gallantly clad; with sic ane repair to his house, that it was ane wonder where the same was gotten that he spendit." It is probable that the style thus maintained by one of his kinsmen served to embitter the relationship betwixt the Earl of Cassillis and Bargany; for a feud arose between the two families, which lasted for many years, and through which the young Laird of Bargany lost his life in a petty skirmish at the Brig o' Doon in December 1601. The powerful alliances which the Cassillis family made with the leading nobles of the time, and the favour with which they were regarded by King James VI, enabled the Earls finally to overbear their rivals, and a new family entirely entered into possession of the estate of Bargany.

Sir John Hamilton of Letterick, natural son of the first Marquis of Hamilton, had a charter of the lands of Bargany on 23d May 1631. He had represented Lanarkshire at the Conventions from 1605 till 1625, and died shortly after the date of this charter. His eldest son, John, was created Lord Bargany in 1639 by Charles I, and led a very chequered life during the time of the Covenanters. His eldest son, by his marriage with the daughter of the eleventh Earl of Angus, succeeded him, and suffered severely at the hands of the Duke of York for his supposed sympathy with the Presbyterian party. He was followed by his second son William, third Lord Bargany who held a commission as Colonel of a regiment of foot-soldiers under General Mackay, and took part in the campaign against Viscount Dundee in 1689.* His son, fourth Lord Bargany, died without issue in 1736, when the title became extinct. The estates devolved upon Johanna Hamilton, only child of John, Master of Bargany, eldest son of the second Lord, who had predeceased his father. She was then the wife of Sir Robert Dalrymple of Castleton, grandson of the first Viscount Stair; and her second son, John, assumed the name and arms of Hamilton of Bargany when that estate was adjudged to him by the House of Lords. He was born in 1715, passed Advocate in 1735, sat as Member for the Wigtown Burghs from 1754 till 1768, was connected by his two marriages with the Earls of Wemyss and Eglinton, and died without issue in 1796. His estates then fell to his nephew, Sir Hew Dalrymple, third Baronet of North Berwick, who thereupon assumed the additional name of Hamilton. The son of the latter, Sir Hew Dalrymple-Hamilton of Bargany and North Berwick, was born in 1774, and represented the shire of Haddington, the shire of Ayr, and the Haddington Burghs in various Parliaments from 1795 till 1826. He married a daughter of Admiral Duncan, Viscount Duncan of Camperdown, and the estate of Bargany devolved at his death, in 1834, upon his only child, Henrietta Dundas, who was then wife of Augustin-Louis de Franquetot, Duc de Coigny, whilst the baronetcy fell to his brother. The eldest daughter of the Duchesse de Coigny is now Countess of Stair; and the estate will pass to the Hon. North de Coigny Dalrymple, second son of the present Earl of Stair.

The house is of considerable size, and although the additions which have been made at various" times have followed no homogeneous plan, the architectural effect is very pleasing. The estate has been conducted with judicious liberality, and more than £30,000 were expended upon permanent improvements between 1862 and 1878.

* MSS. in the possession of Sir Robert Menzies, Bart., at Castle Menzies.

BEACH HOUSE.

BEACH HOUSE may be considered as a model for a modern marine villa. It is situated near the shore at Skelmorlie, and commands a fine prospect of the Firth of Clyde, the Cowal Hills, and the islands of Bute and the two Cumbraes. The house is built in the Italian style of architecture, with bow windows and overhanging eaves. An elegant conservatory is erected at the southern gable, whilst at the opposite end of the building a square cabin has been raised, from the open verandahs of which a magnificent view of the Firth may be obtained. The house belongs to J. Galbraith, Esq., of the well-known Glasgow firm of shipowners, Messrs P. Henderson & Co.

BELLEISLE.

THE lands attached to the mansion-house of Belleisle were at one time a portion of the Barony of Alloway, and belonged for many years to the Magistrates of Ayr. They were alienated, together with several other properties in the neighbourhood, when the Barony lands were disposed of by public roup in 1754. At this time they were known by the name of the Netherton of Alloway, and were purchased by Dr Alexander Campbell of Ayr. About eleven years afterwards (1765), the property fell to Dr Campbell's brother, Archibald, a writer in Edinburgh; who was succeeded by his nephew, John Campbell of Wellwood, in 1775. At the death of the latter in 1787, the estate was acquired by Hugh Hamilton of Pinmore, who extended it by the purchase of some neighbouring fields, and built part of the present mansion-house, bestowing upon it the name of Belleisle. As he died without issue, the estate was left by will to his nephew, Colonel Alexander West Hamilton, second son of the first Laird of Sundrum. During the occupancy of Colonel Hamilton the property was much improved, and the former mansion almost entirely reconstructed and enlarged to its present dimensions. The estate fell to his son, Hugh Hamilton, in 1839, whilst in his minority, and afterwards came into possession by purchase of the late William Smith Dixon of Carfin House, Motherwell, - one of the partners in the well-known firm of Dixon & Co., ironmasters, Glasgow. The house is beautifully situated on an eminence near the Curtecan Burn, on "one of the most enviable sites in the parish," surrounded by plantations and fruitful cultivated fields.

BERBETH.

ALTHOUGH not in itself an imposing building, the mansion of Berbeth is placed amidst a most picturesque country. As the river Doon makes its way from its source in Loch Doon towards the Firth of Clyde, it passes through a deep valley, within which its waters flow by a wild and rocky channel till they emerge at the Loch of Bogton. The contrast betwixt the scenery at this spot and that which prevails in the neighbourhood is very striking. The river, as it rushes through the Glen of Berbeth, is transformed into a mountain torrent, foaming at the base of precipitous cliffs, and almost hidden at some parts by the foliage of the overhanging trees, which spread their branches across its contracted course. The rugged elements of the scene more nearly resemble the ravines and passes of the Isle of Arran than what we might expect amid the fertile fields of Ayrshire. From this point the Doon meanders through the estate of Berbeth, and pursues its course by the classic country which lies between Dalmellington and the coast. The scene has been thus described by a local poet:

> *"Doon, issuing from her slumbering bed of rest,*
> *Is downward through the rocky tunnel prest,*
> *Then dashed against yon shelvy, pointed rock,*
> *Which, unmolested, stands the furious shock,*
> *And turns the torrent to the other side,*
> *Which, in its turn, resists the furious tide;*
> *Here, dashing on the precipices steep,*
> *There, boiling in the dreadful caverns deep,*
> *Now, madly raging o'er the rugged linn,*
> *Mocking the voice of thunder with its din;*
> *Bathing the margin with the foamy spray,*
> *And thus the tortured waters pass away,*
> *Leaving the caverns, linns, and rocks behind,*
> *For banks and channels of a gentler kind."*

Berbeth has been associated with the name of MacAdam for a long period. This family traces its descent from a member of the persecuted Clan Gregor, who sought refuge from the fury of the Campbells of Argyll in the lowlands of Ayrshire. When the name of MacGregor was proscribed, the family adopted the patronymic of MacAdam, and by industry and probity succeeded in acquiring considerable possessions in the country. The daughter and heiress of Quintin Macadam of Craigengillan and Berbeth was married in 1827 to Colonel Frederick Cathcart, third son of the first Earl Cathcart, and brother of Sir George Cathcart, who fell at Inkerman. Colonel Cathcart assumed the name of MacAdam, and the present proprietor, who succeeded in 1878, is Alexander Frederick Macadam of Craigengillan.

BLAIR HOUSE.

THIS is the oldest inhabited baronial mansion in Scotland which has not been rebuilt. Timothy Pont, who surveyed the district of Cunninghame about 1610, described Blair as "ane ancient castell and strong dounioun." Well might he do so, for it had stood there at least three hundred years before he visited the spot, and all that he saw - with additions made in his own century - is extant as a place of residence at the present hour. The structure is thus absolutely unique in the county of Ayr. Nor shall we find many genealogies in Scotland to match that of its laird, for the family he represents have dwelt here in unbroken line for more than six hundred years. The records of the house go back to the reign of William the Lion, and the succession from that day to this is authenticated by documentary evidence. Sir Bryce Blair of that Ilk is named both by Blind Harry and in Barbour's *Bruce*, along with the uncle of Sir William Wallace, as one of the patriotic western barons who were treacherously hanged in the barns of Ayr; while his nephew, Roger, was a steady adherent of the Bruce. The same devotion to the cause of national freedom was exemplified by the William Blair who succeeded to the estates in 1664; the son-in-law of the second Duke of Hamilton, he raised a troop of horse in support of the Revolution, was taken prisoner by Claverhouse, and held an important place in the Convention of Estates from 1669 till 1690. He was one of the Commissioners appointed to effect a Treaty of Union betwixt the two Kingdoms. The famous sea-lion of our century, the Earl of Dundonald, was descended from a younger son, of the House of Blair who married Elizabeth Cochrane, heiress of that Ilk.

Though not without elements of picturesque beauty, the old house has a plain, homely look, and appears more modern than it really is, from the ill-judged expedient of a tradesman who, some years ago, in the absence of the proprietor, washed the external walls with cement, so as to take the rough-cast off. The house stands on a semi-circular plateau of whinstone, which rises from the left bank of the Bombo, one of five streams that water the estate; the little river flows past the northern side of the house, fifty feet below the foundations of the donjon. The precipitous declivity enhances the impressive aspect of the antique dwelling as viewed from the bed of the river. The oblong building of four stories at this side of the house, forming a single square tower, was no doubt the original structure, to which additions have at various times been made. The porch, in the angle on the eastern side, was built by the present proprietor; it conducts to an earlier entrance, over which is carved the date 1668, and the initials of the laird who married the Duke of Hamilton's daughter, and also those of his spouse, as well as the Hamilton arms quartered with those of Blair. The same initials and date are to be seen outside on the gables of the windows in the southern wing. Alongside the entrance, which would seem to have been erected in honour of the Lady Margaret Hamilton, is a yet more ancient door, with the date 1617 on the lintel underneath the arms of Blair impaled with those of Wallace of Craigie; on the dexter side are the initials of Bryce Blair, who succeeded to the estate in 1610 and died in 1639, and his wife, Annabel Wallace. Inside this door is the wicket from which the warrior descried who it was that sought admission before he withdrew the bolts and let down the drawbridge. That there was once a drawbridge here was made evident at the building of the porch, by the discovery of a moat while digging the foundations. In the entrance hall is a figure clad in the veritable armour of Sir Bryce Blair, the patriot of Wallace's time. From the portal we pass through a massive wall into a vaulted chamber, the old guard-room; and a passage leads through the great central wall, which is 14 feet thick, to another oblong vaulted chamber, which probably served as a prison.

In order to facilitate communication between one' part of the Castle and another, Captain Blair cut a passage, 30 feet long and 4 in width, through the central wall. In the turret covering the entrance of 1617 there is a closed-up doorway, over which there is a large granite stone, bearing an inscription with the names of Roger de Blair, the adherent of Bruce, and Mary Mure his wife, the latter of the Rowallan family; this probably indicates the date of the donjon, making it as old as the days of Bruce. The dining-room, on the second story, was a chapel down to the time of the present proprietor's grandfather, Colonel Hamilton Blair, who died in 1782. The portraits in the drawing-room include a charming likeness on glass of the brilliant Duchess of Gordon, noted as the zealous partisan of Pitt and the admirer of Burns; her Grace was aunt of Captain Blair's mother, a daughter of John Fordyce of Ayton. The portrait of Charles I is a copy of the famous picture in the Duke of Manchester's collection at Kimbolton, executed by Lady Cuningham of Fairlie, the younger daughter of Captain Blair; and the literary, as well as the artistic, talents of this lady are illustrated by two MS. volumes, in one of which - *The Shadows of an Old House* - she has related in graceful verse some of the more striking of the family traditions. A picture of Captain Blair's ship, the "Britannia," sailing out of Malta harbour, is a masterpiece of the late Mr Schetky, the Queen's marine painter. Into a series, of large volumes Captain Blair has collected the family papers; these include autograph letters of Mary Queen of Scots, Principal Baillie, and many other people of note. One of the latest is the draught of a letter from Colonel William Blair, the present proprietor's father, to Sir Alexander Boswell, declining to act as his second in what proved to be the fatal duel with Mr Stuart of Dunearn. The armoury, by far the richest collection of the kind in Ayrshire, contains a magnificent sword which formerly belonged to the Dey of Algiers; Captain Blair himself, who was attached to Marshal Beaumont's staff: carried off this trophy from the Dey's palace in 1830. The sword used by Sir Thomas Brisbane at Toulouse is here; he was an intimate companion of the late Colonel Blair, and left this sword to his own friend's son. In the garden Captain Blair has built a museum rich in specimens of natural history and archaeological curiosities, many of the former collected by himself during his years of service in the Royal Navy, from the Greek War of Independence onwards to the engagements at Navarino, the Morea, and Algiers. The collection contains the original face of Thorn's statue of Souter Johnny. The arboreal treasures of the park include one of the largest and most venerable yews in Scotland; and the remarkable manner in which the rhododendron flourishes in the glen at Blair is a problem that has baffled the acutest experts. With characteristic liberality, Captain Blair has thrown open this magnificent park 'to the public. He takes much interest in all philanthropic movements; and in May 1884 he received an illuminated address on the occasion of the opening of the New Public Hall, Dalry, to the erection of which he had largely contributed. Allusion was then made to the fact that he had been in possession of the estate for forty-three years; and the notable circumstance was mentioned that his grandfather, Colonel Blair, had led the Scots Greys at the battle of Fontenoy in 1745. That courageous soldier is described by Lord Mahon (Earl Stanhope) in his History, as "the bravest of the brave."

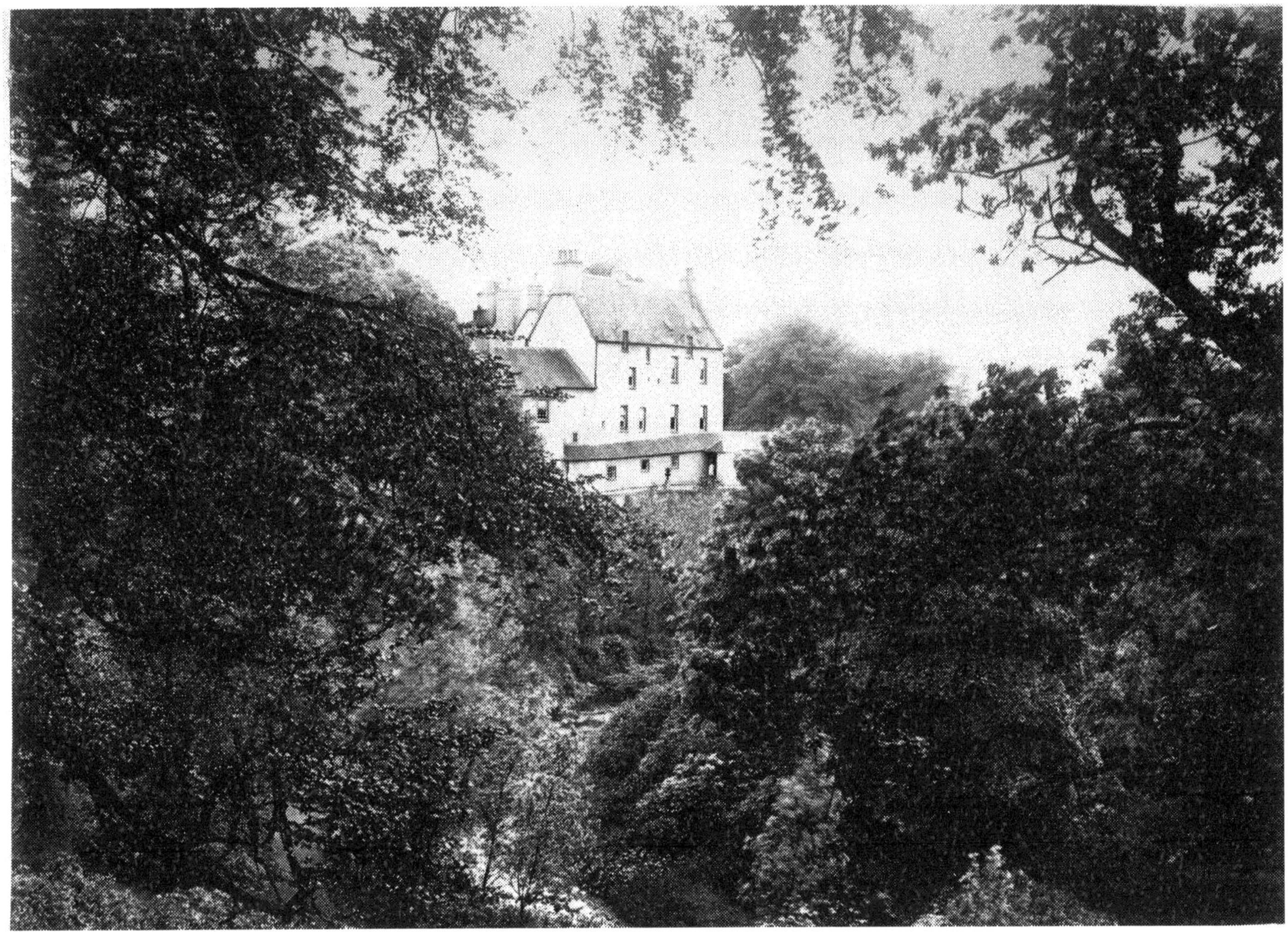

BLAIRQUHAN.

BLAIRQUHAN is the seat of Sir Edward Hunter-Blair, Bart., who is descended from two of the most ancient families in Ayrshire - the Hunters of Hunterston and the Blairs of Blair. These families were united by the marriage in 1770 of Sir Edward's grandfather, James Hunter, second son of John Hunter of Brownhill, with Jane, daughter and heiress of John Blair of Dunskey, a scion of the House of Blair of that Ilk. James Hunter assumed the additional name of Blair, and was a person of some consequence in his day. He was born in 1740, and began his career in 1756 as a banker with Messrs Coutts & Co. of Edinburgh, having Sir William Forbes, Bart. of Pitsligo, as his fellow-clerk. To these two young men the business of the bank was afterwards committed, and to their energy and foresight Scotland largely owes that development of her commerce and manufactures which took place in the latter half of last century. James Hunter-Blair was Member of Parliament for Edinburgh from 1781 till 1784, and Lord Provost of that city from 1784 till 1786. Many of the architectural improvements of Edinburgh, such as the South Bridge, the Regent Bridge, and New University Buildings, were effected or proposed by him; and his name is still preserved in Hunter Square and Blair Street. In 1786 he was created a baronet, and when he died in the following year his remains were interred, with public honours, in Greyfriars Churchyard. He left a numerous family, several of whom became eminent both as civilians and military men. His third son, James Hunter-Blair of Dunskey and Robertland, was Member for the county of Wigtown from 1816 till his death in 1822; and his sixth son, Thomas, achieved renown on the field of Talavera, at Waterloo, and during the Burmese War, reaching the rank of Major-General in 1846, three years before his death. The first Baronet was succeeded by his eldest son, Sir John, who died unmarried in 1800, when the title and estates came to his brother David, father of the present baronet, Sir Edward Hunter-Blair.

The magnificent edifice of Blairquhan Castle was built by Sir David Hunter-Blair in 1824. The old Castle of Blairquhan is said to have been of great antiquity, some parts of it having been built in 1570, but McWhirter's Tower, as it was called, dating back some centuries before that time. For several generations it was in the possession of the Kennedys, a branch of the Cassillis family; and in the time of Charles II. it was held by the Whitefords. The estate was purchased from the latter family by the first baronet, Sir James Hunter-Blair, shortly before his death; but the present mansion was not completed until 1824. Some of the lintels and sculptured stones from the old Castle are built into the new mansion of Blairquhan, which occupies nearly its former site. The ornate Tudor style of architecture has been most successfully carried out in this building, which is most romantically situated. The Girvan Water winds through the policies, and from the windows of the Castle an enchanting prospect of a Lowland landscape, richly varied with stream and woodland and cultivated field, may be seen. The Castle is approached by a long avenue, which passes through some of the finest scenery in the neighbourhood.

James Hunter-Blair, eldest son of Sir David, the builder of Blairquhan, was a Lieut.-Colonel in the Scots Fusilier Guards, and was elected Member of Parliament for Ayrshire in 1852; but when the Crimean War broke out he joined his regiment, and fell at the battle of Inkerman, 5th November 1854. His brother, Sir Edward, the present baronet, succeeded to the title on the death of his father in 1857.

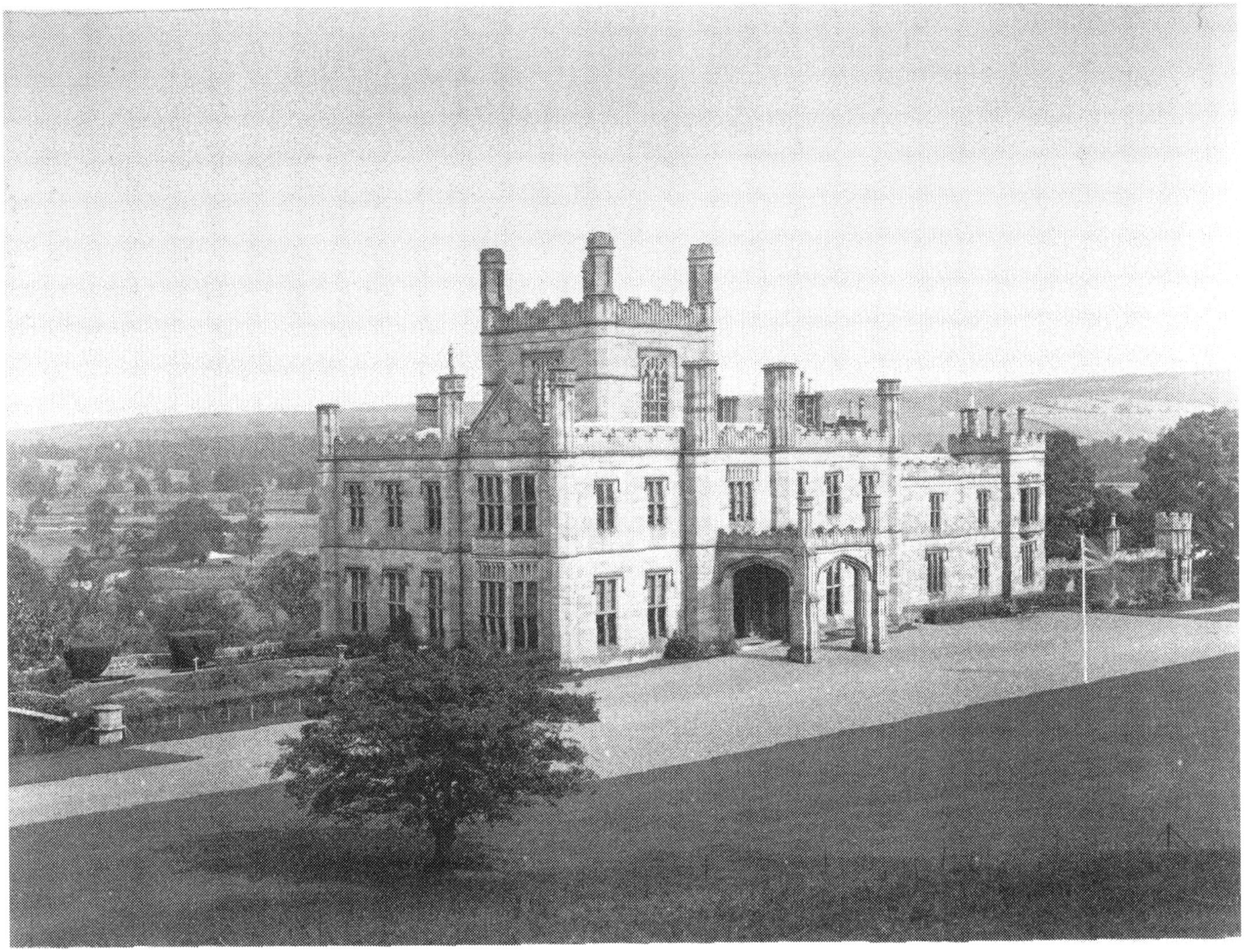

BRISBANE.

THE estate of Brisbane, situated in the parish of Largs, and about two miles north of the latter town, was originally called Kelso-land. Under this name it can be traced back to the thirteenth century, at which time it was in the possession of a family of the name of Kelso. With this family it remained for a long period, until it was acquired by the Schaws of Greenock in 1624. Robert Kelso bought back the territorial estate, circa 1650; but his son, John Kelso, sold the property to James Brisbane of Bishoptoun in 1671, who called his new acquisition by his own name, and whose descendant still occupies the place. The Kelso family is now represented by Commander E. B. P. Kelso, R.N., of Horkseley Park, Essex.

The Brisbane family, though long connected with Renfrewshire, had obtained possessions in the neighbourhood of Largs before the beginning of the fifteenth century; and after the purchase of Kelso-land their territories were united under the title of the Barony of Brisbane. The Lairds of Bishoptoun took a prominent part both in the military and civil service of .the country. Matthew Brisbane fell on the fatal field of Flodden, and his nephew, John Brisbane, was equally unfortunate at the Battle of Pinkie. John Brisbane of Bishoptoun was Member of Parliament for Renfrewshire from 1644 till 1650; and his grandson, John Brisbane, younger of Bishoptoun, represented Ayrshire in the last Scottish Parliament - 1704-1707. As to the latter, a peculiar circumstance is noteworthy. Whilst his mother was Elizabeth, daughter of John Brisbane (*d.* 1635), his wife was Elizabeth, grand-daughter of the same John. He was himself a son of James Schaw of Balliegellie, a scion of the house of Schaw of Greenock, and by the contract of marriage betwixt him and his cousin Elizabeth, the estate of Brisbane was settled upon their heirs-male, and it was provided that he should assume the surname and arms of Brisbane. Kelso-land thus fell once more into the hands of a Schaw, and has continued since in the possession of his descendants.

From this auspicious marriage sprung a race of naval and military heroes. Rear-Admiral Sir Charles Brisbane, K. C. B. - grandfather of the present proprietor - accompanied by two of his brothers, served with distinction under Rodney, Hood, and Nelson. The name of Sir Thomas Makdougall Brisbane of Brisbane, cousin of Sir Charles, is familiar in the ear of every Scotsman who knows the history of this century. During the protracted Peninsular War he became one of the most distinguished commanders under Lord Wellesley; and in 1820 he was appointed Governor of New South Wales, and succeeded in establishing the thriving colony of Queensland whilst he held office. The services which he rendered to science were not less valuable than those by which he had attained to eminence in politics and in warfare. While at New South Wales he established the Observatory at Paramatta, and furnished the necessary astronomical instruments at his own expense, thus making it possible to obtain meteorological observations which have proved of great value to later colonists. His merits were acknowledged by scientists throughout Europe, and he was elected President of the Royal Society of Edinburgh, and bore the honorary degrees of LL.D. and F.R.S. He was created a Baronet in 1836, and raised to the rank of General in 1841. In 1819 he had married Anna Maria, daughter of Sir Henry Hay Makdougall of Makerstoun, and assumed her name in addition to his own, by sign manual, in 1826. His family, consisting of two sons and two daughters, predeceased him; and when he died at Brisbane on 27th January 1860, in his eighty-sixth year, he was succeeded by his kinsman, Charles Thomas Brisbane of Brisbane, who now holds the estate.

The house is a quaint structure, probably of the seventeenth century, with three antique Flemish gables to the front, which break up the sky-line in a picturesque manner. The mansion is in the Vale of Brisbane, and is well sheltered by the hills which rise behind it, and the old trees that have been suffered to remain untouched. The date on the house, which is 1636, is carved deeply on one of the gable stones. The fluctuations in the ownership which took place before this time make it improbable that the "guid housse weill planted," which Timothy Pont describes in 1608, was that which still remains.

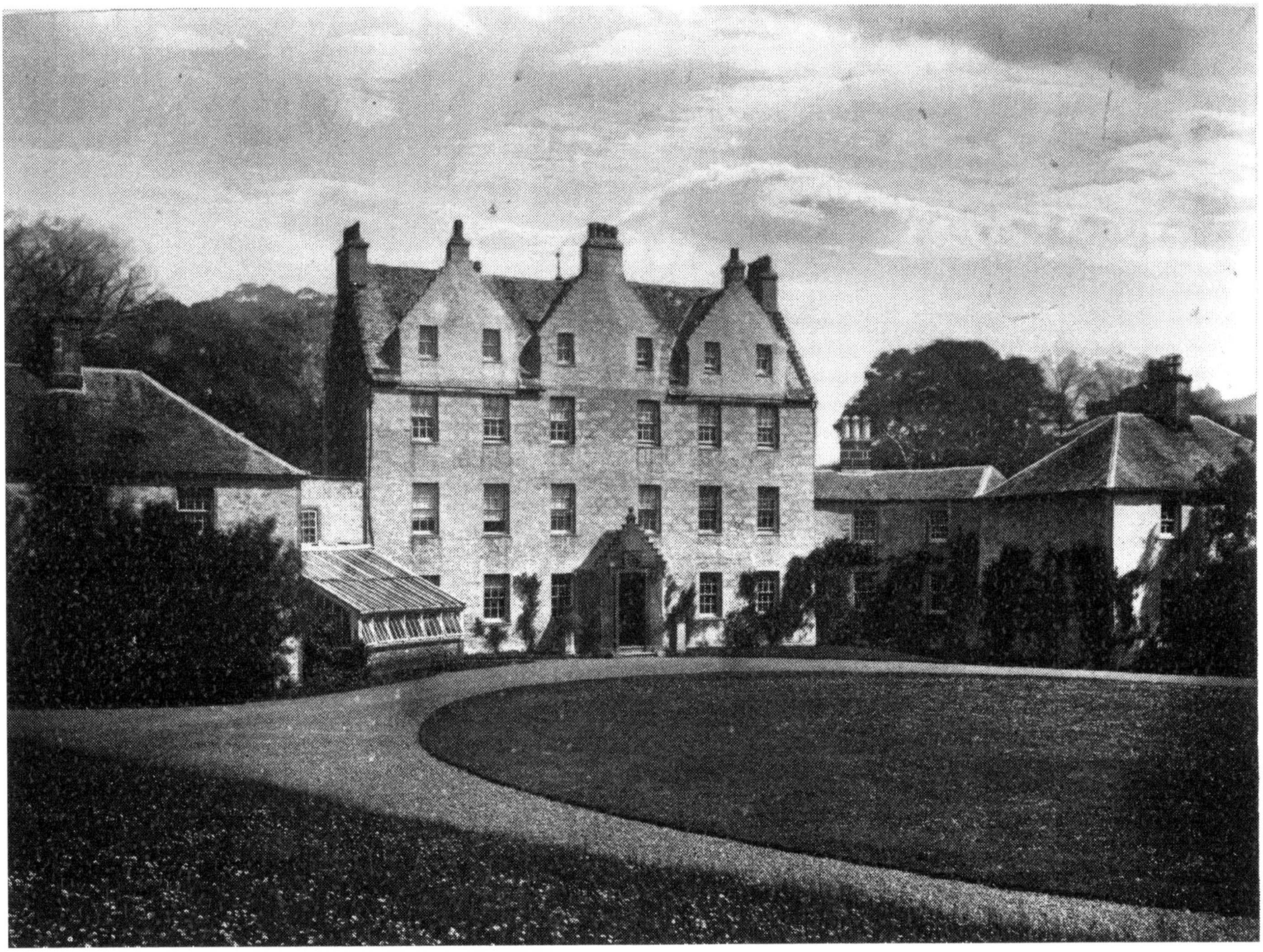

CAMBUSDOON.

WHEN the Barony of Alloway was disposed of by the magistrates of Ayr in 1754, that portion, afterwards known as Greenfield, was purchased by Elias Cathcart of Ayr, the father of Lord Alloway of Session (see *Auchendrane*). From his descendants it was acquired in 1852 by the late James Baird of Auchmedden, who changed the name of the estate to Cambusdoon, and built the present mansion-house in the following year. This imposing pile is in the Scottish Baronial style of architecture, and displays much adaptive ingenuity and a thorough appreciation of such genuine old work of this form as is still extant.

The late proprietor was one of the well-known firm of ironmasters called the Bairds of Gartsherrie. The fact that he became possessed of the estate of Auchmedden, which was for many centuries in the possession of another family of the name of Baird, is apt to mislead the incautious genealogist. James Baird of Cambusdoon was the son of Alexander Baird of Lochwood in Lanarkshire, from whom have sprung the Bairds of Elie, Orie, Closeburn, Stichell, Strichen, Muirkirk, and Knoydart. All these estates are in different counties of Scotland. The eldest son of the Laird of Lochwood, William Baird of Elie, was M.P. for the Falkirk Burghs from 1841 till 1846; and James Baird of Auchmedden and Cambusdoon represented the same constituency from 1851 till 1857. In 1874 James Baird founded the "Baird Trust" - a fund devoted to the extension of the Established Kirk of Scotland. He was twice married, but left no issue at his death, which took place in 1876. His estates were divided between his relatives of Elie, Stichell, Muirkirk, and Knoydart. His widow, daughter of the late Admiral James Hay of Belton, grandson of the first Marquess of Tweeddale, now occupies the mansion of Cambusdoon. The handsome Gothic church which stands near "Alloway's auld haunted kirk " was erected by the late James Baird in 1858, and contains a very fine stained-glass window as a memorial of him.

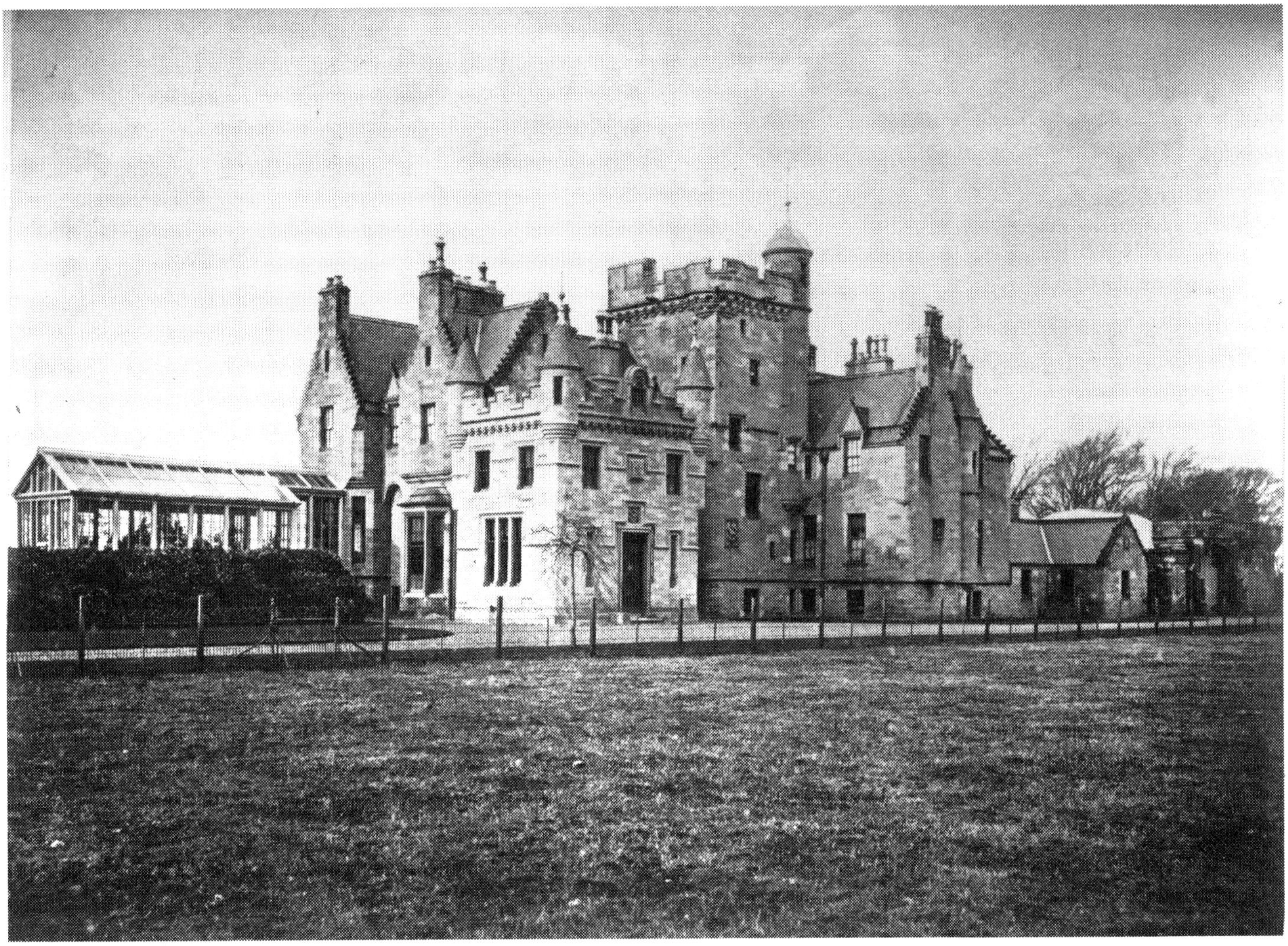

CAPRINGTON CASTLE.

THE date of the building of the first Castle at Caprington is - according to Lord Hailes' phrase - "lost in the mists of antiquity." It is confidently asserted that it belonged to Sir William Wallace, the liberator of Scotland, and was considered an old structure even in his time; and several of his deeds of prowess are connected traditionally with the locality. Few traces of this ancient stronghold, however, will be found in the present castle; though the fact that an important defensible post occupied its site at an early date is beyond dispute. The magnificent mansion of Caprington, as we now see it, has been the gradual growth of many years, and many structural alterations were made in the early part of this century, which serve to give it a more modern appearance than we would expect from its actual age. It stands close by the river Irvine, at a short distance from Riccartoun; and as it is built upon an isolated basaltic rock, which rises considerably above the surrounding country, its position is very commanding. The main entrance is surmounted by a turriform erection, which projects from the line of the front as a semi-sexagon, and presents a very imposing appearance. The access to the castle is made by a spacious archway with flanking towers of solid masonry. The armorial bearings of the Cuninghames of Caprington, fully blazoned, are carved on a stone shield over the central arch.

Caprington belonged to a branch of the Wallace family at the period when we first trace it in local history. It seems to have been a place of some importance in early times, as it is described in a charter, dated 1385, as *Castellum turris fortalicium de Caprington*. At the close of the fourteenth century it was in the possession of Sir Duncan Wallace of Sundrum, and passed into the family of the Cuninghames by marriage shortly after that date, and has remained with the descendants of that House until this day.

The Cuninghames of Caprington trace their descent from the Lords of Kilmaurs, who afterwards became Earls of Glencairn, and were prominent in Scottish history from the time of Macbeth till the expiry of the title in 1796. Sir William de Cunynghame of Kilmaurs, who was titular Earl of Carrick through his marriage with Elinor, grand-daughter of Edward Bruce, granted the lands of Bedland to his third son, Thomas Cuninghame; and Adam Cuninghame, son of the latter, married a daughter of Sir Duncan Wallace of Sundrum in 1400, and thus became first Laird of his name in Caprington. Though not in strict line of descent by heirs-male, the family still holds the estates, which were erected into the Barony of Caprington by a charter of Queen Mary in 1564. Matrimonial alliances have been made during the intervening time which connect the Cuninghames with the noble Houses of Caithness and Eglinton, and with the historic families of Leslie, Hamilton, Johnstone, Murray, Douglas, and Dalrymple.

Several notable names occur in the records of this ancient family. William Cunynghame, Laird of Caprington, represented Ayrshire in the Convention and Parliament of 1617. Shortly after his time the Barony of Caprington passed into the hands of the Glencairn family - the original stock of the Cuninghames; but the estates were bought back by Sir John Cuninghame of Broomhill and Lambruchton - the representative of a younger branch of the Caprington Cuninghames - in 1683. As Sir John's merits have been variously canvassed as partisanship dictated, a slight sketch of him may not be uninteresting.

Sir John of Caprington was the son of John (called William by some genealogists) Cuninghame of Broomhill by his second marriage with Elizabeth, daughter of William Sinclair of Ratter, ancestor of the tenth Earl of Caithness. He was trained to the profession of law, and rose to be a distinguished member of the Scottish Bar during one of its most brilliant epochs. He was Member for Ayrshire in the Convention of 1665, and was created a Baronet of Nova Scotia by patent of 19th September 1669, with remainder to the heirs-male of his body. Bishop Burnet, referring to him in his *History* (*sub anno* 1667), thus describes his character: "Sir John Cuninghame, an eminent lawyer, who had an estate in the [west] country, was the most extraordinary man of his profession in that kingdom. He was Episcopal beyond most men in Scotland, who for the far greatest part thought that forms of government were in their own nature indifferent, and might be either good or bad, according to the hands in which they fell, whereas he thought Episcopacy was - of a divine right, settled by Christ. He was not only very learned in the Civil and Canon Laws, and in the philosophical learning, but he was very universal in all other learning. He was a great divine, and well read in the Fathers and in ecclesiastical history. He was, above all, a man of eminent probity and of a sweet temper, and, indeed, one of the piousest men in the nation. The state of the Church in those parts went to his heart, for it was not easy to know how to keep an even hand between the perverseness of the people on the one side, and the vices of the clergy on the other."

Despite the difficulty, to which Burnet alludes, of steering a safe course in these troublous times, Sir John Cuninghame succeeded in gaining both fame and opulence by the exercise of his great abilities. When the tyranny of the Duke of Lauderdale had become so intolerable in Scotland that Charles II was forced to hear the complaints of the nation against him, Cuninghame was summoned to lay the case for the complainers before the King and Council in 1679. Though the Duke was defended with much forensic skill by Sir George Mackenzie of Rosehaugh, and was a close friend and favourite with the King, the arguments of Cuninghame were irresistible, and resulted in the downfall of Lauderdale's power. Burnet pays the advocate of the people another compliment, when relating this incident, in these terms: "He was a learned and judicious man, and had the most universal, and indeed the most deserved reputation for integrity and vertue of any man, not only of his own profession, but of the whole nation."

The Earl of Glencairn, who was Chancellor of Scotland, had purchased the Barony of Caprington from the creditors of Sir William Cuninghame, the last of the Bedland line, and Sir John acquired it from the Earl in 1683. The baronetcy which had been conferred upon him descended from father to son until the death of the fourth baronet, without issue, in 1829. The title was then conjoined with that of Dick of Prestonfield, and is now borne by Sir Robert Keith Alexander Dick-Cuninghame of Prestonfield, lineal descendant of the second baronet of Caprington. The castle and the chief portion of the estate devolved upon Anne Dick or Cuninghame, daughter of the fourth baronet of Prestonfield, as senior heiress of line; and her second son, William Cathcart Smith Cuninghame, Esq. of Caprington, is the present possessor of them.

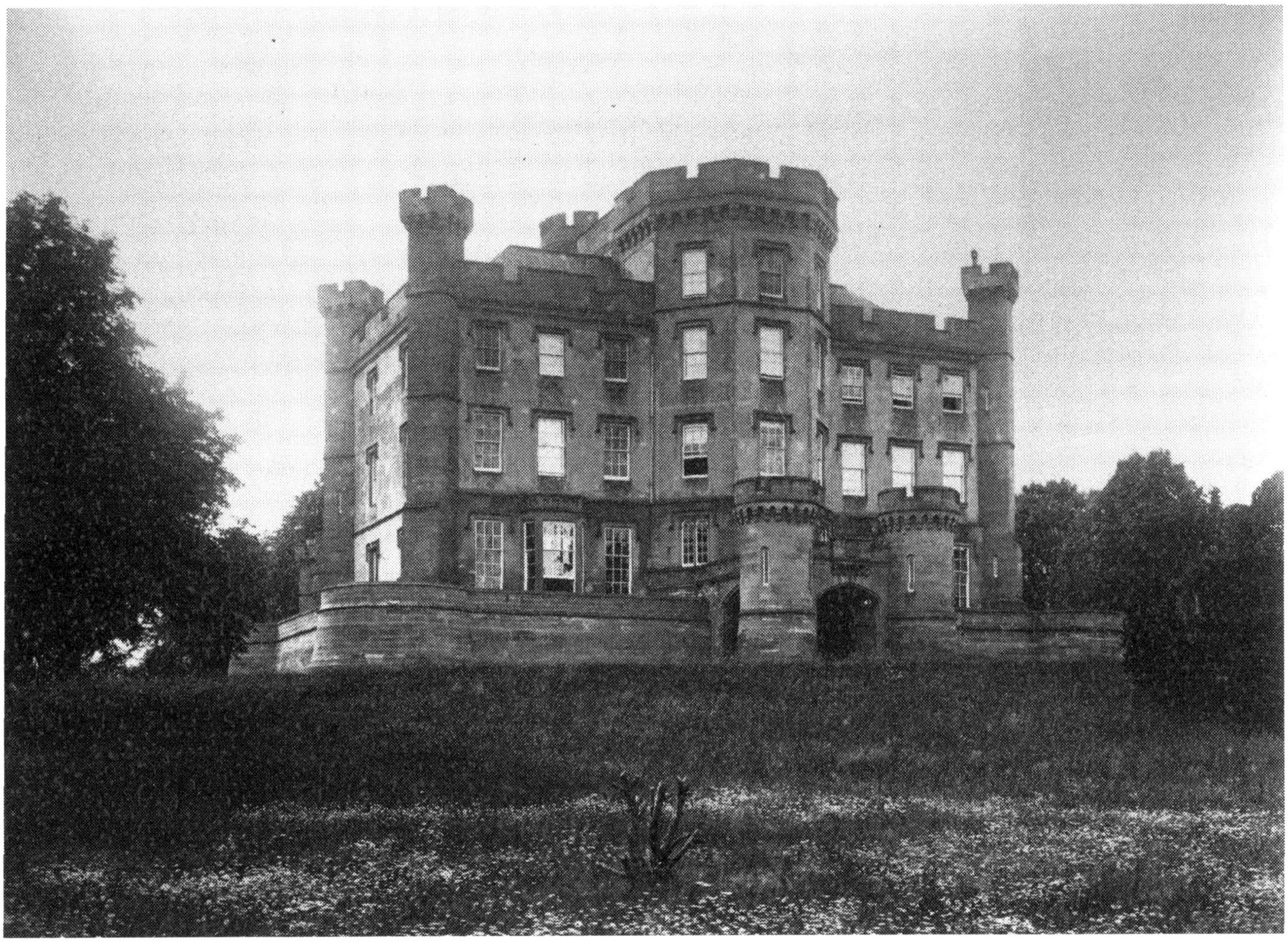

CASSILLIS HOUSE.

CASSILLIS HOUSE, formerly the chief seat of the Earls of Cassillis, occupies a romantic situation on the left bank of the Doon, a few miles from Maybole. The oldest portion of the building at present existing was probably erected by Sir Gilbert Kennedy shortly after he had been elevated to the peerage in 1452 with the title of Lord Kennedy. This part presents all the characteristic features of the architecture of that time, and is still in excellent preservation. Extensive additions to the house were made by Archibald, titular Earl of Cassillis (1794-1832), the eldest son of the first Marquess of Ailsa; and these were completed only a short time before his death. While the alterations were proceeding, a large subterranean apartment with a concealed door was discovered, and many human bones, the relics probably of the victims of feudal tyranny, were found within the place.

The Kennedys, Earls of Cassillis, have been intimately connected with the history of Scotland for many years. The first Laird of Cassillis who can be traced is Sir John Kennedy, son of Sir Gilbert de Carrick, who had a charter from David II (1329-1371) confirming him in the possession of the lands of Castlys, which he had obtained through his marriage with Mary, daughter of Sir Niel Montgomerie. The great-grandson of this Sir John was the first Lord Kennedy to whom we have referred as the builder of Cassillis House; and the third Lord Kennedy was created Earl of Cassillis in 1502. The twelfth Earl was raised to the Marquisate of Ailsa in 1831, and the present holder of the title is fourteenth Earl of Cassillis and third Marquess of Ailsa. Cassillis House belongs to him by inheritance from a long line of noble ancestors.

Reference has already been made to the romantic story of John Faa (see *Culzean Castle*), which is usually associated with Cassillis House; and though the tale will hardly bear critical examination as to its truthfulness, it may be briefly related. John, sixth Earl of Cassillis, was married to Lady Jean Hamilton, daughter of Thomas, first Earl of Haddington, about the beginning of the seventeenth century. The tradition declares that she had been betrothed when young to her lover, Sir John Faa, knight of Dunbar, but that her ambitious father forced her to accept the, more tempting offer of the Earl of Cassillis for her hand. Sir John was sent to the Continent, and when word was brought to her of his murder by bravoes at Madrid, she gave a reluctant consent to the proposals of the Earl. The latter is usually described as of a stern and forbidding aspect, strictly Calvinistic in his religious views, and utterly unsympathetic where romance was concerned. Finding that his lady continued to mourn over the loss of her early love, he conceived an aversion towards her, and seldom permitted her to share either in his duties or pastimes. One day whilst the Earl was absent at a meeting of the Westminster Assembly of Divines, a band of gipsies made their appearance before the door of Cassillis House, and sought to amuse the lady by their songs and dances; and she soon recognised in the leader of the troop her own lost lover, Sir John Faa. Moved by his persuasions, she consented to elope with him; but they had not been long gone when, the Earl returned unexpectedly to Cassillis. No sooner had he' heard of this elopement than he set out in pursuit of his recreant spouse, and succeeded in capturing the whole party at a ford on the Doon, which is still known as the "Gipsies' Steps." The runaways were all brought back to the Castle, and the Countess was compelled to stand at one of the windows whilst the fourteen gipsies and their leader, Sir John Faa, were hanged on the "dule tree of Cassillis." The Countess' Room may still be seen; and it is averred that the Earl caused her to be confined during the remainder of her life in a house at Maybole, and took his second wife ere his first was dead.

The ballad of *Johnnie Faa* follows the details of this incident with tolerable accuracy, but there is nothing in its phraseology to fix it distinctly to the locality of Cassillis. From internal evidence, indeed, it seems to be merely a ballad-singer's romance, which may be referred to almost any date after the introduction of the gipsies to this country. It has been proved also that the Countess of Cassillis, with whose name it is often connected; died in 1642, and was deeply mourned by her husband. As her eldest daughter, Margaret, was married to Bishop Burnet the historian, who had many enemies in Scotland, it has been suggested that this story was invented and tacked on to the pre-existing ballad for the purpose of annoying him. It is certain that the Bishop's description of his father-in-law does not at all correspond with that which is hinted at in this mendacious tale; for he declares that he was "a man of great vertue and of a considerable degree of good understanding; he was so sincere that he would suffer no man to take his words in any other sense than as he meant them." We may therefore safely conclude that the ballad of *Johnnie Faa* is a poetic fiction, coupled with the name of Cassillis by the malice of Bishop Burnet's enemies.

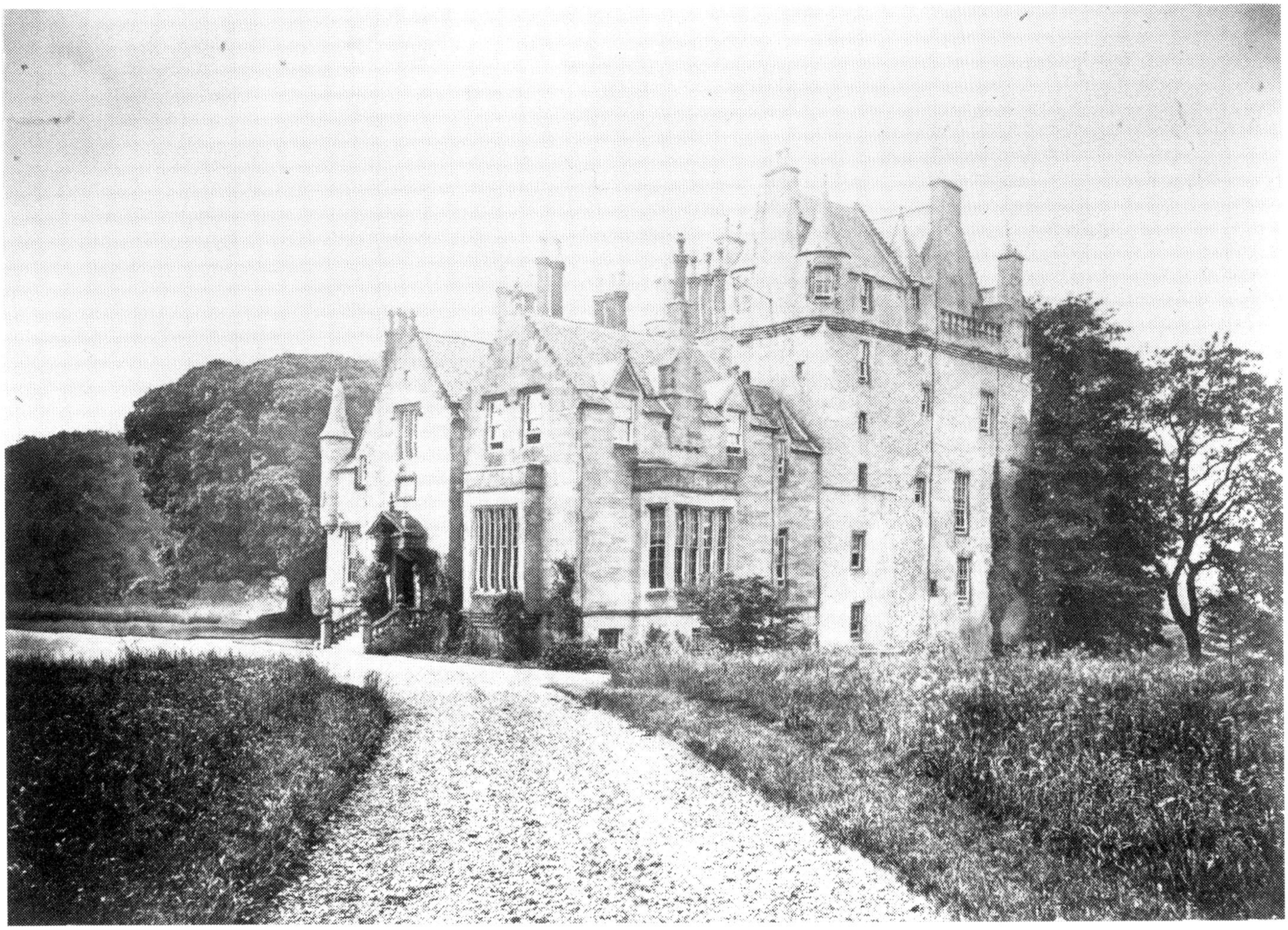

CESSNOCK.

THE quaint, old-fashioned house of Cessnock stands about a mile and a half to the south~east of the town of Galston, In the parish of that name. The streamlet of the Burnawn, a tributary of the Irvine, forms one of those winding links in its course near the building, which are appropriately called "crooks" in Scotland; and the house has been erected on a steep bank, which gives it much value as a post of defence. The house occupies three sides of an irregular square, facing towards the stream, and thus forms a partially-enclosed courtyard. The main entrance is by a doorway in a turret-like structure built at one of the angles; thus following that style of French chateau-architecture which is seen to perfection in the Castle of Glamis. It has been suggested, with some appearance of probability, that the open side of the courtyard was originally defended by a moat or trench cut from the one bank of the Burnawn to the other, so as to leave the house quite insulated.

Cessnock House was long the seat of the Campbells of Cessnock, one of the leading "Westland Whig" families during the seventeenth century. The Laird was married to a daughter of the first Earl of Eglintoun, *circa* 1513, and a later matrimonial alliance connected this family with that of the Earls of Loudoun. The Campbell through whom this last union was made cannot be lightly passed over.

Hew Campbell, son of George Campbell of Cessnock, married the Lady Elizabeth Campbell, younger daughter and co-heiress of George Campbell, Master of Loudoun, and progenitor of the Earls of Loudoun. Hew was born in 1615, succeeded to the estate in 1630, and having chosen the law as his profession, was appointed Lord Justice-Clerk and Lord of Session by the Parliament in 1649, but declined to act in either capacity. It is probable that he was knighted in the latter year, since we find that he sat as Member for Ayrshire under the name of "Laird of Cessnock" in the Parliaments of 1639-41 and 1645-47, and' appears as "Knight" in that of 1649-1650. He had not shown sufficient enthusiasm at the Restoration to establish confidence in his loyalty to Charles II., and severe measures were taken against him without any apparent actions upon his part to justify them. He was specially exempted from the Act of Indemnity of 1662; severe fines were exacted from him; and though he was charged with no special crime, he was imprisoned for two years in Edinburgh Castle. His sympathy with the Covenanters brought him under suspicion twenty years afterwards, and he was charged with having "set on the rebellion of Bothwell Bridge, and chid those who deserted it." The prosecution was conducted by Sir George Mackenzie of Rosehaugh - the "bluidy Mackenzie" of tradition - but the perjured witnesses whom he had suborned were discomfited by the aged Sir Hew in open court. Though acquitted of the charge, the poor knight was carried back to prison, and detained in custody with his eldest son, though both were unconvicted. The Earl of Perth was then Justice-General, and no pains were taken to conceal the fact that he had determined to have Sir Hew attainted, so that he might bestow the forfeited lands of Cessnock upon his own brother, the newly created Viscount Melfort, who had recently married a daughter of Sir Thomas Wallace of Craigie, and wished to increase his possessions in Ayrshire. Foiled at this time, the Earl returned to the charge, and in the following year Sir Hew and his son were accused of complicity in the Rye House Plot, and found guilty. "The old gentleman," says Burnet, "then near eighty, seeing the ruin of his family was determined, and that he was condemned in so unusual a manner, took courage and said the oppression they had been under had driven them to despair, and made them think how they might secure their lives and fortunes." This was held as a confession of guilt, and the lands of Cessnock were declared forfeited, and gifted without ceremony to the Viscount Melfort. The unfortunate baronet, enfeebled by disease, imprisonment, and anxiety, died at Edinburgh in the following year (1686). The triumph of the Drummond family was short-lived; for in 1690 Sir George Campbell, who had shared his father's confinement, was restored to his estate by Act of Parliament, and made Lord Justice-Clerk and one of the Lords of Session. His daughter Margaret was married to Sir Alexander Hume, son of the first Earl of Marchmont, and one of the most distinguished lawyers of his time. Sir Alexander took the name of Campbell in addition to his own when he succeeded to the estate, and was raised to the Bench as Lord Cessnock in 1704. He supported the Hanoverian dynasty vigorously in, 1715 whilst Mar's rebellion was in progress, and terminated his brilliant career as second Earl of Marchmont in 1740. The latter title became extinct on the death of his son, Sir Hew in 1794.

The ancient estate of the Campbells had been alienated by Sir Alexander shortly after the rebellion of 1715, so that he might centralise his property in the Border counties, to which the Hurnes belonged. For some time Cessnock was in the hands of the Dicks, and was acquired from them by the Wallaces of Cairnhill in 1783. It passed afterwards by purchase into the possession of the Scotts of Balcomie; and when Miss Scott, daughter of General John Scott, was made Duchess of Portland by her marriage in 1795, the estate became the property of the Duke, and still remains in his family.

The lineal representative of the Cessnock Campbells is George James Campbell, Esq. of Cessnock and Treesbank. He is directly descended from James Campbell, second son of that Sir Hew Campbell, Bart., to whose misfortunes we have already alluded. The Campbells of Fairfield are also cadets of the same family.

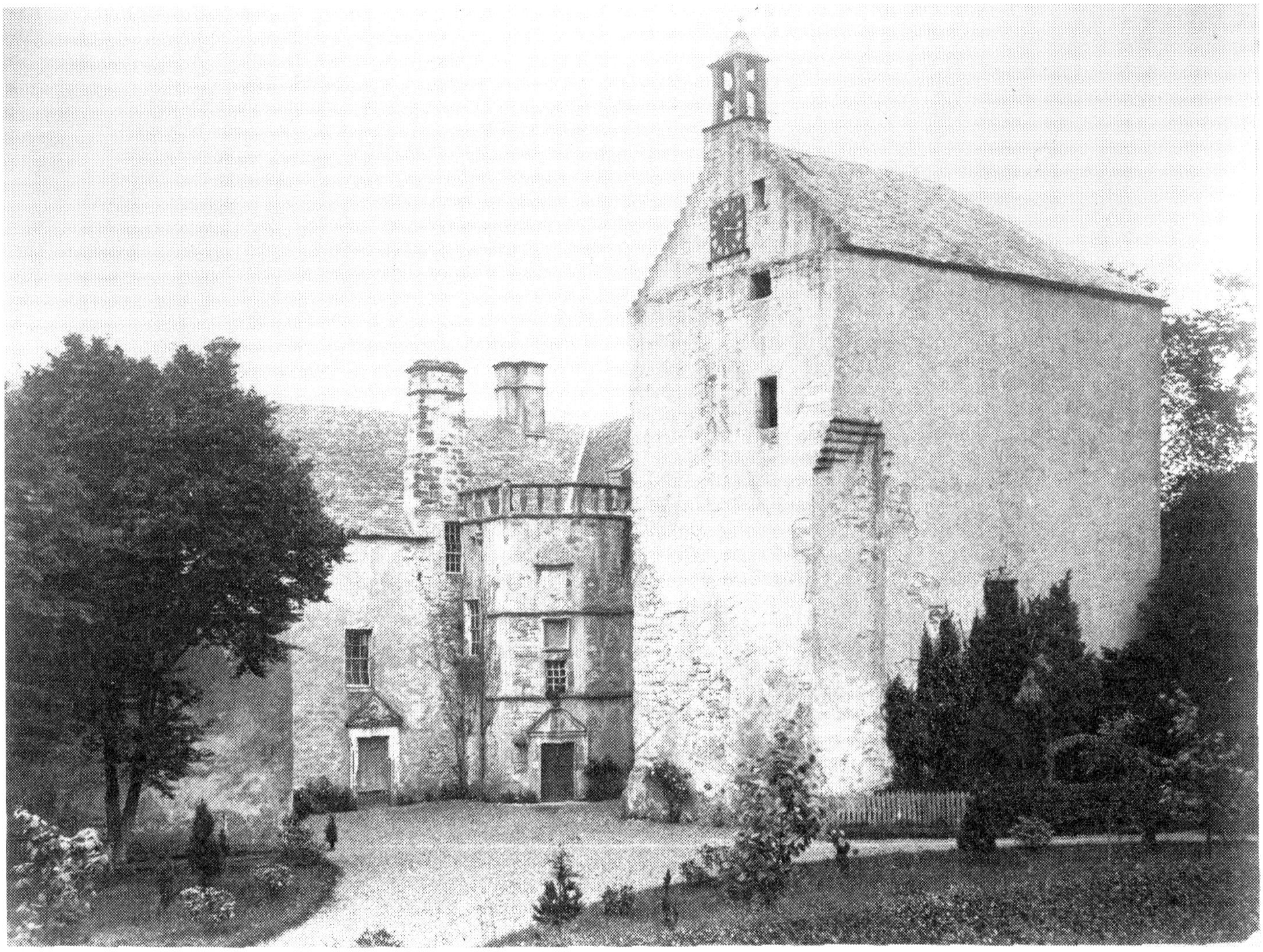

CLONCAIRD CASTLE.

THE Castle of Cloncaird was originally built during the sixteenth century, and is described as having been in the style of feudal mansions of that period, with huge square tower, narrow spiral staircase, and other indications of the time to which it belonged. Towards the close of the sixteenth century it was in the possession of Walter Mure, a scion of the Auchendrane family, and cousin of the unscrupulous Laird of Auchendrane who devised the "Ayrshire Tragedy." This Walter Mure of Cloncaird was the actual perpetrator of the murder of Sir Thomas Kennedy of Culzean, and was assisted in the execution of his dreadful crime by his boon-companion, Kennedy of Drumurchy (see *Old Auchendrane*).

The castle came into the hands of Henry Ritchie, Esq. of Craigton and Busbie, early in this century, and he made extensive alterations upon it so as to fit it for his chief residence. In 1814 the front was entirely re-built and modernised, and it was thus made one of the finest mansions in the county. Mr Ritchie was the descendant of James Ritchie, "merchand burgess" of Glasgow; whose name appears in the Commissary Register in 1674. His family was settled in Craigton, Lanarkshire, in 1746, and his father, James Ritchie, acquired the estate of Busbie, Ayrshire, in 1763. Henry Ritchie was related to the family of the Marquess of Lothian through his mother, Catharine Kerr. He was born in 1777, succeeded to the estates at Busbie and Craigton in 1799, and purchased the Cloncaird property shortly afterwards. As he died without issue in 1843, these estates fell to William Wallace, Esq., his sister's son, and the representative of the Wallace of Cairnhill. The Castle of Cloncaird is now occupied by the widow of Henry Ritchie, who is a daughter of the late Sir James Fergusson of Kilkerran.

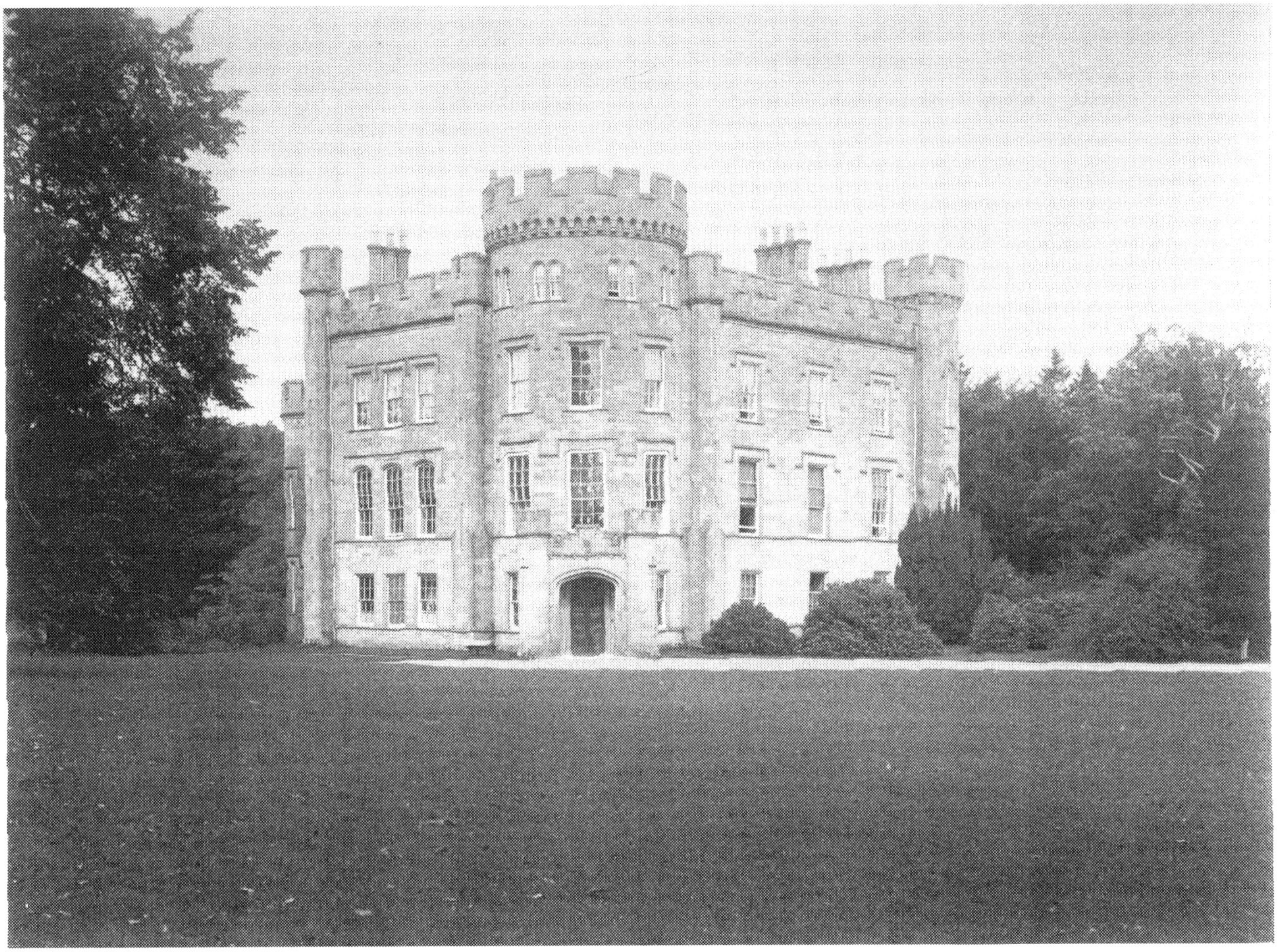

COILSFIELD.

THE mansion of Coilsfield, or Montgomerie, is picturesquely situated upon the right bank of Faile Water, at a short distance from the village of Torbolton. The building is quite a modern erection in the Grecian style, and shows how successfully the architecture of southern Europe can be made suitable even for this northern latitude. The scenery in the neighbourhood is especially fine, presenting a rich variety of sylvan and pastoral country, diversified by fertile plains and pine-clad mountains. It is to this spot that Burns refers in his well-known song on Highland Mary, who was a servant in Coilsfield when he first met and parted with her:

> "Ye banks, and braes, and streams around
> The castle O' Montgomerie !
> Green be your woods, and fair your flowers,
> Your waters never drumlie!
> There Simmer first unfauld her robes,
> And there the langest tarry ;
> For there I took the last Fareweel
> O' my sweet Highland Mary."

The name of Coilsfield was probably derived from the tumulus in the vicinity, which was traditionally declared to be the grave of Coilus or Kyle - a mysterious monarch who belongs to the pre-historic period, and who has given rise to endless disputation amongst Scottish antiquaries. Whilst some of them profess absolute and unquestioning faith in this tradition, others are sceptical enough to deny that such a person as King Coilus ever existed. Explorations made in 1837 conclusively proved that the mound of Coilsfield contained human remains; but, for obvious reasons, these could not be identified. The territorial name, however, can be traced back for nearly five centuries and a half; for we find that in 1343 the lands of *Quyltisfield* (Coilsfield) were granted, for special reasons, to the monks of Melrose by "Johannis de Graham filii," probably a relative of the ancestors of the present Duke of Montrose. The place was held by the monks until the Reformation, but came into the possession of William Cuninghame of Caprington previous to 1590. With this family it remained until the time of Sir John Cuninghame of Caprington (see *Caprington Castle*), who disposed of this portion of his estate to the Hon. Colonel James Montgomerie, fourth son of the sixth Earl of Eglintoun, and ancestor of the twelfth Earl. The family retained the property as the territorial possession of this branch until about 1860, when the lands were sold to the present proprietor. During the rule of the Eglintoun family the Coilsfield branch became important, and several alliances with eminent Ayrshire families were made by the scions of this house. The sixth Earl of Eglintoun, who was the first of the Setons, and therefore the cause of the junction of the earldoms of Wintoun and Eglintoun, established his third son in this locality, and from this earl descended the Montgomeries of Annick Lodge and of Belmont, and the Hamiltons of Pinmore and Belleisle. The earldom descended from father to son with unfailing regularity, until the tragic fate of the tenth Earl - who was murdered by Mungo Campbell in 1769 - threw the succession upon his childless brother, the eleventh Earl of Eglintoun. At the death of the latter in 1796, the title came to Hugh Montgomerie of Coilsfield, whose great-grandson is now fourteenth Earl of Eglintoun and Wintoun.

The twelfth Earl of Eglintoun, who was the first of the Coilsfield family that bore the title, played an important part in the political history of his time (1739-1819) Whilst still Sir Hugh Montgomerie of Skelmorlie, he represented Ayrshire in Parliament, almost without intermission, from 1780 till he attained the earldom in 1796. During this long period he was exceptionally active in his support of the Crown. He raised the regiment of the West Lowland Fencibles, and became their Colonel; was appointed inspector of military roads in Scotland; raised the "Glasgow Regulars" was Lieutenant-Governor of Edinburgh Castle, and a representative Peer; created Baron Ardrossan of Ardrossan in 1806 in the peerage of the United Kingdom. He died in 1819, and was succeeded by his eldest son, father of the present Earl.

The twelfth Earl of Eglintoun disposed of the lands of Coilsfield under peculiar circumstances. Mr Paterson of Ayr died a quarter of a century ago, and left his property to William Orr, Esq., ubder the conditions that he should adopt the name of Paterson, and purchase the estate of Coilsfield, bestowing upon it the name of Montgomerie House. These stipulations have been faithfully regarded, and his eldest son, Robert Paterson Paterson, presently residing at 2 Park Circus, Ayr, is heir-apparent to the property of Coilsfield.

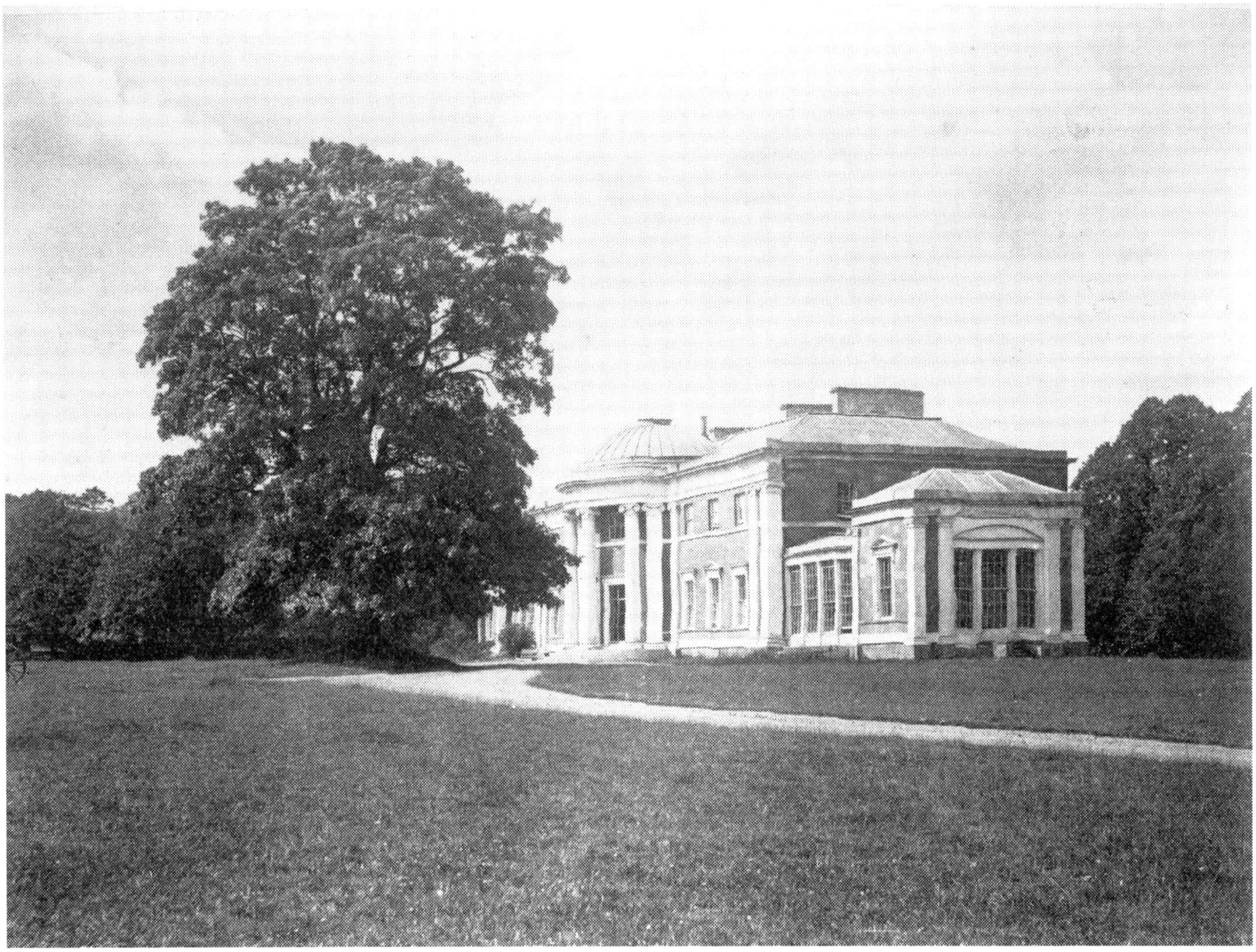

COODHAM.

THE Estate of Coodham, owned in the seventeenth and beginning of the eighteenth century by a family named Baird, and afterwards by the Alisons from whom the Glaisnock stock is descended, was acquired in 1826 by Mrs William Fairlie, of London, the widow of a wealthy Calcutta merchant and banker, who was a native of Kilmarnock, being the son of John Fairlie by Agnes, daughter of Mungo Mure of Bruntwood. About 1831 Mrs Fairlie erected the mansion at a cost, including the improvements in its vicinity, of upwards of £20,000, and, as a tribute to her husband's memory, bestowed upon it the name of Williamfield. The old name, however, clung to the place; and when her son, James Ogilvy Fairlie, became the proprietor, that name was restored. This gentleman's first wife was a daughter of Macleod of Macleod, and his second a daughter of Mr Houison Craufurd of Craufurdland. Coodham became the property of W. H. Houldsworth, Esq., M.P. for Manchester, in 1871, and he has at great expense improved both the estate and house, enlarging the latter, and adding in the rear of the splendid conservatory a beautiful chapel, in which divine service is celebrated by an incumbent according to the Anglican ritual. The services, open to the public of the vicinity, are attended by some of the neighbouring gentry. There is also a burial-place close by, in which a son of Mr Houldsworth's who died young has been interred. In front of the house there is an artificial lake, upwards of a quarter of a mile in length, in which there is an island planted with trees and shrubs. Here water-fowl, both domesticated and wild, may be seen swimming in abundance. The estate is finely wooded, and for the most part walled round; the pillared gateway and lodge on the Ayr road are in keeping with the massive yet elegant mansion within; and, on the whole, few finer places will be met with in the course of a long day's journey.

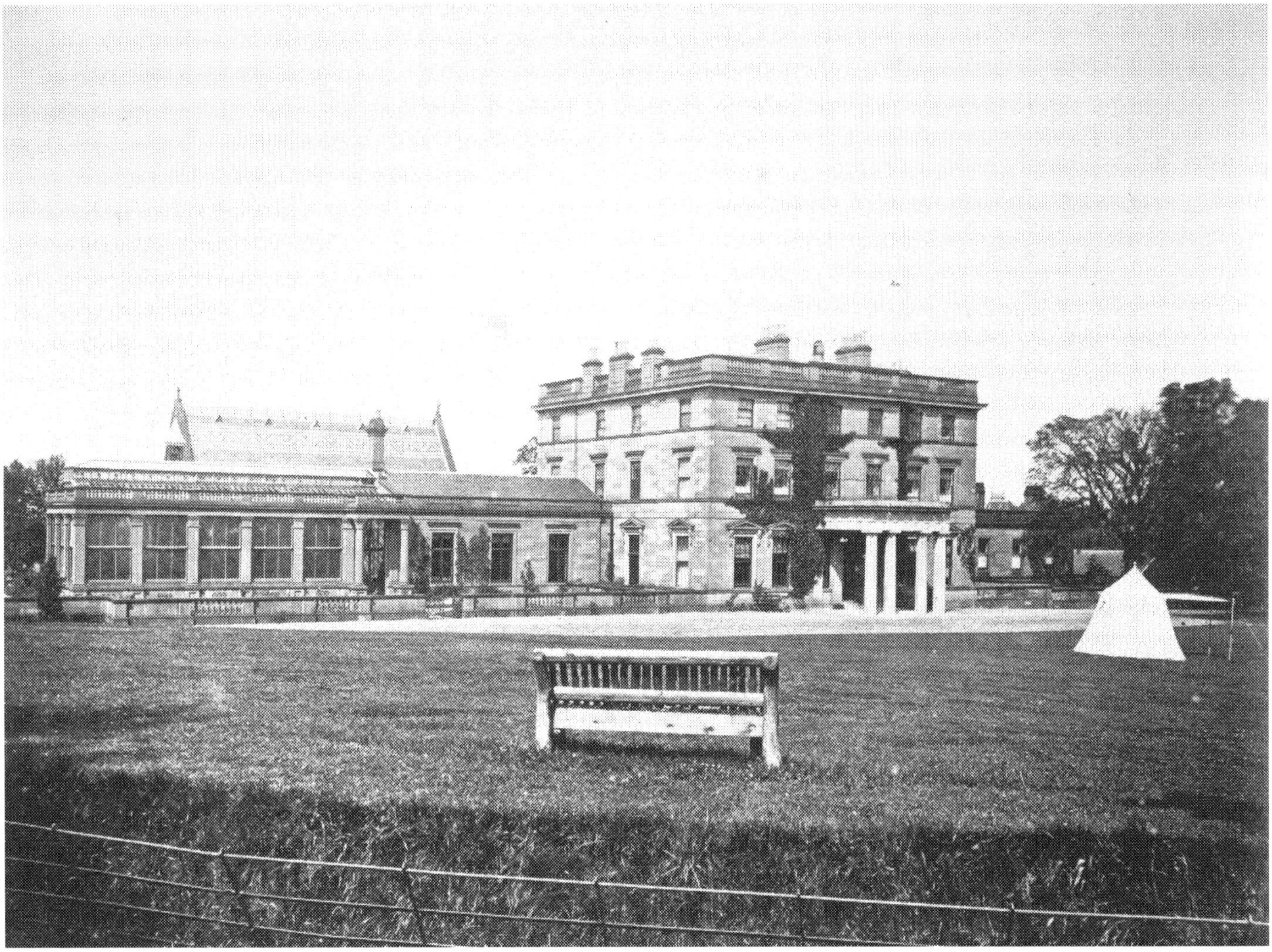

CORWAR.

THE Dhuisk, or Black-water, one of the two chief streams which wind their way through the parish of Colmonell, intersects a tract of country which was within living memory a dreary and desolate waste. About fifty years ago a revolution began to be wrought by a spirited proprietor, Rigby Wason, Esq. of Mayfield, under whose improving hand the bleak moorlands were transformed with almost magical swiftness into fruitful valleys. It is estimated that fully 2000 acres of heathery moor and 200 of deep moss have been reclaimed, and now yield excellent pasturage. In 1838 he commenced the erection of a new and more spacious mansion; and this was the origin of Corwar. It is therefore a house commemorating a beneficent work, which has at once enriched and beautified the district. Mr Wason was an active politician, and the writer of many pamphlets advocating important practical reforms. The estate, in 1883, was sold by the Trustees of the late Mr Wason to the Hon. Hugh Elliot, third son of the Earl of Minto.

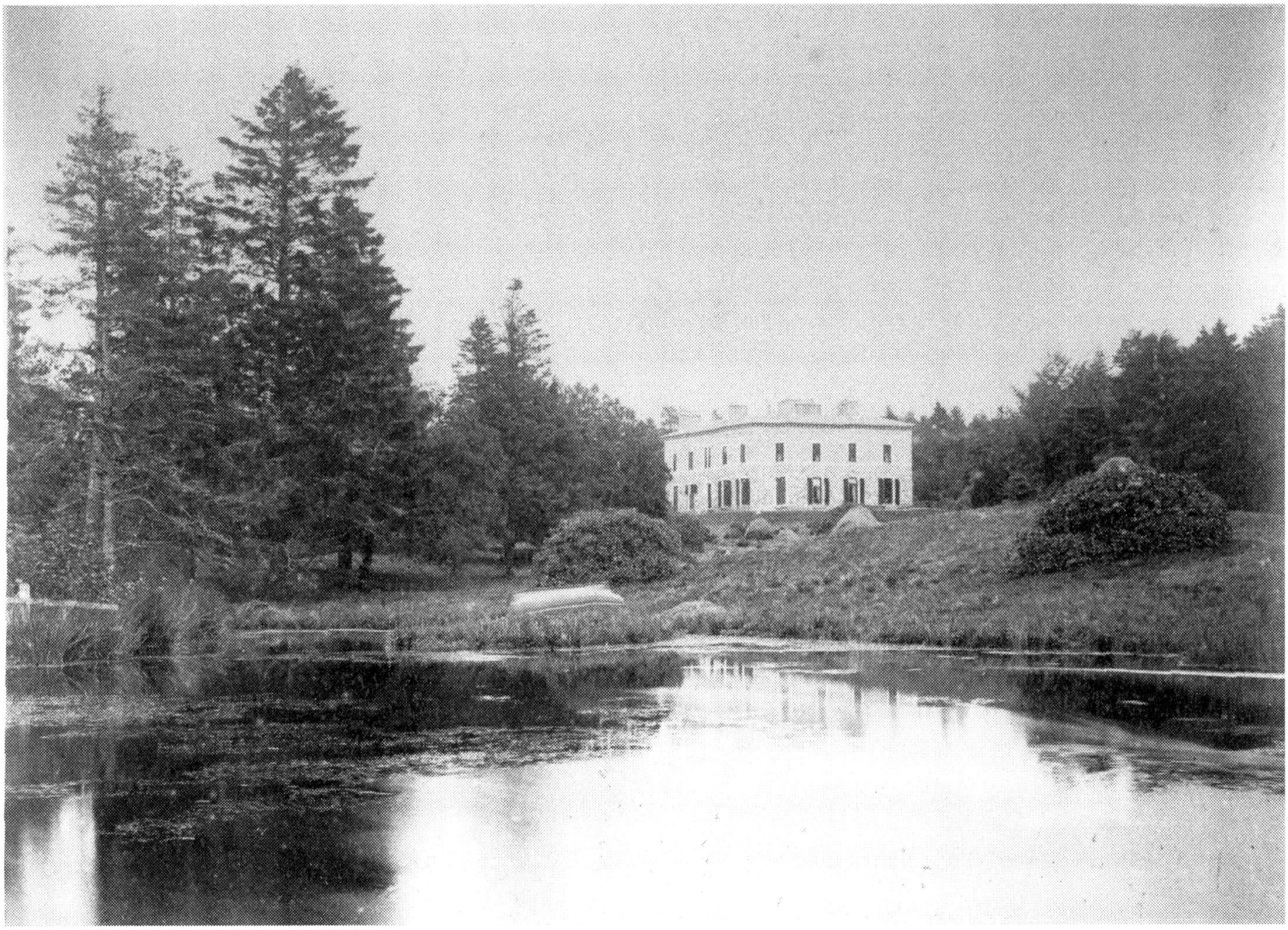

CRAIGIE HOUSE.

IN the fourteenth century, John Wallace of Riccarton, a powerful baron of Ayrshire, whose first wife was a daughter of the House of Eglinton, married the heiress in whom the line of the Lindsays of Craigie had ended; and in the beginning of the sixteenth century the descendant of this couple removed from the old castle of Craigie, whose stately ruins may still be seen in the parish of that name, to Newton Castle. There they dwelt till Sir Thomas Wallace, the fifth baronet, who succeeded in 1730, built Craigie House on the north bank of the river Ayr, a short distance above the town. The old castle of Newton, the seat of the family for upwards of two centuries, had become untenable, a portion of the fabric having been destroyed in a storm about the year 1700. The grandson of the man who reared the new mansion was obliged to part both with his estates and house in 1783, when they became the property of the Campbells, now represented by Mr Richard F. F. Campbell, the popular Member for the Ayr Burghs. His father, James Campbell of Craigie, an advocate at the Scottish Bar, was one of the distinguished band of Edinburgh Whigs which included Jeffrey and Cockburn. No mansion in the west country occupies a more pleasant site; and the park, adorned by many noble trees, can boast baronial dignity as well as sylvan charms.

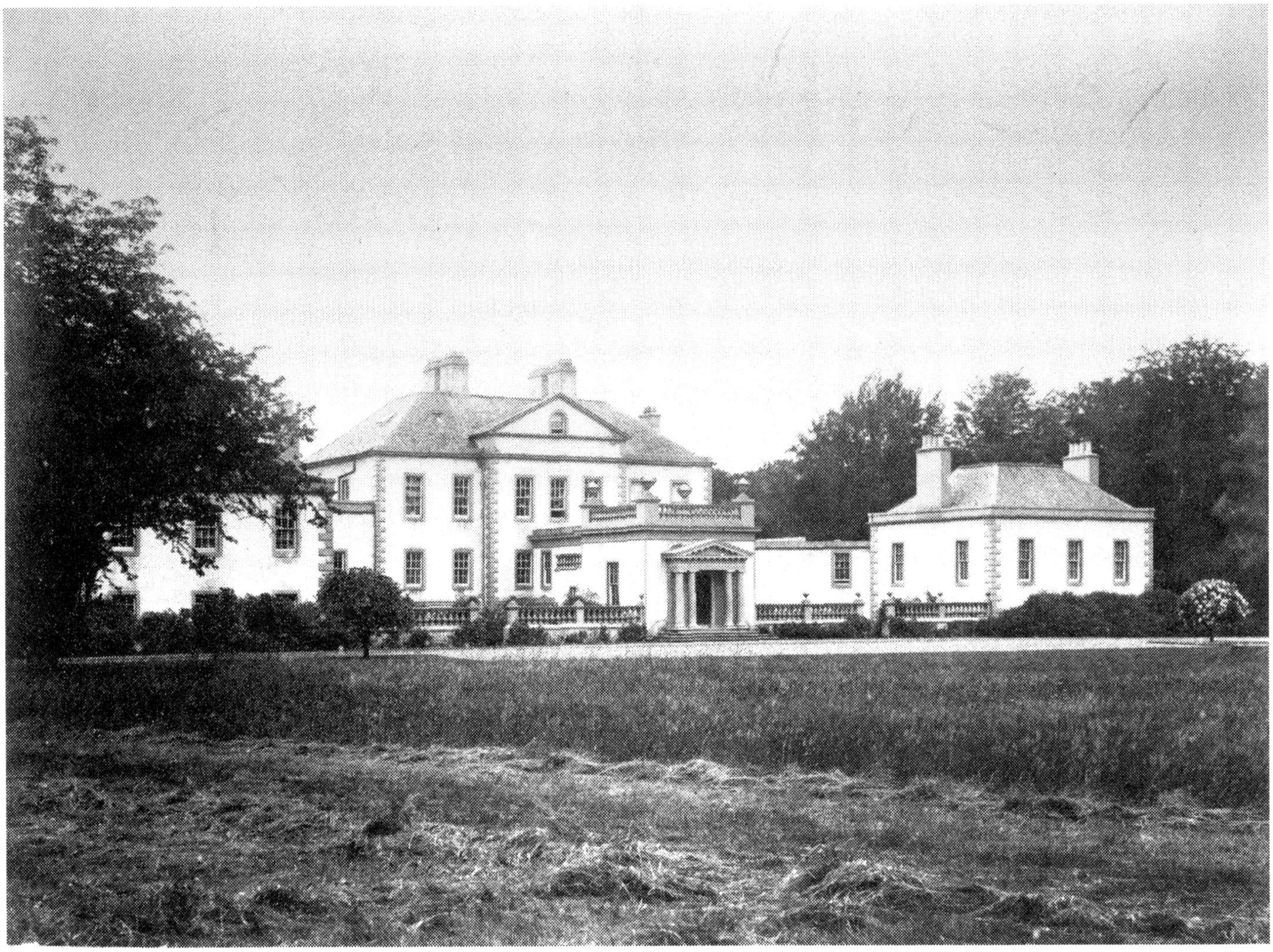

CRAUFURDLAND CASTLE.

OF all the descendants of the Anglo-Danish chief, Thorlongus of Northumberland, who was driven into Scotland by William the Conqueror, few have remained rooted so long on the same lands as the Craufurds of Craufurdland. The first of this tenacious branch of the wide-spread and opulent family of the Craufurds was a grandson of that Sir Reginald Craufurd, Sheriff of Ayrshire, who married the heiress of Loudoun in one of the early years of the thirteenth century; and it was in the reign of Alexander II that this founder of the Craufurdland family flourished. His grandson, the third laird, took part with his cousin, Sir William Wallace, in asserting the independence of Scotland. James I of Scotland made the head of the house a knight; this gallant gentleman had been sorely wounded at the siege of Crevelt in 1423, and was one of the captives released along with his King in the following year. Thomas Craufurd, a scion of this family, represented Glasgow in the Convention of Estates, in 1578. A son of the house was secretary to Mary of Guise, and subsequently to Mary Queen of Scots. The father of this royal favourite had fallen at Flodden. It was the Laird of Craufurdland who attended the last Earl of Kilmarnock on the scaffold - an act of friendly fidelity for which he was degraded to the bottom of the army list. Elizabeth Howieson Craufurd, who died in 1823, united in her own person the representation not only of this ancient family, but also of that of the historic Howiesons of Braehead, which had always been in the male line, till the former came to her mother and the latter to herself. Her son, a noted lay leader on the Free Church side at the time of the Disruption, waited with a silver basin of rose-water upon George IV at the banquet given to his Majesty by the city of Edinburgh - an act of service enjoined in the original grant of Braehead to the Howiesons by James I of Scotland, who had been beholden to the worthy farmer upon whom he bestowed the estate.

Situated on the brow of a steep bank overlooking Craufurdland Water, and surrounded by rich woodlands, with a lovely little loch lying at its foot, the "fair bulding weill planted," which Timothy Pont admired in an early year of the seventeenth century, is now much more attractive. The ancient tower, said to have been built before the days of the Conqueror, had various additions made to it by successive proprietors, all in good keeping with the original fortalice; and the central portion, erected in the present century by the grandfather of the present owner, is a noble piece of Gothic, harmonising at once with the older parts and with the sylvan witchery of the scene.

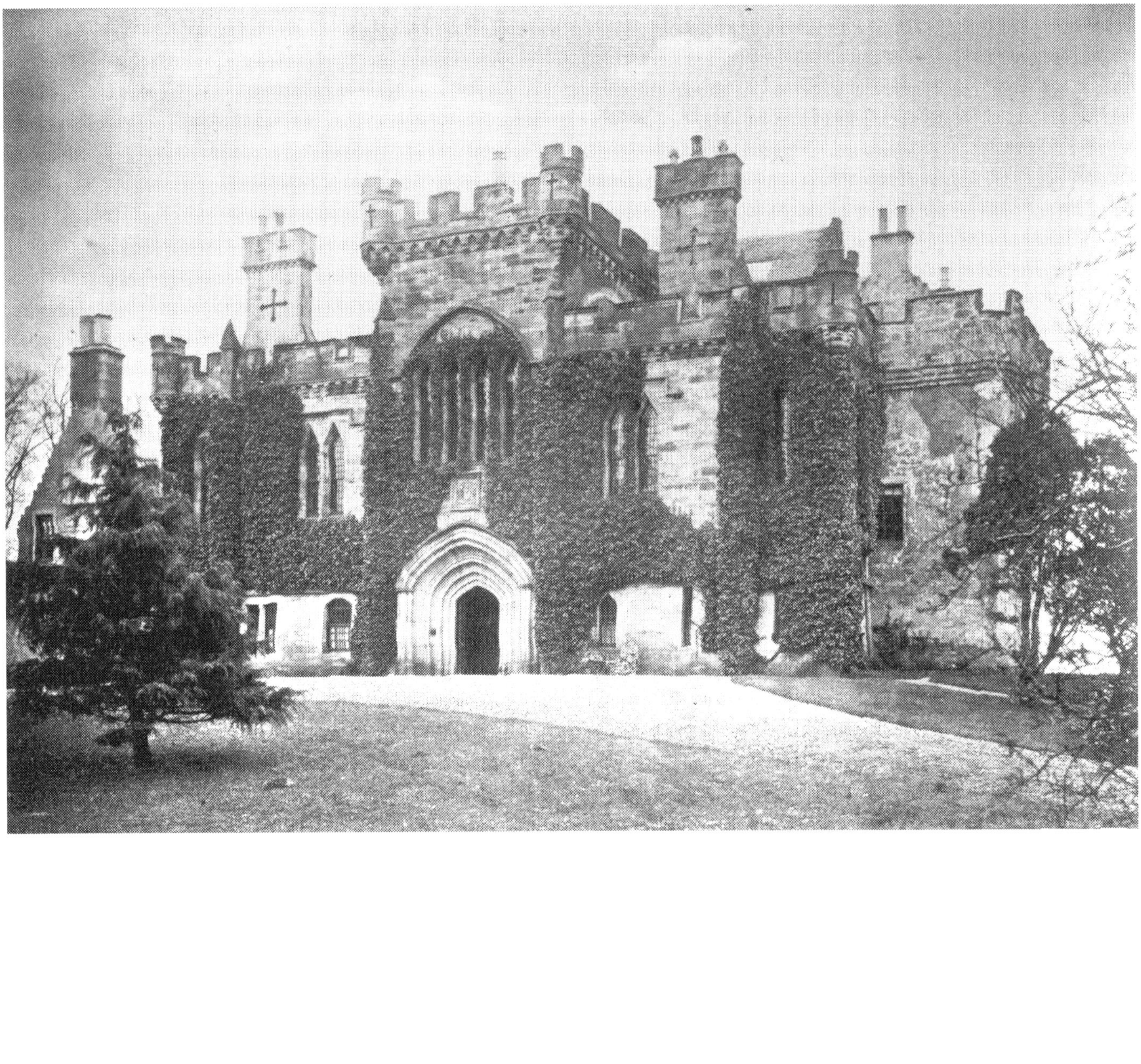

CROSBIE CASTLE.

THERE are five ancient castles in the parish of West Kilbride, all rich in historic associations; but the one that attracts to itself the keenest interest of every patriotic heart is the quaint old-world dwelling of Crosbie, which lies embosomed among fine old woods about a mile to the east of the village. In some instances the traditions relating to the first heroic name in the national history are not beyond a suspicion of the mythical; but there can be no question that this old house was one of the homes of Sir William Wallace - the haven where, in the stormiest days of his troubled life, he found shelter with his uncle, Reginald Craufurd. It was to this castle that the nephew rode back from Kingcase for the bond of peace lying in the charter-chest on that fateful morning of the "Blae Parliament" at Ayr, which was laden with so much bloody treachery, and also with the most momentous issues both for Wallace and his suffering country. Blind Harry has vividly described the events of the day that witnessed the ruthless slaughter by the English of the native leaders, and which closed with the fierce revenge taken by Wallace to the burning of the Barns of Ayr. The Craufurds of Crosbie were immediate descendants from the Loudoun stock of the same name. They rendered memorable service to King Alexander III. at the battle of Largs, and received rich rewards from the king for their faithfulness. The traditional couplet records that

"They had Draffen, Methwein, and rich erth Steuinstone, Cameltoune, Knockawart, and fair Low-o-doune."

Reginald Craufurd of Auchenames - probably a son of Wallace's uncle - is witness to a charter by Robert the High Steward in 1358. Robert Craufurd was the husband of Margaret Douglas, sister to that Master of Angus who married the widow of James IV; and either he, or a succeeding head of the house, fell at Flodden. A sister of Bishop Burnet became the wife of William Craufurd; and the great-grand-daughter of Sir Robert Walpole was the mother of the present proprietor. John Craufurd of Kilbirnie sat as Member for Ayrshire from 1693 until he was created Viscount Garnock in 1703; and Patrick Craufurd of Auchenames and Crosbie occupied a similar position from 1741 till 1754. John Craufurd of Drumsoy and Auchenames, the elder son of the latter, was Member for Old Sarum in 1768, for Renfrewshire from 1774 till 1780, and for Glasgow Burghs from 1780 till 1790. He was the intimate friend and associate of Fox, and received his share of abuse for his fidelity to the cause of that statesman. The present Laird of Auchenames and Crosbie, Edward Henry John Craufurd, was Member for Ayr Burghs from 1852 till 1874. Under a recent re-grant of arms and supporters, he is recognised by the Lord Lyon as head of the Craufurd family.

The tower of Crosbie which Pont describes was partly taken down and rebuilt after the visit of the old topographer, and when undergoing some still more recent repairs it narrowly escaped destruction by fire; latterly it has been used as a shooting lodge, and it is now let to a tenant. The family possess an elegant cottage residence in the immediate vicinity of the ancient Castle of Portencross, and that picturesque ruin is also their property, having (together with the Ardnele and Portencross estate on which it stands) been acquired in 1737 by Patrick Craufurd of Auchenames and Crosbie from Lord Kilmarnock, who suffered in 1745. On the beach close by it may be seen a cannon removed from one of the large ships of the Spanish Armada, which was-wrecked upon the shore of West Kilbride in 1588.

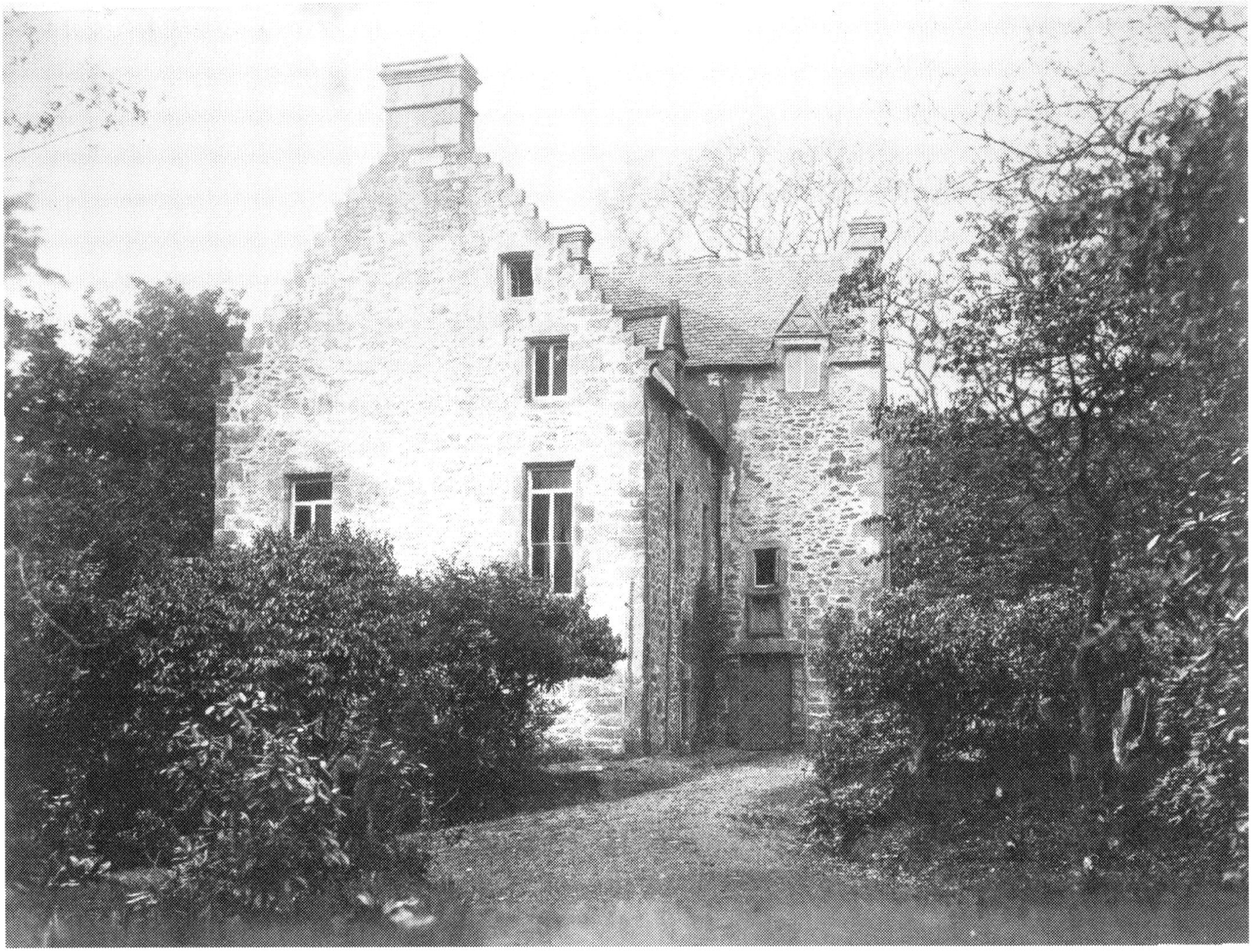

CULZEAN CASTLE.

THE picturesque coast-line south of Ayr, as well as the country lying behind that rocky rampart, is studded with memorials of the ancient and illustrious house whose ascendancy in feudal times over that region of Scotland is indicated in the old rhyme:

"'Twixt Wigton and the town of Ayr,
Portpatrick and the Cruives of Cree,
Nae man need think for to bide there
Unless he court Saint Kennedie." *

Dunure Castle, a massive ruin with a fishing hamlet nestling at its feet, was the original seat of these "Kings of Carrick." Cassillis House, on the banks of the Doon, was a later abode indicative of progress in refinement; though it is true that if the savage stronghold by the sea has its gruesome story about the roasting of the Commendator of Crossraguel Abbey by Earl Gilbert, the tragic incidents recorded in the ballad of *Johnnie Faa* are assigned by tradition to Cassillis House, and an Earl who, while assiduous in his attendance at the Assembly of Divines at Westminster, was unkindly as well as imprudently neglectful of his spouse. Both of these stories however, must be taken *cum grano salis*; the Commendator was no doubt roughly handled to make him disgorge a part of the church property in his care, but the roasting is questionable. As for the legend of the Countess of Cassillis and her gipsy lover, it has been distinctly disproved. But there can be no question that in the course of the nearly seven hundred years in which this family have dominated Carrick, it has produced many notable men. Sir James Kennedy married a daughter of Robert III. Gilbert, the third son of the first baron, and a grandson of the King's daughter, wrote *The Praise of Age*, and was held in high esteem as a poet by his distinguished contemporaries and friends, Dunbar and Lindsay. Gilbert, the second Earl of Cassillis, was a man of fine gifts; and it was his son Quintin, Abbot of Crossraguel, who held the famous three days' disputation with John Knox at Maybole. Gilbert, the third Earl, on the other hand, assisted in furthering the Reformation; and it was as his lordship's guest at Cassillis that George Buchanan wrote his deadly satire against the Franciscans. The sixth Earl was still more distinguished as a friend of Protestantism; it was his daughter who became the wife of Bishop Burnet.

Earl David, who built Culzean Castle about 1777, had the merit of rearing a residence worthy of a family history like this. For situation there are few, if any, castles in the three kingdoms that can be said to surpass it. Seated on the verge of a great basaltic cliff, a hundred feet in height and almost perpendicular, overhanging the sea, it commands an extensive sweep of prospect, with a distance singularly diversified. In front lies the picturesque island of Arran, the gem of the Clyde, with the Holy Isle of St Molios guarding one of its nearest bays; to the right the view stretches to the very head of the firth, embracing the verdant isles of Cumbrae and Bute, and terminating in the mountains of Argyll; to the left the Atlantic opens between the Mull of Kintyre and the distant coast of Ireland; while the line of the horizon is intersected by the majestic Ailsa Craig, sitting like a sentinel in mid-ocean, from which the chief of the Kennedies derives his title as a British peer. When Dr Stoddart, a writer of taste familiar with the British Islands, visited the spot in the closing year of the last century, he declared it to be, beyond comparison, the noblest coast view he had ever beheld; adding that Culzean Castle itself was "a suitable accompaniment to such a view."

The house is a modern imitation, by Robert Adam, of the Gothic style; it presents along the verge of a precipice a range of lofty castellated masses that harmonise most admirably with the rocky site, the outline of the building being well varied with round towers and angular projections, while subordinate masses are formed by the offices and other detached buildings. The high grounds are clothed with plantations, chiefly of fir, the tree that most befits such a scene; underneath the Castle the bold and massy rocks are penetrated by deep caverns, six in number, which used to be peopled by the popular imagination with supernatural beings, as is attested in the *Halloween* of Burns. On the landward side, and immediately below the Castle, are the gardens belonging to the old house of Culzean, formed out of rock into three terraces; upon whose walls are planted a rich variety of shrubs and trees, some of which are seldom found growing in the open air. The policy extends to about 700 acres, and is interspersed with many fine old plantations. The original castle of Culzean was built by Sir Thomas Kennedy, younger son of Gilbert, third Earl of Cassillis, who was murdered in 1602 at the instigation of Mure of Auchindrane. This tragic story is fully related in Pitcairn's *Criminal Trials*, and it forms the subject of Sir Walter Scott's drama of *Auchindrane; or, The Ayrshire Tragedy*.

*This is the version quoted by Sir Walter Scott; but the traditional form of the lines current in the locality, and probably the authentic version, runs thus:-
"'Twixt Wigton and the toun o' Ayr,
And laigh doun by the Cruives o' Cree,
Nae man shall get a lodging there
Unless he court the Kennedy."

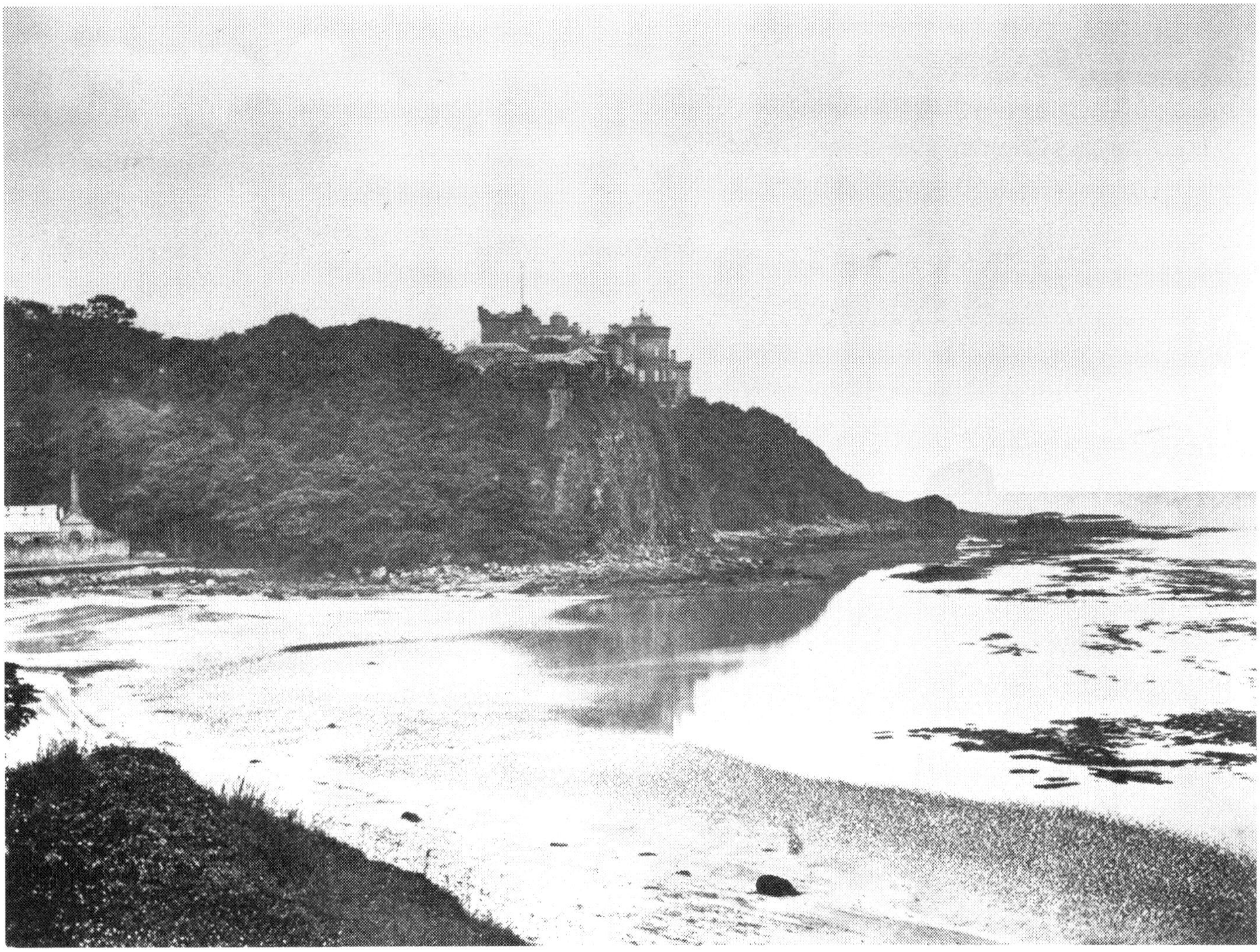

DALJARROCK.

THE estate and mansion-house of Daljarrock are situated near the river Stinchar, and about three miles from the village of Colmonell. The house was built about the middle of last century, and occupies a well-chosen site, which is completely sheltered by the surrounding trees, many of which are of considerable age. The larger portion of the estate consists of arable land. It comprises 1927 acres, and was purchased from R. T. Kennedy, Esq., in 1875, by Captain Hamilton of Pinmore, the present proprietor.

Though there is no special story connected with Daljarrock, it is placed in the midst of a country teeming with historic memories. The ancient Castle of Craigneil, in the neighbourhood, dates back to the thirteenth century, and is still pointed out as one of the hiding-places of Robert Bruce, whilst he was wandering as a homeless fugitive through Carrick and Galloway. The ruined towers of Knockdaw, Carleton, and Pinwherry preserve the recollection of feudal days; whilst there are many memorials of the "Killing times " amongst the Covenanters to be found in the kirkyards of the district. The principal mansions in the vicinity are Pinmore, Corwar, and Knockdolian, views of which are to be found in this volume.

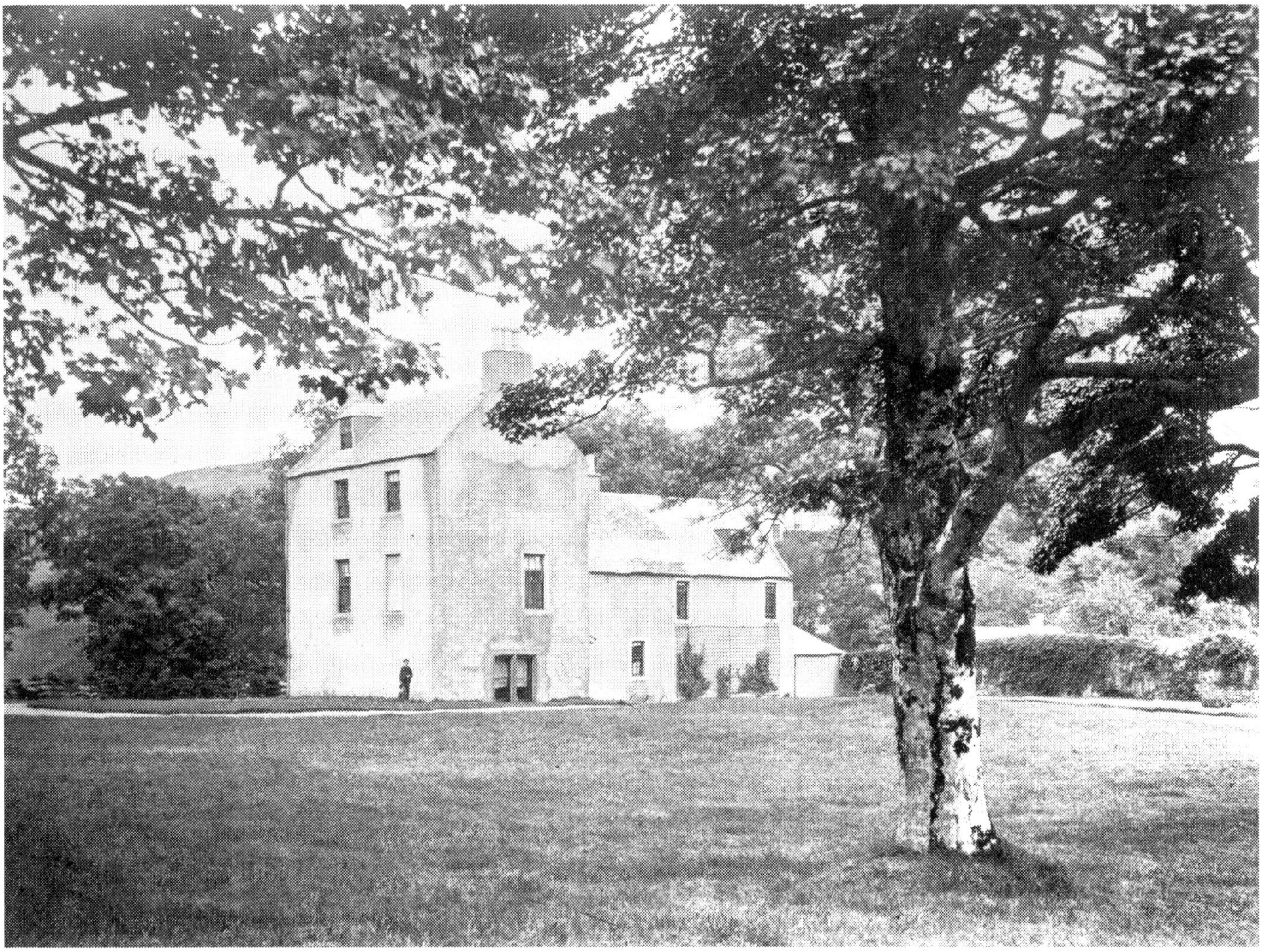

DALQUHARRAN.

THERE is reason to believe that the House of Bargany was the senior branch of the Kennedys; and the Dalquharran family, originally of Kirkhill, in the parish of Colmonell, was derived from the ancient stock which includes among its illustrious women the Princess Mary, daughter of Robert III, who became the wife of Sir Gilbert Kennedy of Dunure. Sir Thomas Kennedy of Kirkhill, who fought at Worcester, was the immediate ancestor of another Sir Thomas, who became Lord Provost of Edinburgh, and who acquired the estates of Dalquharran, Girvanmains, and Dunure. His son was a Baron of Exchequer, who before receiving that appointment had been advocate to Queen Anne, and whose brother Francis, his successor, was the friend and companion in exile of the Chevalier. Thomas, the son of this Francis, and a man distinguished for his public spirit, was the builder of the new mansion of Dalquharran, and also of the harbour of Dunure - the latter a project which involved an enormous expenditure, but unfortunately failed to realise the purpose of its founder. This enthusiastic improver was succeeded by his son, Thomas Francis Kennedy, who was admitted a member of the Scottish Bar in 1811, and who represented the Ayr Burghs from 1818 to 1834. Having held office in several Liberal Ministries, he was chosen a member of the Privy Council in 1837, and appointed paymaster of the Civil Service in Ireland, 1837-50. The active associate of Cockburn, Jeffrey, and the other distinguished Whig leaders in Edinburgh in the early years of the century, he outlived them all, and retained to the very last the warmest interest in public affairs, and especially in the political and social advancement of his native country. In one of the closing years of his life he published a volume of his correspondence with Cockburn, which throws a flood of light on the important public events with which he was personally associated. He married the only daughter of Sir Samuel Romilly, the distinguished law reformer, and survived till 1879; and their only son, Francis-Thomas Romilly Kennedy, born in 1842, is the present proprietor. The old Castle of Dalquharran, a ruin though still very entire, is pleasantly situated on the margin of the Girvan, the stream that flows through the richly-wooded valley from which Dailly parish derives its name; it is a stately tower, which Abercrombie, writing about 1686, declared to be the best house in a district that is peculiarly rich in noble mansions. In its immediate vicinity is the still more splendid house erected by Thomas Kennedy about a hundred years ago, and which is one of the most massive specimens of domestic architecture to be seen in the district of Carrick, and added to in 1881 by F. T. R. Kennedy.

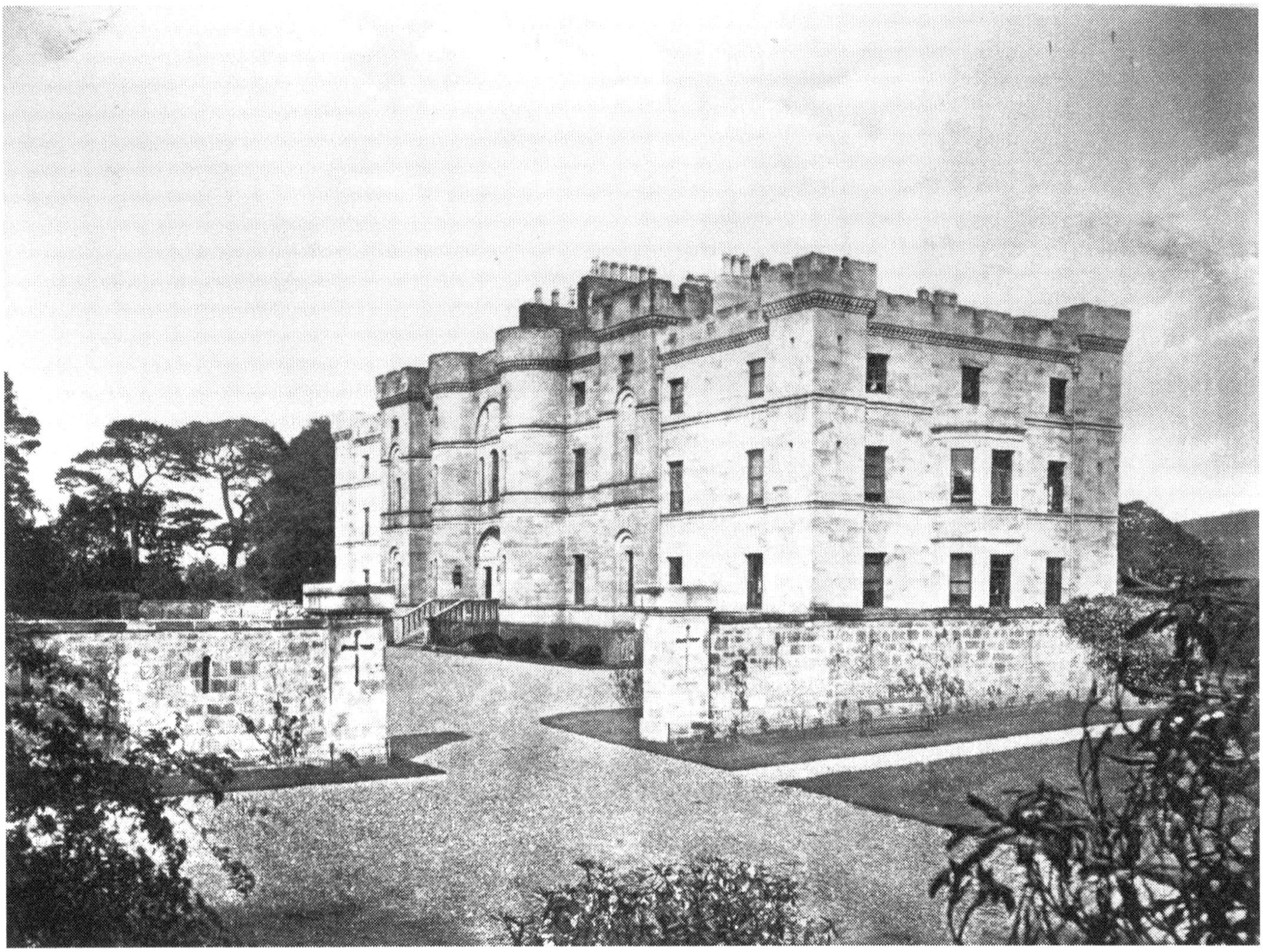

DUMFRIES HOUSE.

DUMFRIES HOUSE, one of the seats of the Marquess of Bute, is in the parish of Old Cumnock, on the left bank of the Lugar Water. It was built in 1754-1759 by William Dalrymple, fourth Earl of Dumfries, and has come to the present Marquess of Bute as heir to that earldom. The architects of the building were John Robert, and James Adam; the plans prepared by them being still preserved at Dumfries House. The following docquet is written at the foot of the elevation of the south or principal front: "This is the elevation referred to by contract betwixt the Right Honble. the Earl of Dumfries and Jno. Robt., and Jas. Adam, architects, subscribed by them at Edinburgh, 24th April 1754, and by the Earl of Dumfries at Leiffnorris, 16th May 1754." Signed, "Dumfries, Jno. Robt., and Jas. Adam." From this it would appear that the architects were also contractors for the building. It is built of a particularly close-grained sandstone of fine quality, and is remarkable as a good specimen of masonry. The corners and carvings are still as clear and well defined as the day they were finished. Amongst the treasures which the building contains, special mention is made of a very fine old tapestry with which the drawing-room is hung, and which is said to have been presented to one of the Earls of Dumfries by Louis XIV of France. Within the policies of Dumfries House the ruins of the ancient Castle of Terringzean are still to be seen, and though it shows faint traces of either strength or opulence, the fortalice has given a sub-title to the Earls of Loudoun for many generations. The present Marquess of Bute has a double claim upon this locality, since his mother was a daughter of Flora Muir, Countess of Loudoun and Baroness of Terringzean.

The former house, destroyed after the building of the present mansion, was situate near the existing stables, where the foundations yet remain. This was probably the site of the "Ward of Lochnorris."

The estate upon which Dumfries House stands was originally called Leifnorris or Lochnorris, and belonged to a branch of the Craufurds of Loudoun in 1440. This family held the estate continuously until it was purchased by William, second Earl of Dumfries, in 1635. At that period the residential mansion was a tower, called the Ward of Lochnorris, which stood on the estate, but no signs of its location are now visible. It had possibly fallen into ruins before the property came into the possession of the Earls of Dumfries. The Craufurds of Lochnorris played an important part in the history of their day, and were connected with the leading Ayrshire families of the time, participating in the most important political movements of the period. Their power in the district declined after the Earl of Dumfries purchased their property, and their descendants can be traced with difficulty even in the lands over which they ruled.

The earldom of Dumfries had a very chequered existence. The first earl was descended from Sir Robert Crichton of Sanquhar, who was summoned as Lord Crichton to the Parliament of 1485. The story of the sixth Lord Crichton forms one of the romances of the peerage. This nobleman, whilst on a visit at Lord Norrey's seat in Oxfordshire (Rycott) about 1605, lost his eye in fencing with one John Turner, a master of the science of defence, which so enraged him against Turner that he laid elaborate plans for his destruction. His machinations were repeatedly foiled, but he at length succeeded in procuring an assassin called Carlyle to take the life of his enemy in cold blood. For this crime Carlyle and a companion-in-guilt were tried, convicted, and executed; and as Lord Crichton of Sanquhar was deeply implicated in this tragedy, he was brought to trial and ultimately hanged on a gibbet erected in Great Palace Yard, before the gate of Westminster Hall, in June 1622. The succession to the title reverted to the descendant of the second Lord Crichton, who was created first Earl of Dumfries in 1622. The title came into the Dalrymple family for a short time through the marriage of Penelope, daughter of the second Earl, with the second son of the first Earl of Stair; but it was ultimately settled by marriage in the family of the Stuarts of Bute, the present Marquess, John Patrick Crichton-Stuart, being the seventh Earl of Dumfries.

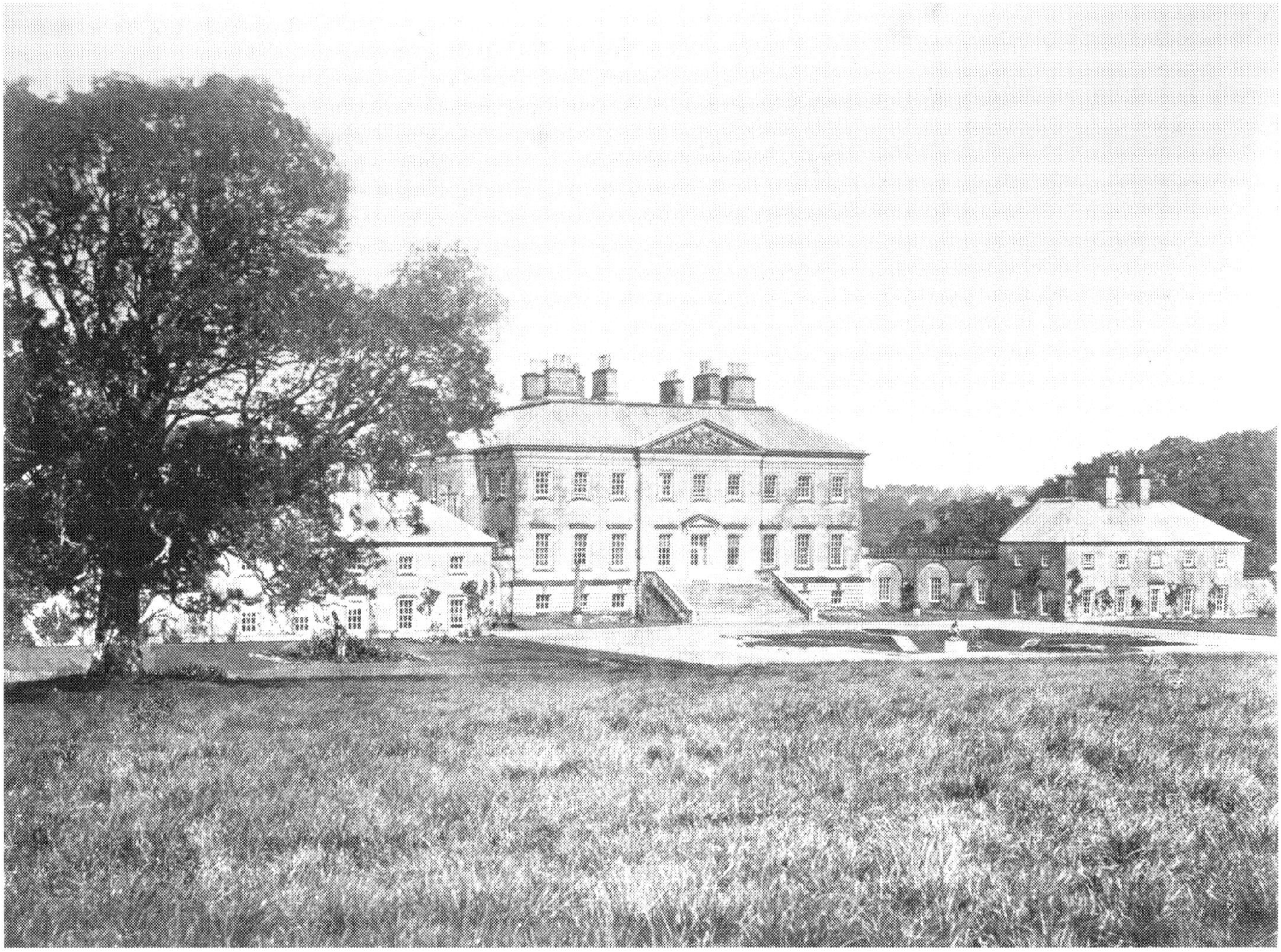

DUNLOP HOUSE.

THOUGH now a bare upland region, the lands of Dunlop were at one time covered with a great forest; and the huntsman to Godfred Ross, who held these lands under the De Morevilles, and in the reign of David II was Sheriff of Ayr, became the founder of the family of Dunlop of that Ilk. The house of the old huntsman probably stood near, if not on the site of the ancient Castle, which Pont pictures as fortified with a deep fosse of water, and surrounded by luxuriant orchards. Over its hall door, on a stone that may now be seen above the inner door of the entrance-hall of the new mansion, there were the dates 1599 and 1601, with the armorial bearings of the family on a shield between. Pont tells us that the stronghold continued in his time to be called Hunthall, a reminiscence of the origin of the sturdy stock who flourished there for full five hundred years, making allowance for an interval in which they iost their hold, on account of their espousing the side of Baliol in the struggle for the Scottish crown. Neil Fitz-Robert de Dunlop signed the Ragman Roll in 1351. A daughter of the house became the wife of James Stuart, Sheriff of Bute, a great-grandson of Robert II. James Dunlop, though in 1614 he had married Dame Margaret Hamilton, daughter of one bishop and widow of another, resisted the attempts of Charles I to introduce Episcopacy, and was followed in this respect by his nephew, James, who suffered both fines and imprisonment for his attachment to the Presbyterian cause. That nephew's son, Alexander, paid still heavier penalties for his fidelity to conscience, being obliged to flee to America after the engagement at Bothwell Brig; and a son of this stanch Covenanter, Francis Dunlop, was one of the witnesses at the Union to the disposition of the Scottish Regalia in Edinburgh Castle, and served as lieutenant-colonel of a cavalry regiment raised against the Chevalier in 1715. The wife of his eldest son, a lineal descendant of a brother of Sir William Wallace, finds a place in literary history as the friend and correspondent of Robert Burns. The fifth of this lady's seven sons, General Dunlop, who served in the American War, in India, and under Wellington in the Peninsula during the campaign of 1811, was the representative of Kirkcudbright in three Parliaments, - 1812-1826; and his son, Sir John, who married the eldest daughter of the Earl of Rosebery, was Member for Ayrshire from 1833 till 1839, during the stormy period which followed the passing of the first Reform Bill. 'With the death in 1858 of his son Sir James, the second baronet, the title became extinct. It was Sir John who built the modern mansion in 1834. It is one of the finest examples in the county of the Old English style, and bears the unmistakable stamp of the genius of Thomas Hamilton, the architect to whom we also owe the classical gem erected on the banks of the Doon in memory of Burns. The little rivulet that flows past the mansion, called Clerkland Burn, divides the parish of Dunlop from that of Stewarton. On the death of the second baronet the place passed into the possession of Thomas Dunlop Douglas of Dunlop, who died in 1869, and was succeeded by his nephew, Thomas Douglas Cuninghame Graham, son of the late William C. C. Graham of Gartmore, the present possessor.

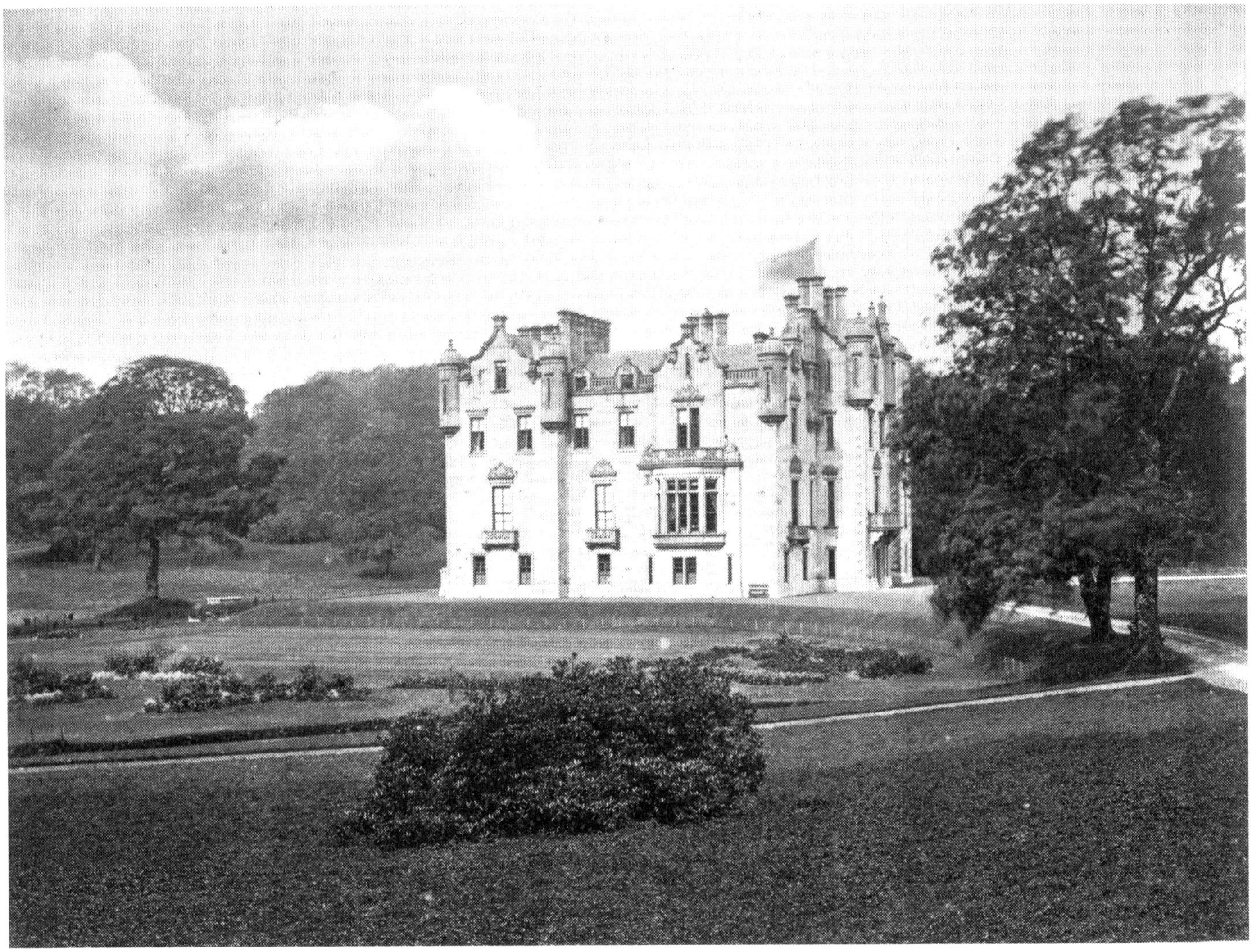

EGLINTON CASTLE.

FEW of our great historic families have held through the centuries a warmer place in the popular heart than that of Montgomerie. From the old ballad hero, Sir John, who took Hotspur captive with his own hands at Otterburn, and so won the niece of King Robert II for his bride, down to that thirteenth Earl who flashed upon our own century the light of all that was most gracious and poetic in the ancient chivalry, they were men of distinguished abilities and the most fervent patriotism. "The gude Schir Hew of Eglyntoun," lamented in the verse of Dunbar, was one of our earliest bards; Alexander, the sixth Earl, "Greysteel," with two gallant sons by his side, fought under the blue banner of the Covenant; Alexander, the tenth Earl, whose kindly countenance looks out upon us to-day from the canvas of Sir Joshua, was a leading pioneer of that agricultural revival, towards the close of the eighteenth century, which transformed the face of Scotland. In the happy periods of peace, as well as on the field of war, the men of this house came to the front; and at each successive epoch of the National History, they were identified in sympathy and effort with the common people. For well on to six hundred years Eglinton Castle has been the chief seat of this the most illustrious branch of the House of Montgomerie.

A stately baronial structure, second to few in Scotland for dignity, it has yet a cheerful and winsome look, with still more of beauty than of stateliness. The site has something to do with this, so have the noble trees in whose midst the building is embowered, as well as the waters of the Lugton, that flow past the rear of the Castle; but still more must the agreeable effect be ascribed to the genius of the unknown architect, to the soft grey tone of the walls and towers, and to the masses of ivy by which a portion of the structure is clothed. The whole presents a perfectness of pictorial effect, a complete unison, on which the eye rests with delight. Almost up to the very threshold sweeps the emerald turf; an iron-bound chestnut of enormous girth, which has braved the blasts of more than two hundred winters, casts its shadow across the broad carriageway nearly to the porch; the association of man's handiwork with nature is close and intimate, the one blending into the other without a single inharmonious note.

The Castle, as it now stands, was built by Earl Hugh, soon after his accession to the Earldom in 1796; and there is a tradition that the name of the architect was Paterson. It was originally intended to preserve a circular tower which stood in the centre of the old castle; to this the staircase was sacrificed; and though it was afterwards found necessary to remove the tower, the general plan remains unaltered. The central tower is 100 feet high, the smaller towers 70. Never, perhaps, was the style of the feudal fortress more happily combined with the light and conveniences of a modern dwelling. The porch was built by the father of the present Earl about thirty years ago. He also erected the iron bridge which spans the Lugton within a few yards of the Castle. Its parapet is a repetition of the pointed Gothic arch, surmounted by a battlement, and relieved in the centre with foliated pinnacles.

The entrance hall of the Castle contains six suits of armour, including two that were worn at the famous Tournament in the August of 1839, a futile attempt to revive the amusements of the age of chivalry, which cost its author a sum of not less than £40,000. Amongst the other objects of interest in the hall is a chair, made in 1818 from the oak roof of Alloway Kirk; it was in this chair Lord Eglinton sat when he presided at the Burns' Festival on the Banks of Doon in 1844, at which he gave thrilling utterance to the emotion awakened in the heart of "repentant Scotland" towards the Poet-farmer of Mossgiel. In the saloon, a circular apartment, into which several of the main rooms converge, the walls are draped with the banners of the knights who tilted at the Tournament. In the gentlemen's morning room are several family portraits, including one Raeburn; but the Castle is less rich in these on account of a grievous accident by which the portraits in the old Castle were destroyed by fire whilst the present edifice was being erected. The old portraits still extant are limited to the small collections which existed at Auchans, Skelmorlie, and other minor seats of the family, from which they were brought to Eglinton after the fire. One of these is a portrait of the Lady Montgomerie of Skelmorlie, a daughter of Douglas of Drumlanrig, whose beauty was celebrated in two sonnets by the author of *The Cherrie and the Slae*. The curtains in the large Drawing-room are made of damask from the pavilion of Lady Seymour, the Queen of Beauty at the Tournament; and in the north Drawing-room, besides a portrait by Reynolds of Lady Jean, the first wife of the eleventh Earl, there is a picture by Walter Severn of a Scene in Venice, said to represent Queen Victoria going to a masked ball. In the Dining-room there is a portrait of Mary Seaton, one of the "Four Maries" of the ballad, taken along with her parents when she was a child. A necklace which she got from her royal mistress is still in the possession of the Eglinton family, and is occasionally worn by the present countess. Another family portrait of interest in the same room is that of Susanna Kennedy, third wife of the ninth Earl, the greatest beauty of her day, to whom Allan Ramsay dedicated his *Gentle Shepherd* and who at 85 gave Dr Johnson a welcome at Auchans, which he regarded as one of the crowning honours of his life. This portrait represents her before marriage; in the Library there are other two portraits of the same notable woman, the first taken when she was a wife, the second when she was a widow. A head of Rubens, by himself, is the choicest of the artistic treasures in the Castle. The Library is specially rich in local literature; and in the same noble apartment which contains the books there are two magnificent pieces of silver plate, with representations of scenes at the Tournament-the one presented to the Earl by visitors, and the other by three hundred citizens of Glasgow. On the second story of the Castle there are six suites of bedrooms, which were furnished as they stand by the late Earl for the reception of five Duchesses who were all his guests at the same time.

The policies and gardens are the loveliest in that district of Scotland. They extend to 1346 acres, of which 624 are grassy glades, 650 plantations, 12 gardens, and 60 roads. Within the stone wall surrounding the park there is a drive of six miles; another drive, two miles in length, reminds the visitor of Versailles. The grounds were laid out, as we now see them, by Alexander, the tenth Earl, the agricultural reformer. The gardens were planned by Tweedie, an intelligent writer on landscape gardening, who finished them in 1801. The bowling-green, a little to the west of the Tournament Bridge, 190 feet long and 96 in breadth, is the finest. in Britain. The stables, built a hundred years ago, appear from the mason marks on some of the stones to have been constructed, in part at least, from the ruins of the neighbouring Abbey of Kilwinning. In a retired spot among the woods there is a marble monument, with a pathetic inscription, erected by Earl Hugh in memory of a little grandson, who died at the age of six; and in another nook, on the edge of the Lugton Water, is "Lady Jane's Cottage," built by Lady Jane Hamilton, an aunt of the late Earl, under whose care he was placed in boyhood; and who in that cottage was wont personally to train the peasant girls of the neighbourhood in domestic economy.

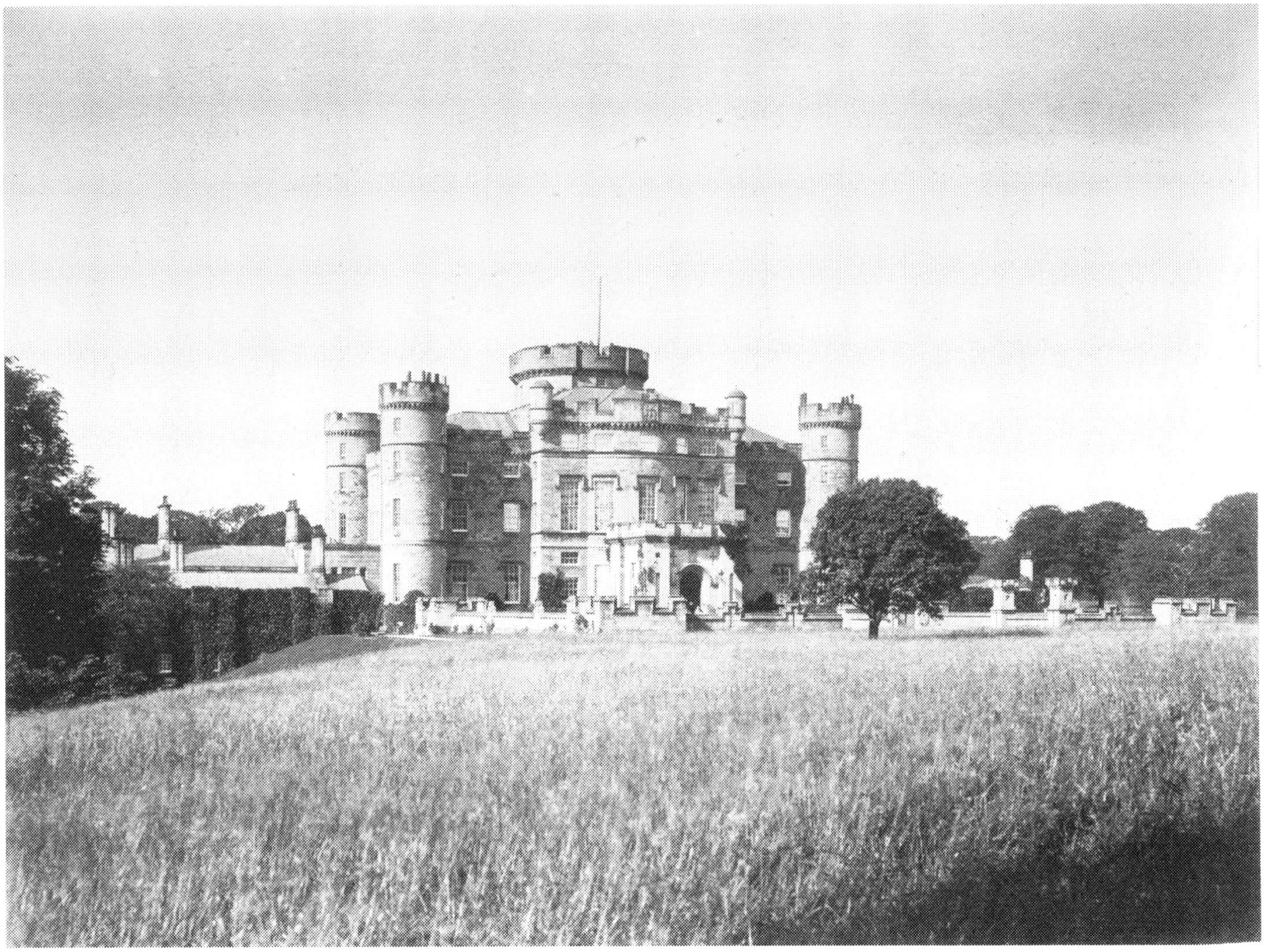

ENTERKINE.

IN the charming landscape which may be viewed to great advantage from the Bridge of Stair, one of the most striking objects is the mansion of Enterkine, standing out in fine relief from the massive woods in which it is embosomed. Next to the great House of Darnley, in which the Barony of Torbolton was vested from 1361 till the Reformation, one of the oldest families connected with this region was that of the Dunbars of Enterkine, who flourished in the first half of the seventeenth century, but whose property afterwards passed into the possession of a branch of the Cuninghames of Caprington. In 1830 it was acquired by John Bell, Esq., who for many years was one of the most active leaders of the political life of, Ayrshire, as well as in the local government of the county. From the records of the Enterkine Cuninghames, it appears that their representative in the years immediately preceding the Revolution of 1688 held the office of "furnisher of the News-Letter" to the burgh of Ayr - a post of greater dignity, it would thus appear, when the newspaper was weak than it became when the newspaper grew strong. He was succeeded, as he had also been preceded, in the post by the head of another Ayrshire house, Craufurd of Craufurdstone.

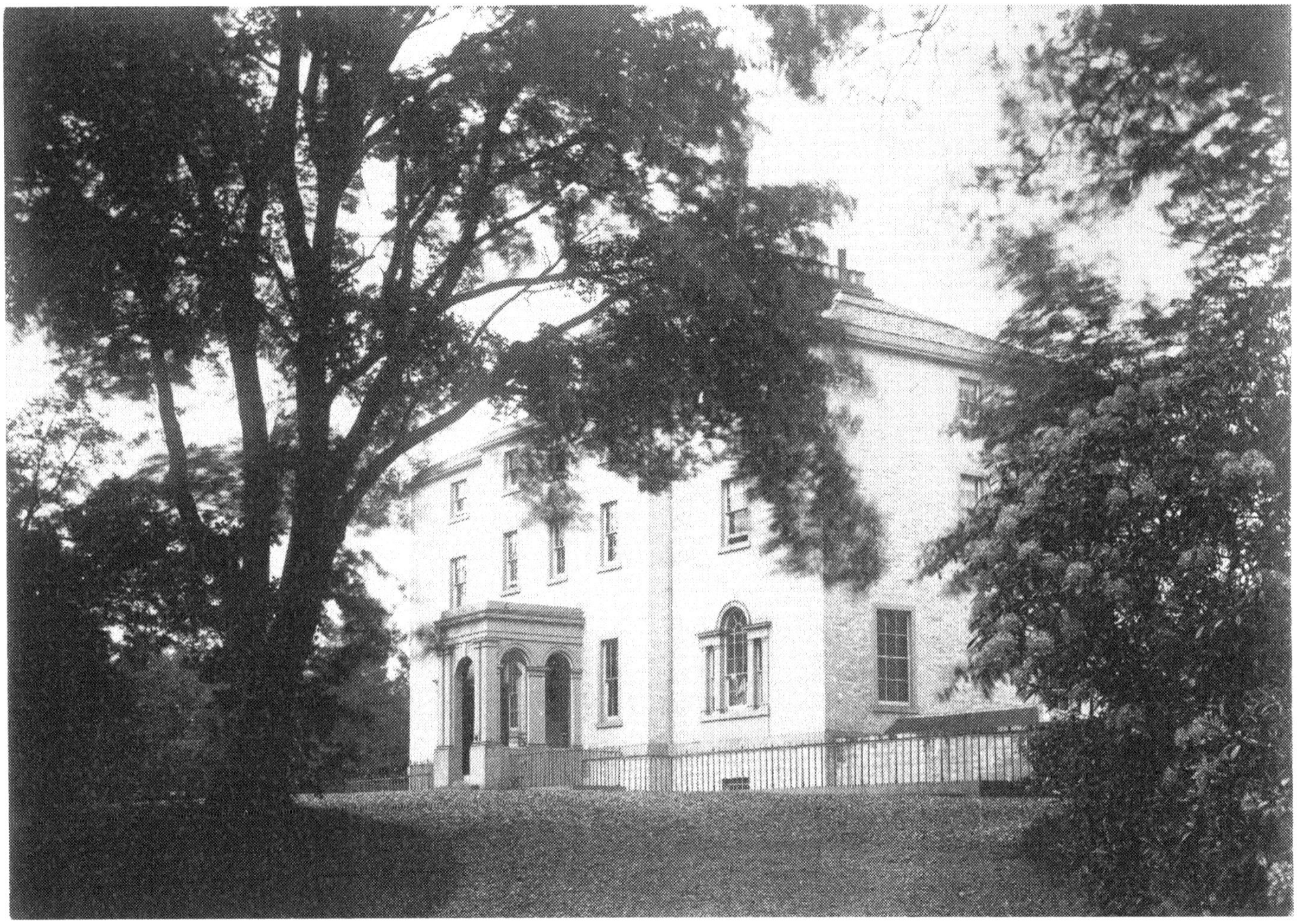

FAIRLIE HOUSE.

THE family of Fairlie of that Ilk is supposed to have belonged originally to the Rosses of Tarbet, and to have assumed the surname of Fairlie after the purchase of the estate so named on the shores of the Firth of Clyde. There are few traces of the members of this family to be found earlier than the sixteenth century; and the fact of the existence of distinct families of the name both in Aberdeenshire and at Berwick before this period has led to much genealogical confusion. The square tower of Fairlie Castle, the ruins of which are still to be seen near Largs, was described by Pont in 1608 as "a strong toure and werey ancient, beutified vith orchardes and gardins;" and we may hence conclude that the family had attained to considerable importance in the county before this time. The lands were sold to John Boyle of Kelburne, ancestor of the Earls of Glasgow, in 1650, and still belong to his descendants.

Thomas Fairlie settled at Irvine shortly after this time, and became progenitor of the Fairlies of Coodham and of Holms. Another branch of the same family, denominated Fairlies of Bruntsfield, from their possessions in Midlothian, came into Ayrshire about this period; and William Fairlie had acquired the lands of Little Dreghorn from the Fullartons before 1689. His son changed the name of this estate to Fairlie, and thus became Fairlie of that Ilk. He had sasine of the barony of Fairlie in 1704. His grand-daughter Margaret was married in 1741 to Sir William Cuninghame of Robertland; and the eldest son of this marriage, who succeeded to the title in 1781, assumed the additional surname of Fairlie. He is now represented by his great-grandson, Sir Charles Arthur Cuninghame-Fairlie, who is tenth baronet since 1630.

Fairlie House was built early this century by Sir William Cuninghame-Fairlie as a family seat. It stands on a gently-sloping bank near the water of Irvine, and is "an elegant, commodious, and remarkably well-constructed modern mansion." It is now occupied by Lieut.- Colonel Duncan Stewart.

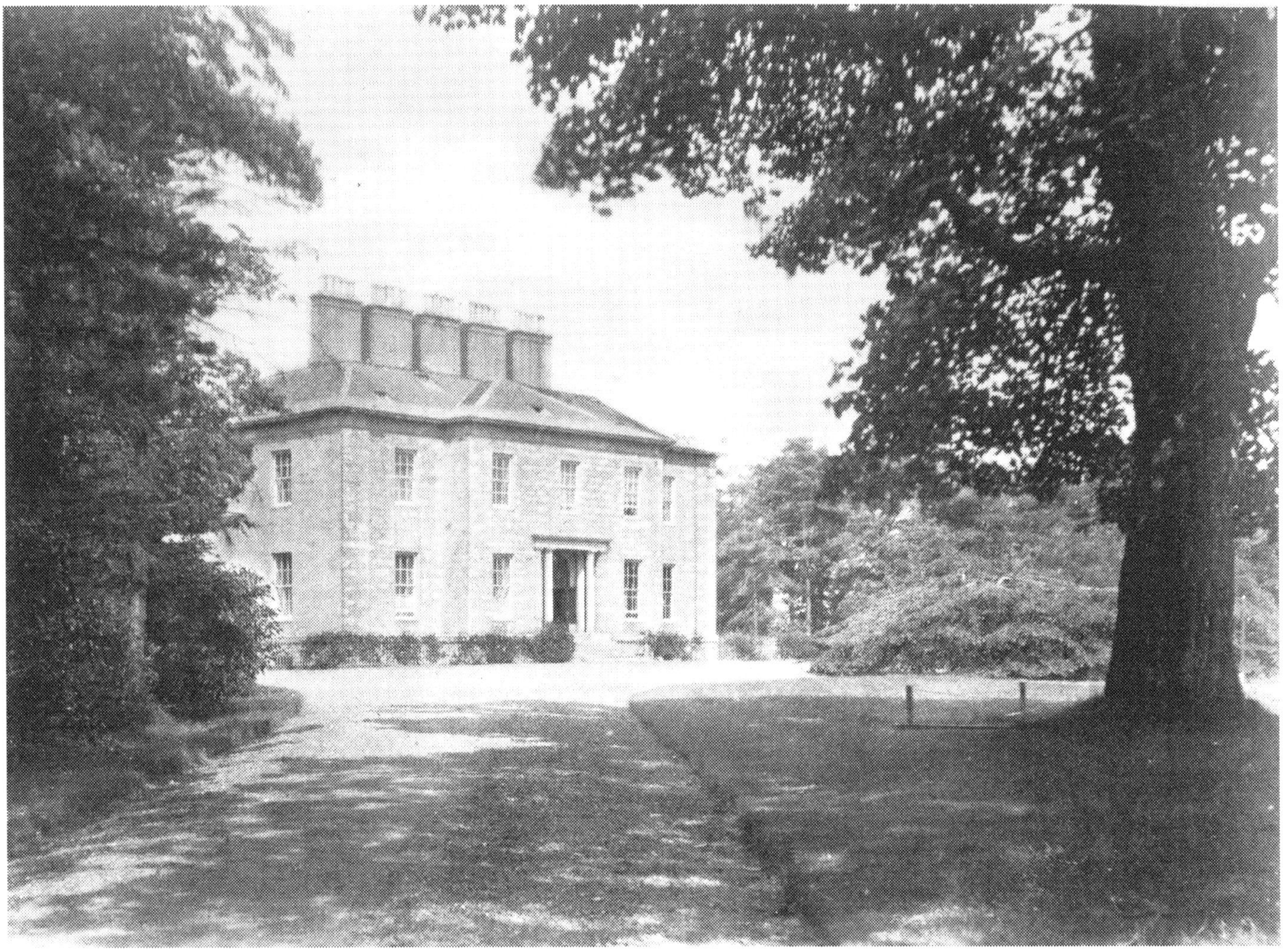

FULLERTON HOUSE.

THE estate and mansion of Fullarton are in the parish of Dundonald, a short distance eastward of the village of Troon. For many centuries the estate was in the possession of the Fullartons of that Ilk; but in, 1805 it was acquired by the third Duke of Portland, and has since that time formed the principal Scottish property of that family. The present mansion-house was built by William Fullarton in 1745, and was not unworthy to form the seat of one of the most ancient families in Ayrshire. For two hundred and fifty years before this time the Fullartons had lived at Crosby Place, which latterly became known as Fullarton House; but the new house of Fullarton far eclipsed it in splendour, as may be still judged by a comparison of the relics of the former mansion with the existing one. Considerable additions were made to the building by Colonel Fullarton, son of the original builder; and wings were added to the first structure and its whole plan altered after it came into the possession of the Duke of Portland. The approach has been re-constructed, and what was formerly the back of the house has been changed into the front, so as to make the principal windows look towards the Firth of Clyde and the Island of Arran.

It has been suggested that the name of Fullarton has been derived from the office of Fowler, probably held by some remote ancestor, whose house, or Fowlertoun, has been assumed from the territory as their name by his descendants. A similar origin is assigned to the family of the same name in Angus, one member of that race being required to supply Robert I with wild-fowl when he visited the Castle of Forfar. Apart from the traditional theory, it can be proved from existing documents that Alanus de Fowlartoun was in possession of the lands of Fullarton shortly before his death in 1280. From him the heritage descended, almost without intermission, from father to son until 1710, when William Fullarton, the architect of the mansion, succeeded his grandfather, George Fullarton, brother-german of his immediate predecessor. During this long period matrimonial alliances were made with some of the foremost Ayrshire families, including those of Wallace of Craigie, Blair of Blair, Mure of Rowallan, and Cuninghame of Cuninghame-head.

The Fullartons took a leading part in the political struggles of the seventeenth century in Scotland. James Fullarton of that Ilk, described as "Laird of Corsbie," sat as Member for Ayrshire in the Conventions of 1643-44 and 1648; was made head Sheriff of Ayr in 1645; and seems latterly to have cast in his lot with the Presbyterian party, and suffered for his adherence to it. Two of his sons were charged with having been present at Bothwell-Brig, but the accusation was not put to trial. One of the latter was the father of the Fullarton who built the existing mansion. The eldest son of William Fullarton was the first and last laird of that name who could claim this mansion as his birthplace. His mother was Barbara, daughter of William Blair of Blair; and he was born in 1754, five years before his father's death. He was educated at Edinburgh, and early showed a desire for travel, which he had many opportunities of encouraging. In 1775 he was appointed principal Secretary to the embassy of Lord Stormont - afterwards second Earl of Mansfield - at Paris. From this time onward his life was divided between the arduous labours alike of the senate and the field. His Parliamentary career was begun as Member for Plympton in 1779-80; he represented the Haddington burghs 1787-96, Horsham 1793-96, Ayrshire 1796-1802, and also in the following Parliament, until he was appointed Commissioner for the government of Trinidad in 1803. In 1780 he initiated his military services by raising the 98th regiment of infantry, which was afterwards honourably distinguished at China and the Punjaub; and in 1793 he organised the 23d Light Dragoons, - known as "Fullarton's Light Horse " - and the 10lst regiment of infantry. He made himself conspicuous as the prosecutor of General Picton, Governor of Trinidad, who was accused of putting a Creole girl to the torture, and after a protracted series of trials, lasting from 1804 till 1808, was declared not guilty, as the old Spanish law permitted the employment of judicial torture. Before this decision was announced, Colonel Fullarton's career was unexpectedly terminated. He died at London on 13th February 1808, aged fifty-four years. His services to science and agriculture have been generally acknowledged, and he was regarded as a munificent patron of literary genius. As he died without male issue, the representation of the family fell to his second cousin, Colonel Stewart Murray Fullarton of Bartonholm, who married his daughter Rosetta, and whose two sons succeeded him. The mansion and estate, as already mentioned, were purchased by the third Duke of Portland in 1805; and it was here that that nobleman introduced some of those improvements in agricultural draining which have been generally adopted since his time throughout Scotland.

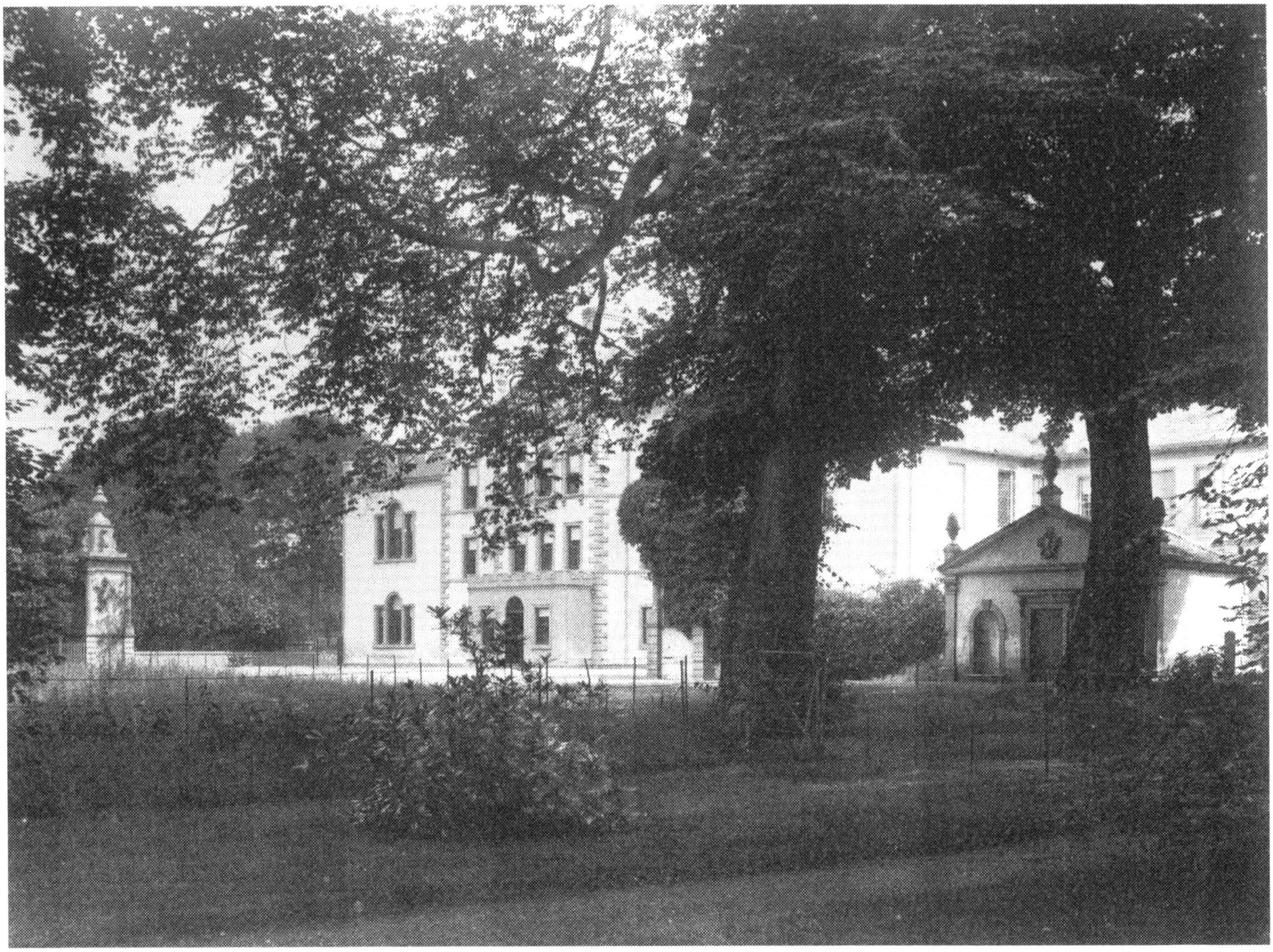

GARRALLAN HOUSE.

THE estate of Garrallan, which lies in the parish of Old Cumnock, can be traced to the possession of the Campbells of Loudoun in the middle of the sixteenth century. Sir Matthew Campbell of Loudoun, father of Sir Hugh, first Lord Loudoun, granted a charter of the lands of Garrallan in 1562 to Hew Campbell of Bogoroch, a scion of the family of Campbell of Shankston, and a near relative of the Loudouns. Hew Campbell died in 1602, and left the property to his eldest son and namesake. The latter was succeeded in 1648 by his grand-daughter, Margaret Campbell, who was married to George Douglas of Waterside, and whose son and grandson successively inherited the estate. Patrick Douglas, the last named, died in 1819, leaving one daughter, Jane, who married Hamilton Boswell, a descendant of the Auchinleck family. The father of the latter - John Boswell of Knockroon - had been compelled to part with his patrimony, in consequence of the disastrous failure of the Douglas & Heron Bank; and when Hamilton Boswell married the heiress of Garrallan, he assumed the additional name of Douglas. His eldest son, John Douglas-Boswell, succeeded to the estate on the death of his mother in 1862, but died without issue in the following year. The present proprietor is his brother, Patrick Charles Douglas-Boswell, Esq. of Garrallan.

Garrallan House is old and picturesque, and has been frequently added to. There are stones in the walls and gables bearing initials, coats of arms, and various dates from 1660 to 1868. The house is situated on rising ground, and commands an extensive view of the valley of the Lugar, the village of Auchinleck, and the beautiful woods surrounding Dumfries House.

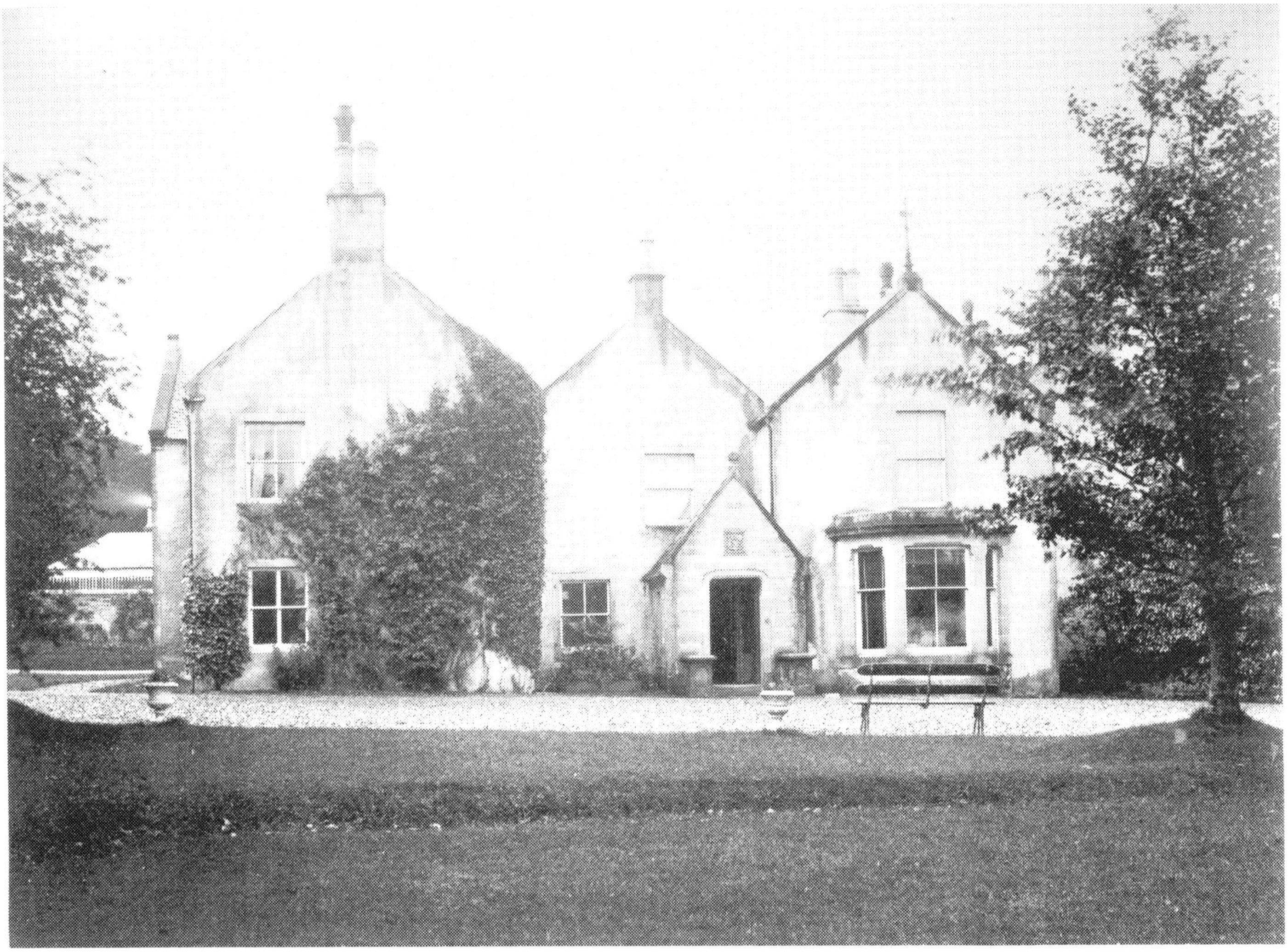

GIFFEN HOUSE.

WILLIAM PATRICK, Esq. of Roughwood and Woodside, a descendant of the ancient family of the Ayrshire Patricks, acquired the mid-superiority of Giffen In 1855 from the late Earl of Eglintoun and Wintoun. He was succeeded in 1861 by his nephew, Henry Gardiner Patrick, the present Laird of Giffen, who built the large and handsome mansion called Giffen House shortly after his accession. The building is in the Scottish Baronial style, and from its elevated position and picturesque arrangement, it gives an old-world charm to the surrounding landscape. Giffen House is situated on the farm of Bankhead, a little over two miles from the old Castle of Giffen, whose ruins are of historical importance.

The precise period when Giffen Castle was built cannot be accurately ascertained. The Barony of Giffen was included in the grant of the whole lands of Cuninghame made by David I (1124-53) to Hugh de Moreville; and in a charter granted by Walter de Mulcaster to the Abbey of Dryburgh before 1233, reference is made to certain lands which he had formerly granted sub castro de Giffen, which shows that a castle of some kind was in existence before this date. In 1608 Timothy Pont refers to "Giffin-castell, a stronge old housse;" and the place he saw was probably that square tower, forty feet high, which fell to the ground in 1838, leaving little but the lines which mark its foundation. It is probable that this place was inhabited by the lord of the manor so late as 1722; but after that time it fell into disrepair, and as it formed a convenient quarry for dyke builders it was soon reduced to ruins.

For many years after the De Morevilles and De Mulcasters had disappeared from Cuninghame, the Barony of Giffen remained in the possession of the Scottish King; and in 1370 it was gifted by Robert II to Sir Hew de Eglintoun, the progenitor of the present Earl. With this family it remained for many generations; for as it was the custom to present it to the second son of the family and his heirs-male, it reverted to the gift of the existing lord when direct heirs failed. For this reason many of the cadets of the Montgomerie family brought the name of Giffen into prominence in the Parliamentary history of the kingdom. Henry Montgomerie of Giffen, second son of the sixth Earl of Eglintoun, who obtained the barony by charter in 1636, was Member for Ayrshire in the Parliament of 1640-41. At his death, without issue, in 1643, the barony reverted to the seventh Earl, who gifted it to his second son, Francis. The latter took a prominent share in the politics of his time. His term of service in Parliament as Member for Ayrshire extended, without intermission, from 1690 till 1710, and thus embraced the crucial period during which the Union of the Parliaments was effected. For his share in this Union he did not escape without popular rebuke; yet he managed to resign the representation of the county to his son, John Montgomerie of Giffen, who was Member for Ayrshire in the United Parliament from 1710 till 1727. Having entered the Army, he rose to the rank of Lieut.-Colonel, and held several important offices at the court of George II. He died at New York, whither he had been sent as Governor in 1760; and as he left only one daughter, Beatrix, who died unmarried, the remnant of the original property which still remained fell again into the hands of the Earl of Eglintoun. Giffen had been acquired by Sir John Anstruther, of the Balcaskie family, in 1722; but it was regained gradually by the Earls of Eglintoun, and finally sold, as has been stated, to the ancestor of the present possessor.

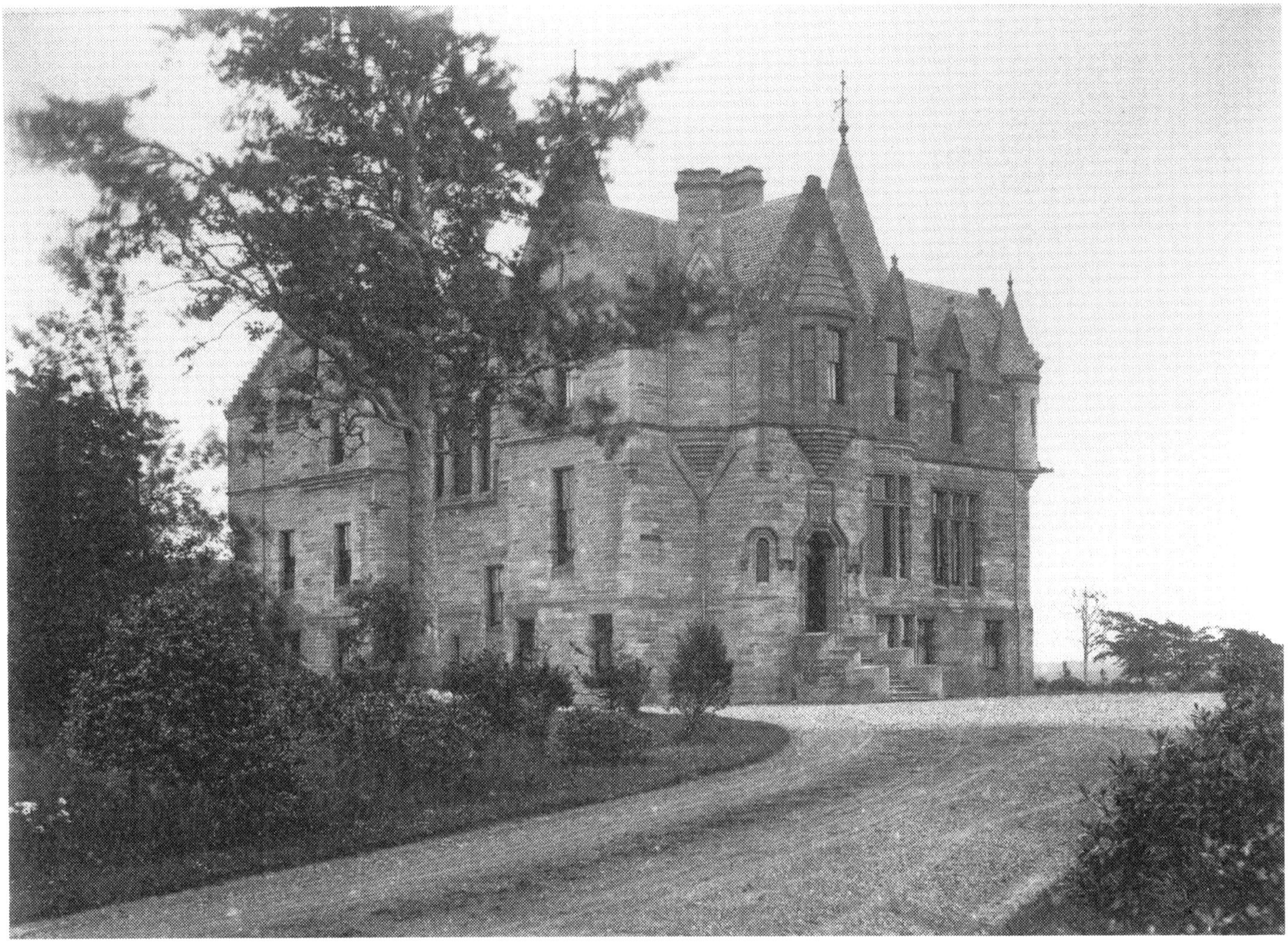

GIRGENTI.

THE estate of Bonnyton, upon which the mansion of Girgenti now stands, was acquired from Thomas Reid of Stacklawhill in 1827 by Captain John Cheape, who erected the present building shortly after that date. He belonged originally to the Fifeshire family represented by George C. Cheape, Esq. of Strathtyrum, and was the seventh son of James Cheape, Esq. of Sauchie, in Clackmannanshire. He retired from the army in 1827, and erected the house of Girgenti in the midst of what was then little better than a piece of waste land, and devoted himself to the improvement of his property. The quaint and whimsical dwelling which he built is now surrouned by an extensive garden, and many of the trees which he planted have reached a goodly stature. He died unmarried in 1850.

His only sister, Marianne, was married to Sir Alexander Campbell of Ardkinglass in 1792 and became the third wife of the eleventh Earl of Strathmore in 1817. She died without issue in 1749, a short time before her brother. Captain Cheape had made his will, leaving her life-rented in his property; but as she had predeceased him, the place was sold after his death for the behoof of several infirmaries in Scotland, according to the terms of his testament. It was purchased at that time by William Broom, Esq., ironmaster, Glasgow, and is now the property of Alexander Cochrane, Esq., of Verreville, Lanarkshire.

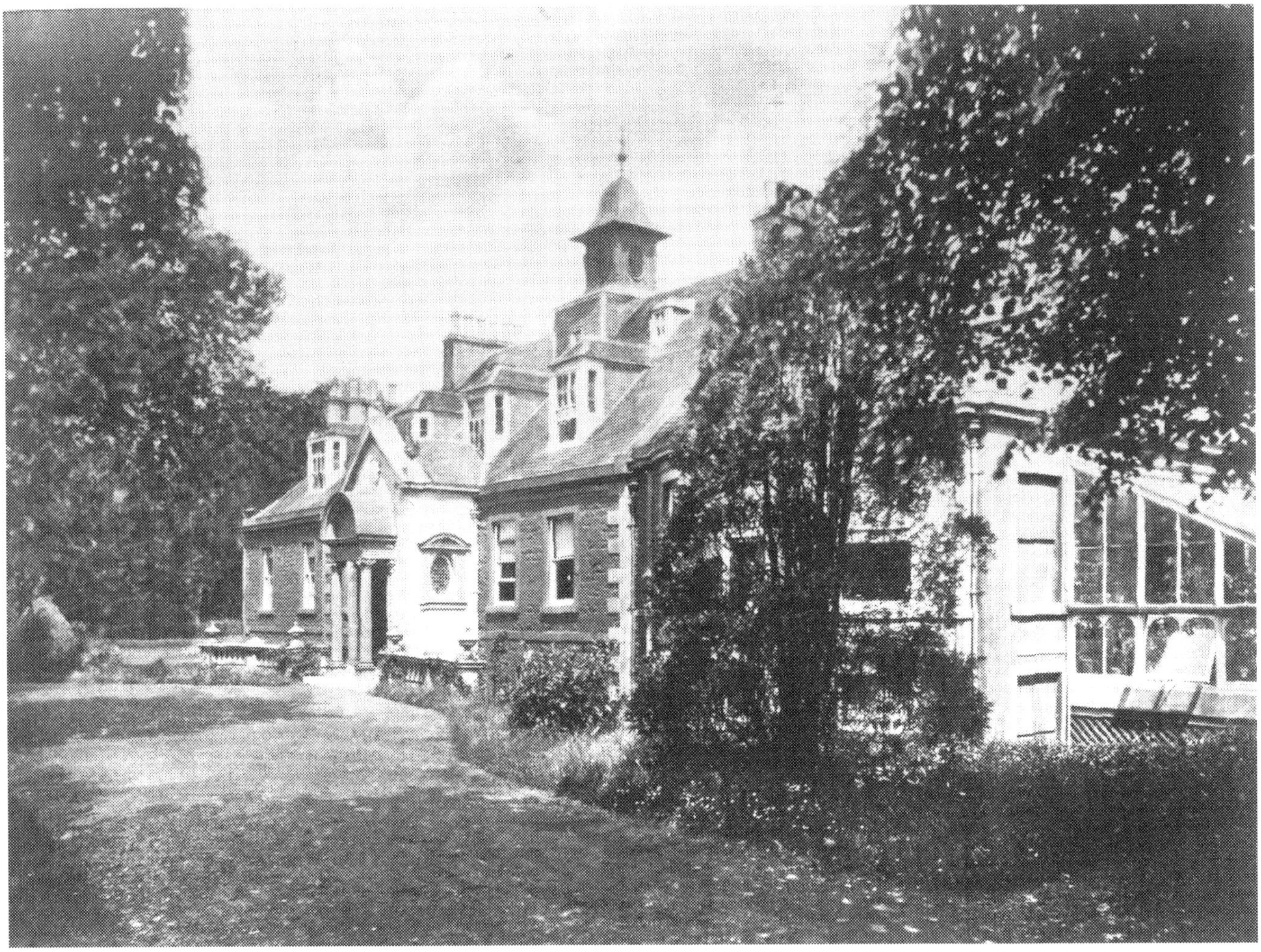

GLENAPP HOUSE.

THE estate of Glenapp, in the parish of Ballantrae, was acquired by the late Earl of Orkney about 1830, and he improved the place considerably by planting hardy trees on the waste lands. In 1864 he disposed of the estate to James Hunter, Esq., the present proprietor, for whom the mansion of Glenapp was built in 1870. The designs for this magnificent Scottish Baronial castle were prepared by the late David Bryce, R.S.A., and the work was completed under his superintendence shortly before his death. Mr Hunter has been a Deputy-Lieutenant of Ayrshire since 1868, and is otherwise connected with the county through his marriage with a member of the Houldsworth family.

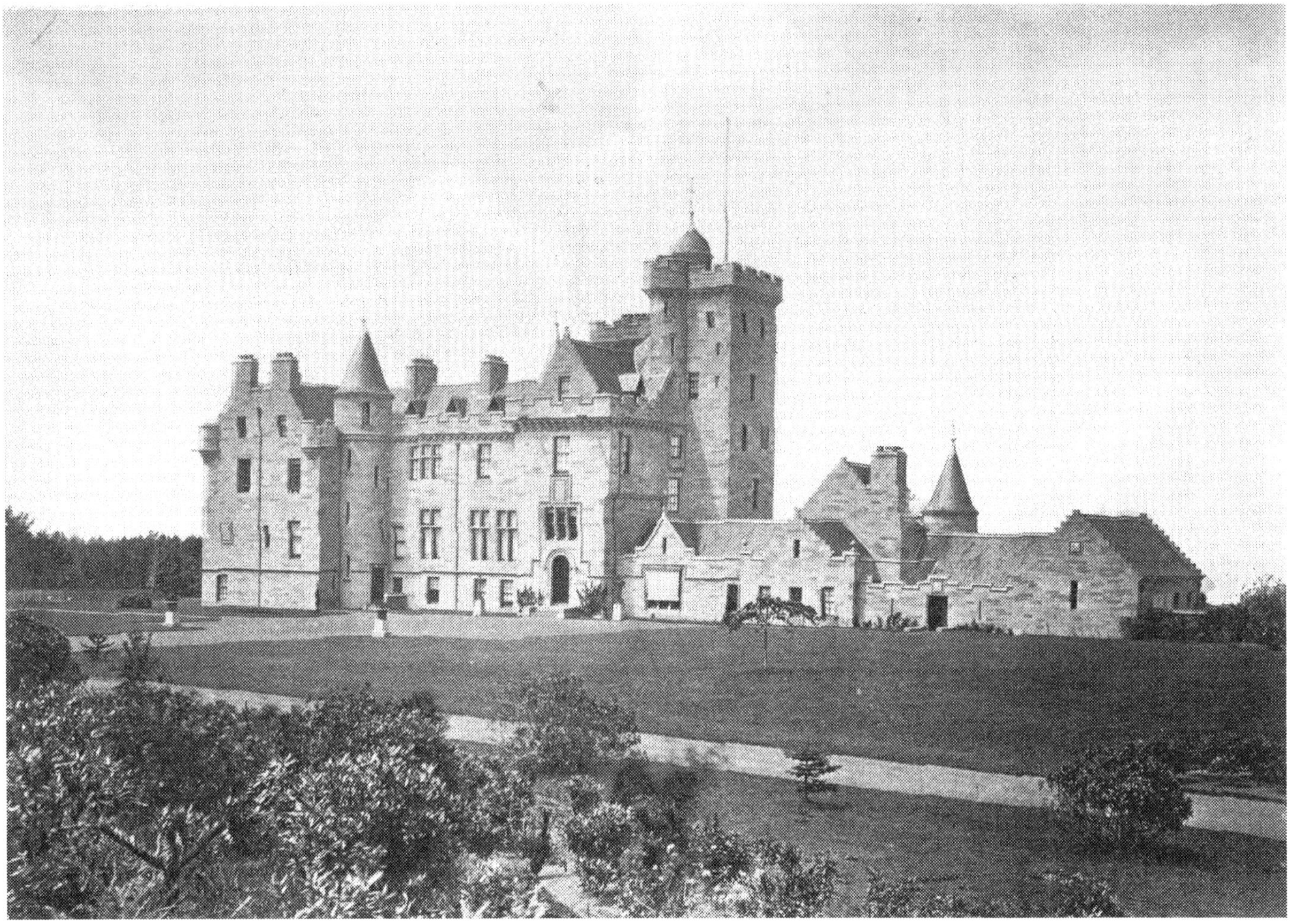

HILLHOUSE.

HILLHOUSE is situated in the parish of Dundonald, about three miles from Troon. It is now In the possession of Robert Mure McKerrell, Esq., Major of the First Ayrshire Rifle Volunteers, who succeeded to the estate as thirteenth Laird of Hillhouse in 1882. The name has been associated with this property since the middle of the fifteenth century, and tradition connects the family with the famous Sir John McKirel, who distinguished himself at the battle of Otterburne five hundred years ago, by wounding and capturing Ralph Percy (Hotspur's brother), who was second in command of the English host. It is supposed that the McKerrells came originally from Ireland,-possibly with Edward Bruce,-and settled in this quarter early in the fourteenth century: the estate of Hillhouse, however, along with others in the neighbourhood, was in the possession of the Cathcart family up to about 1500, at which date Martin McKerrell, an ancestor of the present Laird, resided at Hillhouse, holding it from the then Lord Cathcart as superior. Martin McKerrell had a son, John McKerrell, who also resided at Hillhouse; and his son, William McKerrell, who was born in 1552, eventually acquired possession of the estate, and was the first Laird of Hillhouse. He became Sheriff-Clerk of Ayr, and from him the estate has descended in the family in the male line, without any intermission, until the present day. During this long period the McKerrells have been connected with the well-known families of Chalmers of Gadgirth, Fullarton of Dreghorn, Fairlie of Fairlie, Mure of Rowallan, Craufurd of Newfield, Campbell of Treesbank, and many others. Although they took no prominent part in the political strife of their time, they were not inactive in defence of their country: Lieutenant-Colonel William McKerrell, afterwards the ninth Laird of Hillhouse, had the honour of raising, at Paisley, the first volunteer corps embodied in Scotland during the French Revolutionary war, at the time when the threatened invasion of 1803 was striking terror to the hearts of British subjects, and anticipated the anti-Gallic movement of our own time. His son, John McKerrell, the tenth Laird, attained distinction in the service of the East India Company, and rose to be Master of the Mint at Madras. He died unmarried, and was succeeded by his brother Henry, who, dying childless, was succeeded by his cousin-german, William, the late Laird, whose cousin is now Laird of Hillhouse.

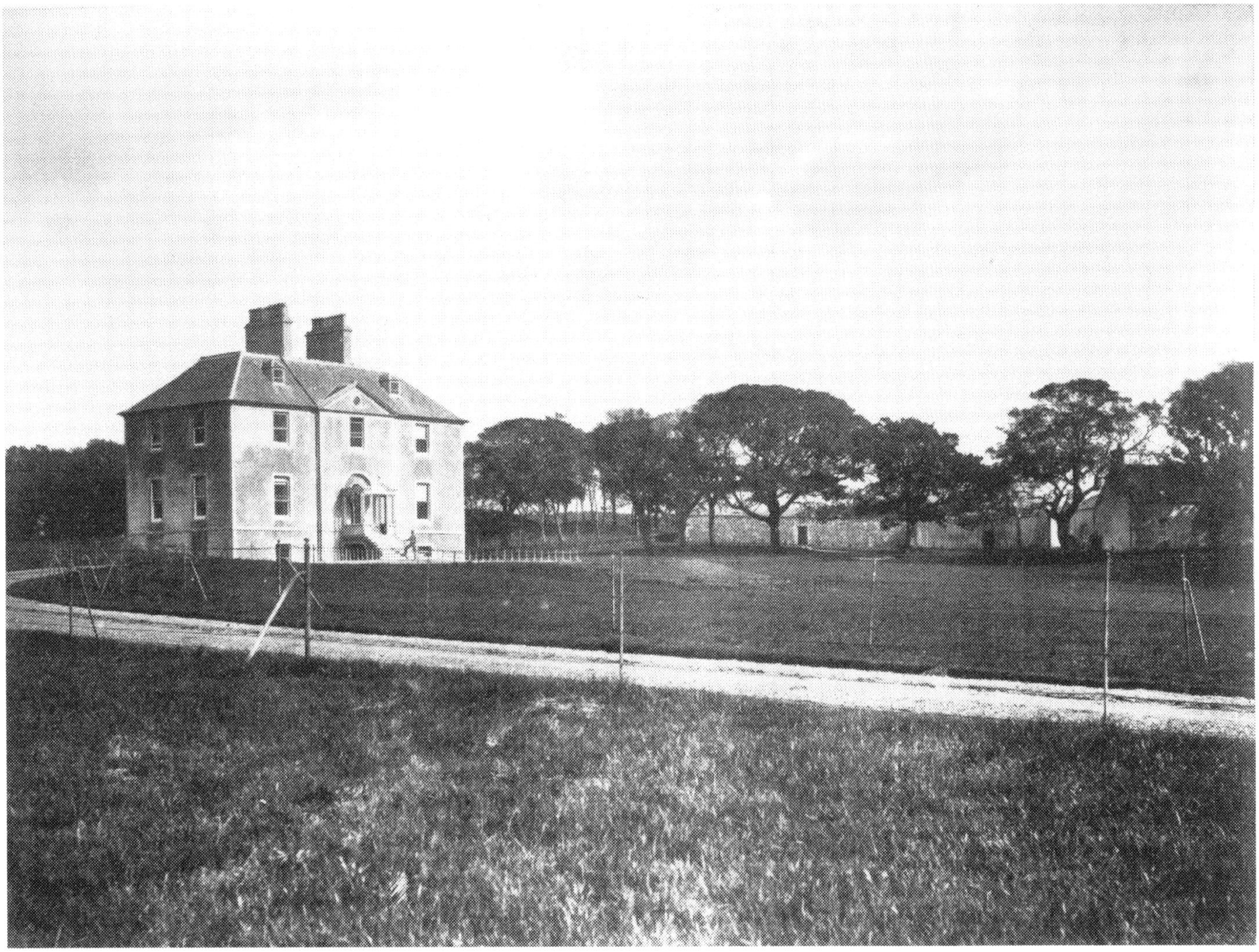

HOLMS.

HOLMS is the seat of William Fairlie, Esq., a descendant of the family of Fairlie of that Ilk. Thomas Fairlie, a cadet of that family, settled at Irvine in the middle of the seventeenth century. His grandson, John Fairlie, born 1717, had three sons - James, Mungo, and William - who went abroad in pursuit of fortune, and were all singularly successful. The eldest returned from Jamaica, and purchased the estate of Bellfield, in his native county, where he died. William, the youngest son, died in London, where he had settled on his return from Calcutta; his widow erected the mansion of Coodham, naming it Williamfield in memory of him. The second son, Mungo, came back to Ayrshire in 1796, and bought the estate of Holms from the trustees of his deceased relative, Patrick Clark. Mungo Fairlie died unmarried in 1819, and his nephew, Lieut.-Colonel James Fairlie of Bellfield, succeeded him. The present proprietor, William Fairlie, Esq. of Holms, is the second son of the latter, and came into the estate on the death of his father in 1858. The Barony of Holms belonged at one time to the Earls of Marchmont, through the Campbells of Cessnock; and the estate was purchased from the last Earl by Mr Clark in 1770 (see *Cessnock*).

The mansion of Holms is situated on an eminence overlooking the valley of the river Irvine, near the village of Galston. It is in the Tudor style of architecture, and is surrounded by many noble trees, which add greatly to the grandeur of its appearance.

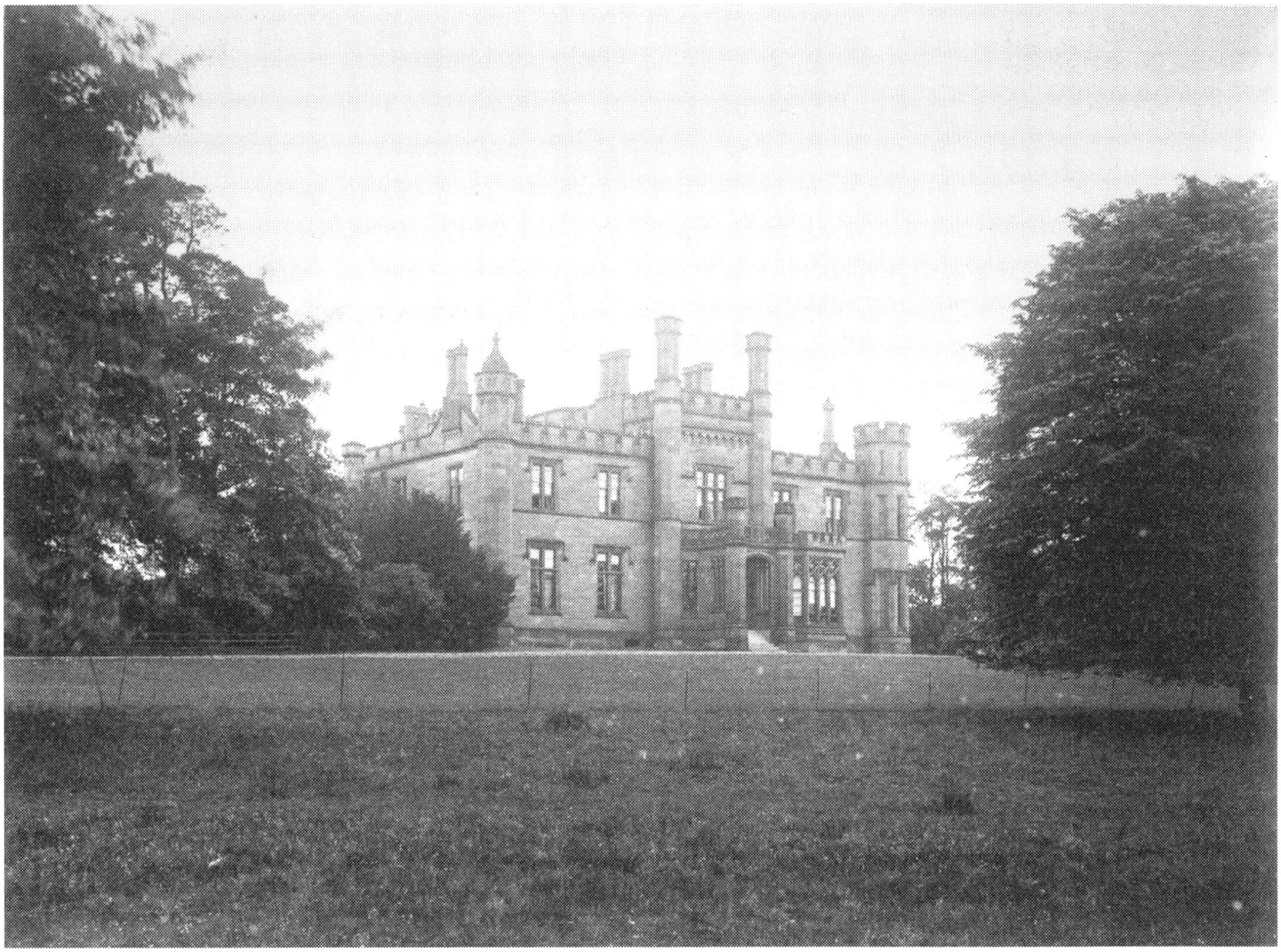

HUNTERSTON.

AS early as the year 1080 there was a Norman Hunter settled on the coast of Ayrshire opposite the Cumbraes, one of the Anglo-Normans who had come northward in the train of David I, and who doubtless gave his name to the lands which his descendants have continued to hold down to the present hour. Deriving his surname from his office, "Praefectus Venatorum Regiorum," he must have been one of the first residents in Scotland who bore an appellation continued to his descendants. His office of royal forester became hereditary, the last mention of it being made in a charter granted by James V, dated 31st May 1527, by which the Little Cumbrae was conferred on Robert Hunter of Hunterston and his heirs, in respect that his ancestors had been the hereditary keepers of the island. As early as 1116 the name of William Hunter occurs as witness on an inquisition by David, Prince of Cumbria, regarding lands pertaining to the Church of Glasgow. Aylmer de la Hunter appears in the Ragman Roll, 1296. In the family archives, in excellent preservation, is a charter that was granted by Robert II to William Hunter in 1374. From a younger son of the house in the seventeenth century were descended the Hunters of Long Calderwood - a branch of the family which produced Dr John Hunter the anatomist, his brother William, the founder of the Hunterian Museum at Glasgow, and Joanna Baillie, the poetess.

The ancient seat of the Hunters was originally in the form of a parallelogram, having its entrance to the westward, its eastern front resting upon the borders of a morass. The greater part of this fortalice has entirely disappeared, a farm-steading now occupying a portion of its site - the only remains of the old stronghold being the massive square tower, in perfect preservation, which formed its north-eastern extremity; to the southward, and attached to it, is the former dwellinghouse, the cottage shewn in the illustration being on the northern side. The new manor-house, a plain building of four stories, erected about eighty years ago, has an elegant interior, and is now being considerably altered and enlarged. Amongst many fine trees which surround the castle, a giant ash, known as the "Resting Tree," is specially worthy of mention.

By his marriage with Christian Macknight, eldest daughter of William Macknight Crawfurd of Cartsburn, county Renfrew, Mr Hunter, dying in 1880, left two daughters - Jane and Eleanora. He was succeeded by his elder daughter, Jane, who in 1863 married Lieut.-Colonel Gould Weston, a direct descendant of the ancient Staffordshire family of that name, seated at Weston-under-Lyzard in the reign of Henry II. This officer distinguished himself in the Indian service by extirpating the Thugs and Decoits who infested the kingdom of Oudh, and earned the praises of Outram for his skill and bravery during the siege and at the capture of Lucknow. In conformity with the provisions of the Hunterston entail, Lieut.- Colonel Weston assumed in 1880, under Royal Licence, the additional surname and arms of Hunter of Hunterston. Lieut.-Colonel Hunter-Weston has two sons - Aylmer Gould, born in 1864, a lieutenant in the Royal Engineers; and Reginald Hugh, born in 1869. The late Mrs Cochran-Patrick, wife of R. W. Cochran-Patrick of Woodside and Ladyland, county Ayr, the eminent archaeologist and M.P. for North Ayrshire, was the younger daughter of the late Mr Hunter.

The famous "Hunterston Brooch" was discovered in 1826 on this estate at the foot of the Hawking Craig. It is undoubtedly the finest fibula ever found in Scotland, and is the only one known to exist in this country bearing runes. The possessions of this family were formerly far more considerable, including Holy Isle near Arran, the little Cumbrae, and lands in the counties of Ayr, Bute, Lanark, and Forfar, now of very considerable value. Hunterston is beautifully wooded, and the garden near the old Castle, notable alike for its size and antiquity, contains some evergreens and shrubs of great size and beauty.

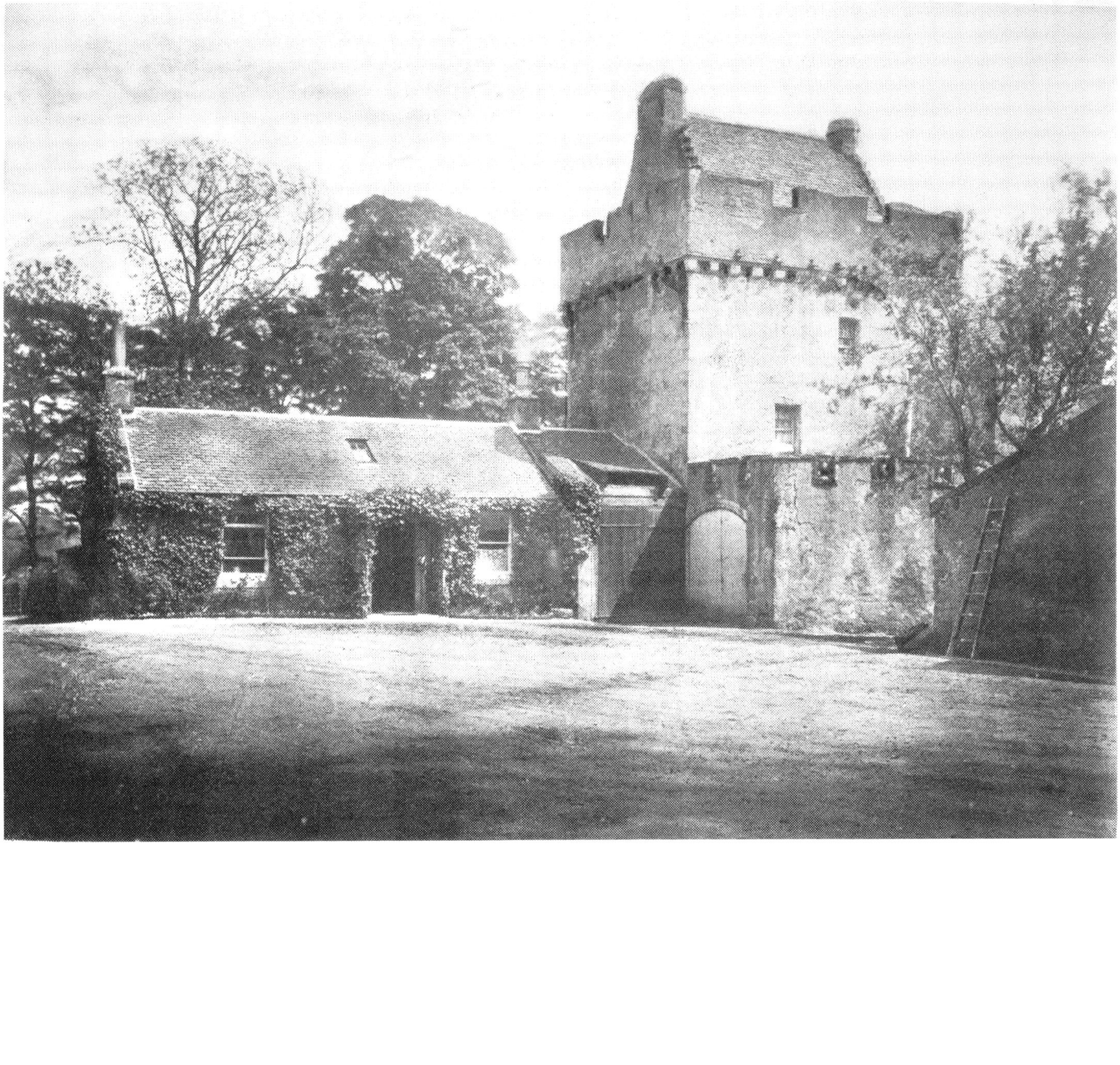

KELBURNE CASTLE.

NESTLING in a richly-wooded gorge in the hillside, under the shelter of a ridge that rises abruptly behind it, and with luxurious pleasure-grounds sloping down to the Clyde, the baronial mansion of Kelburne occupies a site picturesque in no ordinary degree. Originally it resembled the neighbouring castle of Fairlie, now a ruin, the supposed residence of Hardyknute, the hero of the familiar ballad; but the Boyle family must have been gifted with aesthetic qualities, if we may judge by the charms with which their old home is now invested. As the voyager examines it from the sea, his attention is powerfully arrested by its scenic beauty; while the visitor to the valley looks out, through leafy glades, upon most exquisite views of the loveliest of all our British rivers. The place has belonged from time immemorial to the Boyles, who five hundred years ago held the office of coroner for the Largs district, but rose to still greater dignity when David, one of the Commissioners in promoting the Union, was created a peer in 1699. In that year he was made Lord Boyle of Kelburne, and in 1703 he became the Earl of Glasgow. The second wife of this nobleman was the daughter and heiress of the last Sir William Mure of Rowallan, and one of their children became mother of the fifth Earl of Loudoun. The third Earl of Glasgow, a brave soldier who was wounded at the battles of Fontenoy and Lawfeldt, is commemorated by a monument erected by his widow near the castle, in a romantic spot on the banks of the rivulet that runs through the ravine to the sea. This memorial consists of a female figure, in white marble, placed in a niche, and represents "Virtue lamenting the loss of one of her favourite sons." The fourth Earl was advanced in 1815 to the honour of a British peerage by the title of Lord Ross of Hawkhead; his first wife was a daughter of the Earl of Errol, and his second a daughter of Sir John Sinclair of Ulbster, Bart. The present earl, whose wife is a daughter of the third Lord Abercromby, is the founder of the Episcopal college at Millport, and is distinguished not less for his benevolent and many amiable qualities than for his love of literature and earnest desire to further the interests of religion. Pont's description of the castle as "a goodly building, well planted, having very beautiful orchards and gardens," is still more applicable to it to-day than it was before Earl David enlarged the place to make it more suitable to the dignity to which his sovereign had promoted him. In the *Baronial and Ecclesiastical Antiquities of Scotland,* Billings refers specially to Kelburne Castle as having "the only ancient metallic termination to the turret" which he had met with, and alludes to the fact that it "distinctly shows the finishing personality and nationality of Scotch architecture - the crest of the Laird surmounted by the thistle." He speaks also with admiration of "the ingeniously ornamented sun-dial, where every inch of surface is made to tell the story of time under every possible contortion of form and position, and where its pinnacle, by a series of gnomes, imitates the crocketting of Gothic architecture."

The Boyles of Kelburne have frequently represented their district in Parliament. John Boyle of Kelburne was Member for Buteshire from 1678 till 1685, and his brother James represented Irvine in the Convention of Estates from 1681 till 1686. David Boyle, son of this Member for Buteshire, succeeded his father in that office in 1689, and continued in it till he was created Lord Boyle in 1699. David Boyle of Maress, grandson of the second Earl, and afterwards Lord President of the Court of Session, was Member for Ayrshire from 1807 till 1811; and the late Earl of Glasgow (1792-1869) held the same honourable position from 1839 until he succeeded to the peerage in 1843.

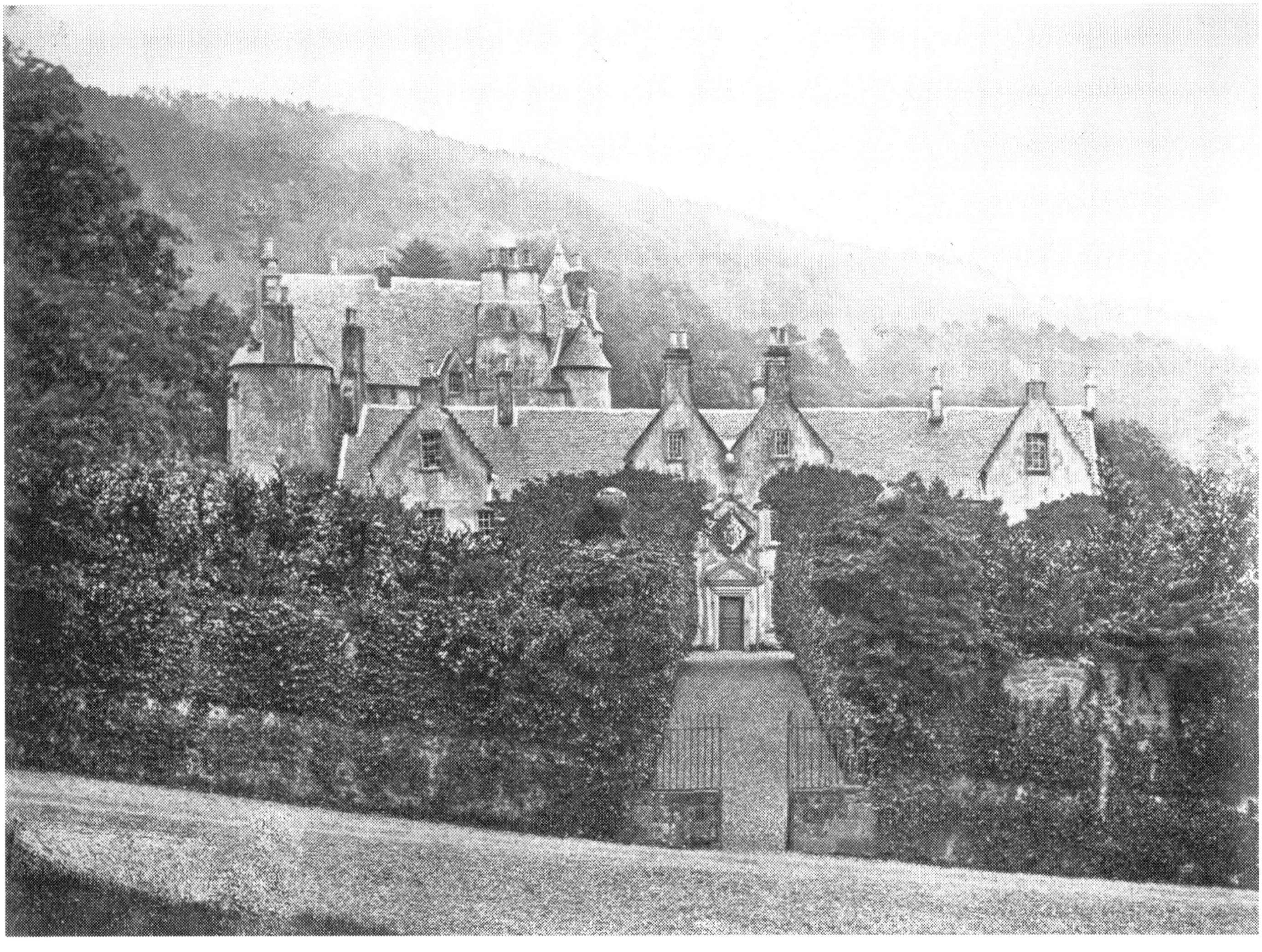

KILKERRAN.

THE lands of Kilkerran came into the possession of the Fergusson family in the early part of the fourteenth century, and remain with the present representative to this day. Fergus Fergusson obtained a charter of them from Robert the Bruce, and from him they descended to Sir John Fergusson, knight, who suffered severely for his adhesion to Charles I, during the troubled reign of that monarch. Sir John's grandson and namesake had won a leading position at the Scottish Bar, and was able to relieve the estate of the heavy burdens which had been put upon it. He was created a Baronet in 1703, and died in 1729. His son and successor rose to eminence as a Lord of Session under the title of Lord Kilkerran, receiving the latter appointment in 1749, ten years before his death. His third son, George Fergusson, distinguished himself as an advocate by his defence of the rebels of 1745, and was afterwards well known on the Bench by 'his title of Lord Hermand. The eldest son of Lord Kilkerran was Sir Adam, third baronet, who sat in Parliament from 1774 till 1796, in all twenty-two years, during eighteen of which he represented Ayrshire. On the death of the Earl of Glencairn without issue in 1796, Sir Adam claimed the earldom, but was defeated on a technical point in the House of Lords. He died without issue in 1813, aged eighty-one, and the succession then devolved upon his nephew, who was grandfather of the present baronet.

Sir James Fergusson of Kilkerran has spent an active life in the service of his country. He was born in 1832, entered Parliament as Member for Ayrshire in 1854, and continued to represent that constituency- except during 18S7-59 - until 1868. As Captain of the Grenadier Guards he took part in the Crimean Invasion, and was wounded at Inkerman. He was appointed Under-Secretary for India in 1866; transferred to the Home Department in the following year; was Privy Councillor in 1868; Governor of South Australia, 1868-73; of New Zealand, 1873-74; and has been Governor of Bombay since 1880. Few Scottish politicians have been privileged to fill such varied offices with equal credit in so short a time.

The mansion of Kilkerran has been built at various times, though the greater portion of it exhibits signs of that style of architecture which prevailed during the eighteenth century. It is probable that the front part, with its urn-surmounted, pediment and alternated corner-stones, was erected principally by Lord Kilkerran; whilst Sir Adam Fergusson would likely complete the building, as we now see it, in the course of his long life. The public duties of the present laird have compelled him to spend the best of his years far from his ancestral home.

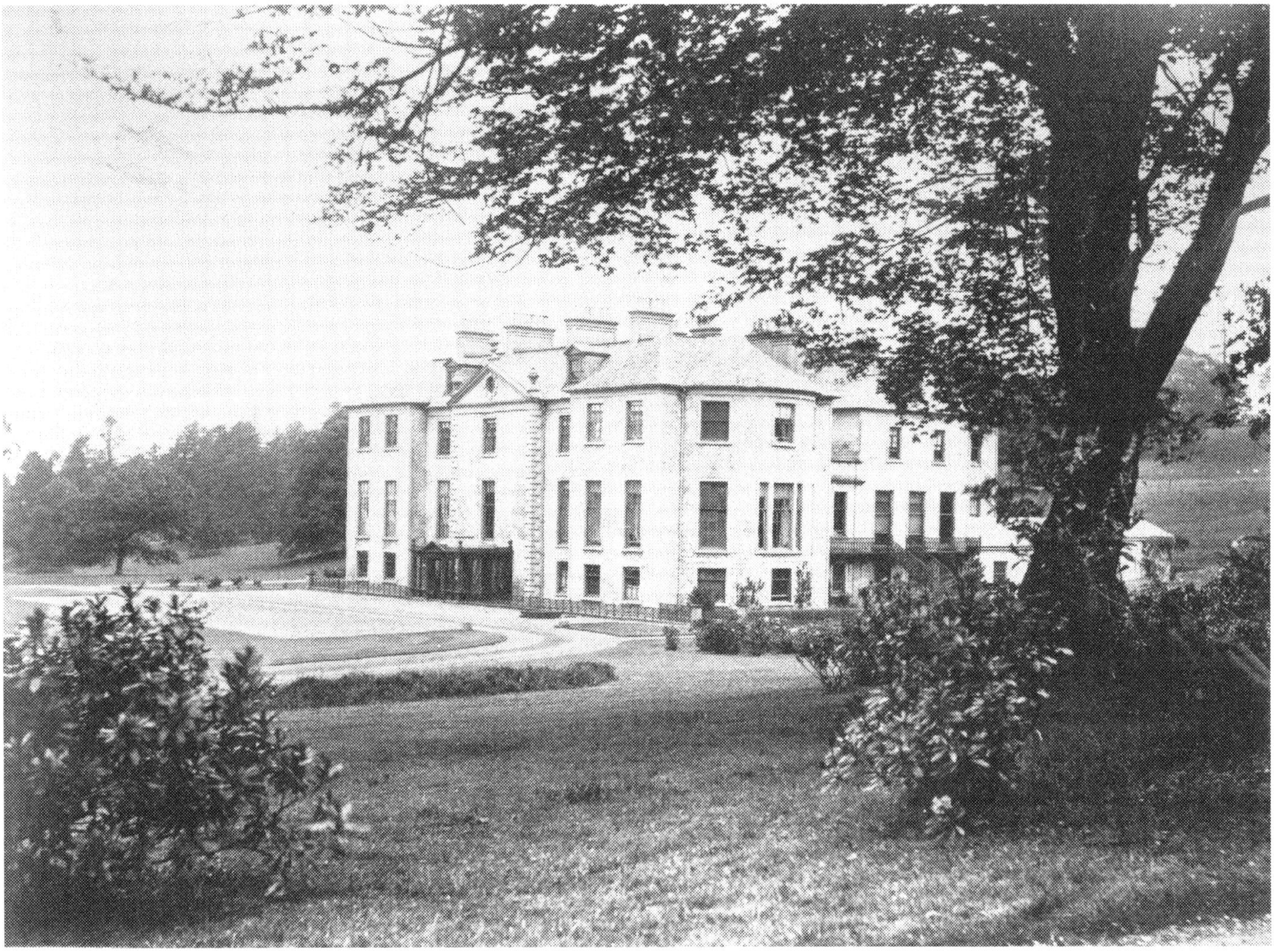

KILLOCHAN CASTLE.

THE Cathcarts of Carleton, whose Scottish seat is at Killochan Castle, are descended from the same ancestor as the Earls Cathcart. The first of the present Cathcarts of Carleton was a grandson of the second Lord Cathcart, and obtained the territorial title through his mother, Margaret, daughter and heiress of Alan Cathcart of Carleton. His father was slain at Flodden, and he became himself the progenitor of the Cathcarts of Greenock. From him descended Hew Cathcart, "Laird of Cairltoune," who represented Ayrshire at the Convention of 1625. His grandson was Member for Ayrshire in the Parliament of 1702-7, and was created a Baronet of Nova Scotia in 1703. Sir Andrew, fourth baronet, who was a grandson of Sir Hew, died at Killochan in 1828 in his 90th year - not 87th as usually stated - and was succeeded by his grand-nephew, Sir John Andrew Cathcart, father of the present proprietor. The late baronet held a commission in the 2d regiment of Life-Guards, and was appointed Deputy-Lieutenant of Ayrshire in 1835. He married Lady Eleanor Kennedy, grand-daughter of the first Marquess of Ailsa, and was succeeded by his eldest son, Sir Reginald Archibald Edward Cathcart, sixth baronet, in 1878. The Castle of Killochan, which was probably built by Robert Cathcart of Carleton in the early years of the sixteenth century, is a most interesting example of the baronial architecture of that period, and is in excellent preservation. The ruins of the original Castle of Carleton, from which the title of the family came, may still be traced upon the summit of Carleton Hill in the parish of Colmonell.

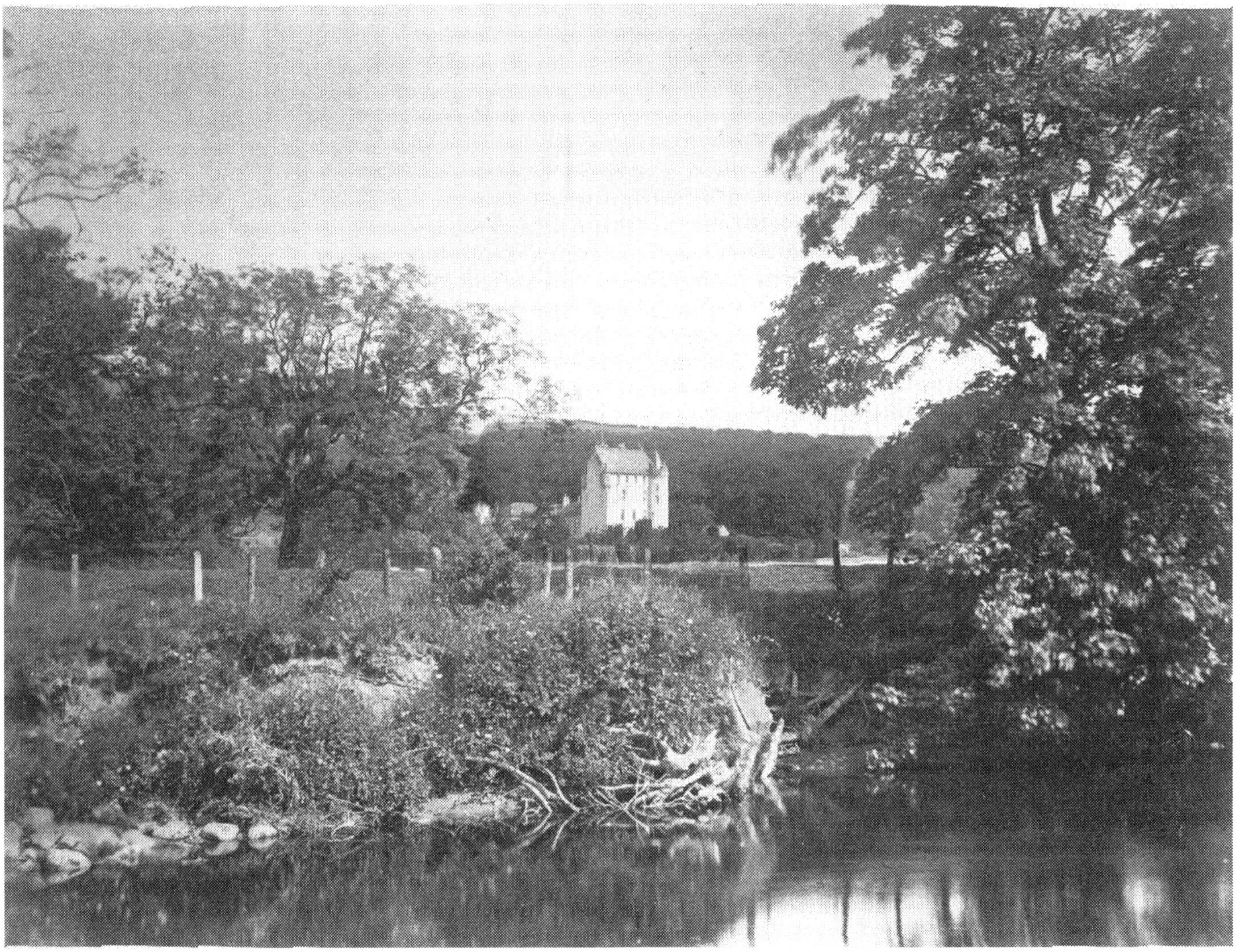

KIRKHILL.

THE new mansion of Kirkhill is built in close proximity to the ruins of its predecessor, and serves thus to preserve the historical traditions associated with the ancient name. The modern house was built about forty years ago by the late Lieut.-Colonel Barton, and is now the property of Mrs B. Farquhar Gray of Glentig and Ballaird. It is situated near the quaint village of Colmonell, in the parish of that name.

The ruined castle was originally one of the seats of the Kennedy family, and still bears the date 1589, with the arms and initials of Thomas Kennedy and his wife Janet, by whom it was erected. The estate was acquired shortly after the Reformation by Gilbert, third son of Alexander Kennedy, third Lord Kennedy of Bargany, and remained in the possession of the Dunure family till 1843. It was then purchased by Lieut.-Colonel Barton of Ballaird, and at his death became the property of his nephew, J. Farquhar Gray, Esq. of Glentig. The latter place had been a seat of a cadet of the Bargany family so early as 1504, and thus the two properties were united after a lapse of several centuries.

The most eminent name amongst the Kennedys of Kirkhill is that of Sir Thomas Kennedy, who was Lord Provost of Edinburgh in 1680-84, and made a large fortune by trafficking in arms and ammunition during that warlike time. Lieut.-Colonel Barton, who introduced a new name into the history of the estate, claimed to be a lineal descendant of Booth de Barton, one of the military companions of William the Conqueror. He served under the Duke of Wellington throughout the Peninsular War; and distinguished himself specially at Waterloo. He was gazetted Brevet-Major in 1819, and Lieut.-Colonel in 1837; and when he retired from military life to reside at Kirkhill, he had served in the 12th Lancers for the long period of forty years.

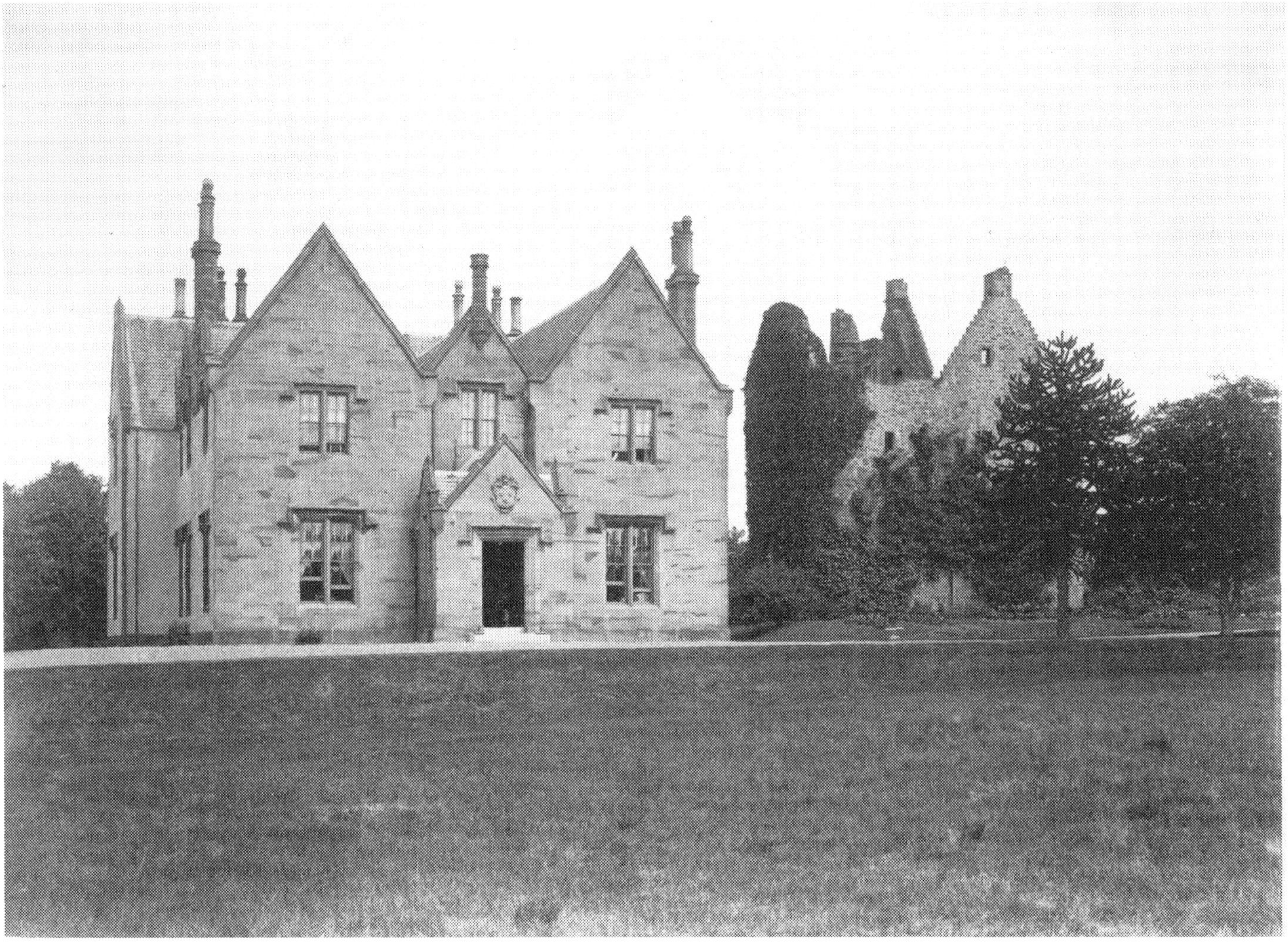

KNOCK CASTLE.

THE modern mansion called Knock Castle was built shortly after 1850 by Robert Steele, Esq., of Greenock, who had purchased the ancient estate on which it stands from John Wilson of- Auchmedden. In 1858 the mansion and greater portion of the estate were acquired by George Elder, Esq. of Knock, the present proprietor, who is third son of the late George Elder of Kirkcaldy, and was appointed a Deputy-Lieutenant of Ayrshire in 1871. Knock Castle occupies a commanding position near the shores of the Firth of Clyde, not far from Brisbane House.

The old Castle of Knock, the ruins of which may be seen at a short distance from the new house, appears from the style of its architecture to have been erected early in the sixteenth century. The first notice of the estate that has been discovered dates from about 1380, when John Frazer, third son of Hew Frazer of Lovat, married the heiress of Knock, whose name cannot be traced. The Frazers remained in possession of Knock from this time till 1674, and during that long period the families of the Earls of Lennox, Boyle of Kelburne, Craufurd of Auchinames, and Brisbane of Brisbane, were connected with them by marriages. Alexander Frazer of Knock chose the losing side in the contest betwixt the Covenanters and Montrose, and suffered severely in his estate after the defeat at Philiphaugh. His four daughters - Jean, Grisel, Agnes, and Janet Frazer - were returned as his heiresses-portioners in 1674; but were forced to dispose of the property shortly afterwards to Sir Robert Montgomerie of Skelmorlie. The grandson of the latter sold the lands to David Boyle of Kelburne - afterwards first Earl of Glasgow - in 1696, and he excambed them with the Laird of Brisbane for the lands of Killingcraig. The estate of Knock, with the old Castle, was sold by the late Sir Thomas Makdougall-Brisbane, in 1835, to George Wilson, whose nephew, John Wilson of Auchmedden, succeeded. The last-named proprietor did much to improve the lands, and repaired the castle so as to prevent that interesting relic of feudal times from falling to decay. Though it is no longer the "prettey duelling seatted one the mane occeane and veill planted," which Pont described, it still displays some tokens of its former grandeur and importance.

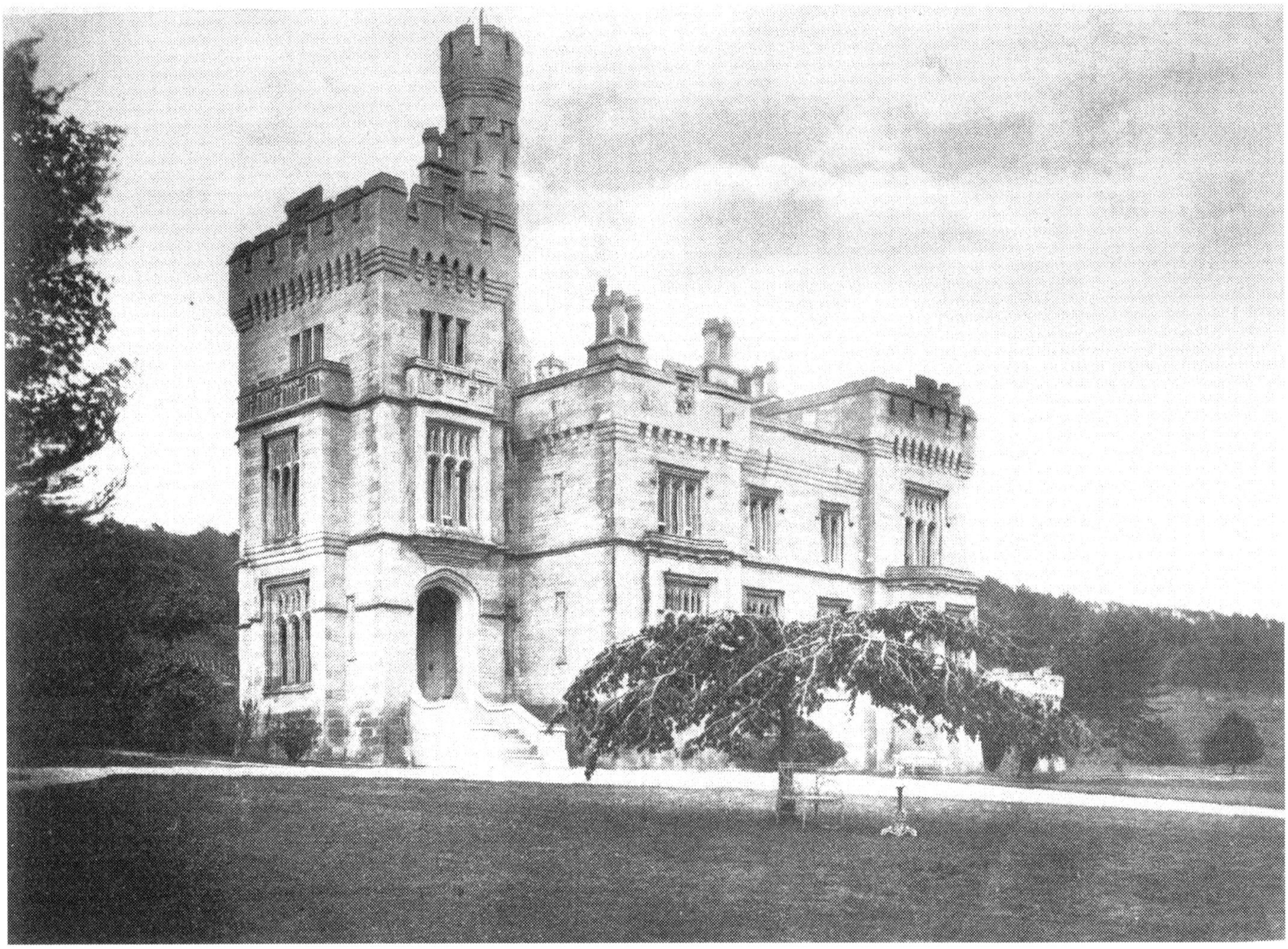

KNOCKDOLIAN CASTLE.

THE ruins of Knockdolian Castle, situated near the present mansion, mark the seat of a branch of the Cathcart family. James Cathcart of Barneill was a younger son of Cathcart of Carleton (see *Killochan Castle*), who obtained a charter of the lands of Easter Barneill from James I. in 1601, and purchased the estate of Genoch in Wigtownshire in 1618. His great-grandson, John, the first Cathcart of Knockdolian, who acquired the estate by purchase from Fergus McCubbin in 1715, was a descendant of the two powerful houses of Kennedy of Culzean and Agnew of Lochnaw, and was himself allied by marriage with the Cochranes of Dundonald. He died in 1779 at an advanced age, and was succeeded by his son Robert, who only survived till 1789. John Cathcart of Genoch and Knockdolian (1768-1835) was an advocate of some eminence, and increased his influence by his marriage with a daughter of Lord Rockville of Session, who was a younger son of the second Earl of Aberdeen. His eldest son, Robert (1797-1840), entered the service of the East India Company, and died unmarried at Agra, Bengal. He was succeeded by his only surviving brother, the late Alexander Cathcart of Knockdolian (born 1800), in whom the direct line of this family terminated. The estate now belongs to William McConnel, Esq., who acquired it in 1872.

The modern mansion of Knockdolian is situated near the base of the peculiar conical hill from which its name is taken, and on the right bank of the Stinchar. It was built by Alexander Cathcart of Genoch and Knockdolian in 1842, and several additions have since been made to it. Many of the trees in the neighbourhood are of great age; and the site of the house has been chosen with considerable taste.

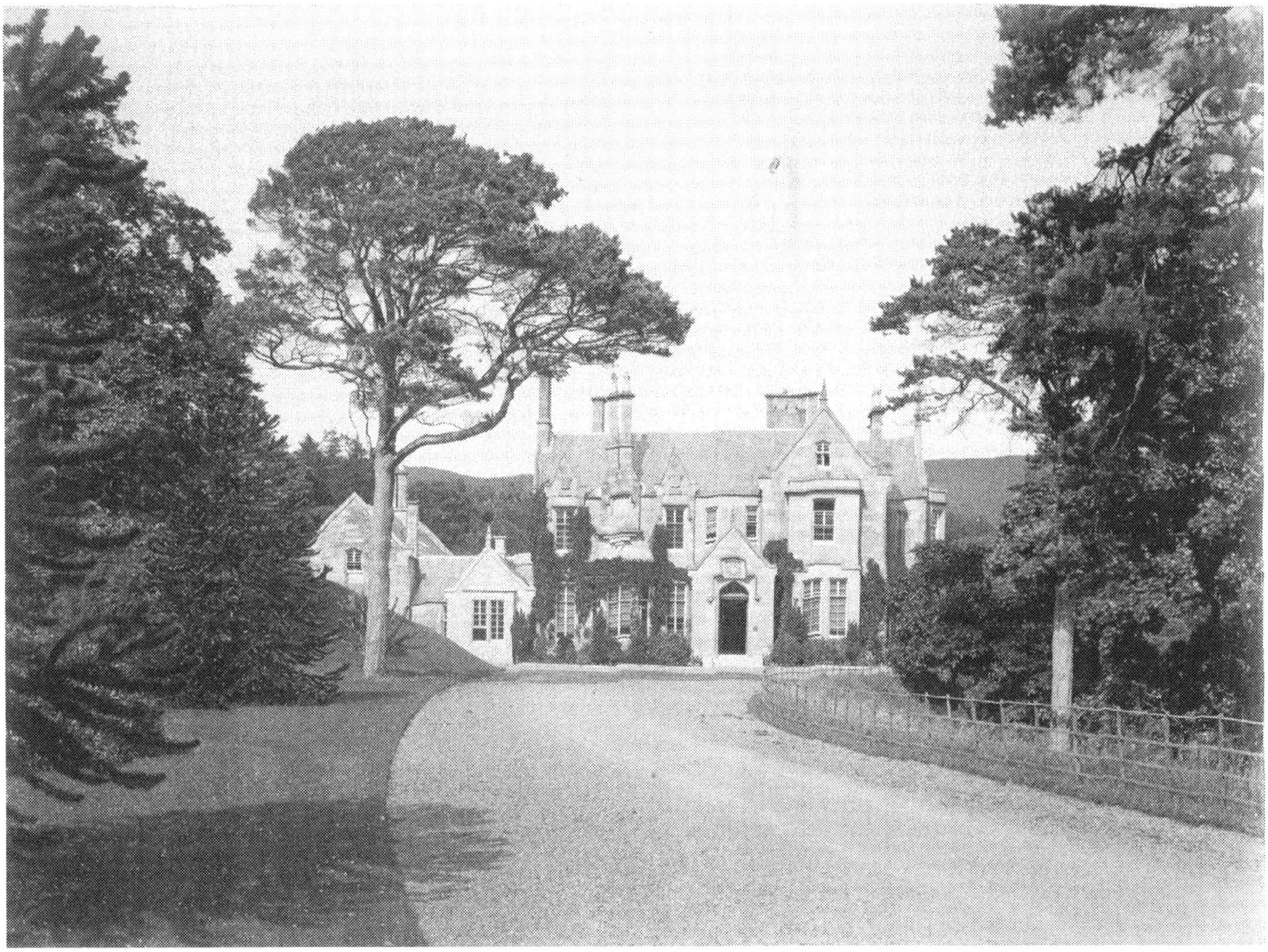

LAINSHAW.

LAINSHAW - or, as it was formerly called, *Langschaw* - was at one time a portion of the Lordship of Stewartoun, and therefore the original seat of the family which afterwards bore sway in Scotland as the race of Stewart. The baronial castle of Stewartoun was described by Pont in 1608 as "a stronge old Dounijon, the ancient inheritance of ye predicessors of our Scotts Kings;" and it is likely that the Lordship was considered of much value, since the Royal Family retained their power over it very tenaciously, and bestowed it only as a special mark of favour. Stewartoun became the inheritance of James, the High Steward, in 1283; and the right of his successors to dispose of it arbitrarily was exercised nearly three hundred years afterwards. Robert III granted it to Archibald, Earl of Douglas, and afterwards resumed it, so that he might bestow it as a dowry on the Earl's daughter, Elizabeth, when she was married to John Stewart, Earl of Buchan (*ob.* 1424). The bestowal of the Lordship seems to have been always given under strict reversionary limitations, as it came into the gift of the Crown several times. There is a special interest connected with the fact that "the landis and lordship of Stewartoun, with the feu maills," were presented as a bridal gift by Queen Mary to "her hienes' familiar servitrice,' Mary Livingstoun, on the occasion of her marriage to John Sempill, son of "the great Lord Sempill," whom she described as "her daylie and familiar servitor." Mary Livingstoun was the first of the famous "Four Maries" to enter the state of wedlock, and she only felt herself at liberty to break the vow of celibacy which these damsels had made when the Queen disclosed her own intention of wedding Lord Darnley. The marriage took place at Holyrood on 5th March 1565 - not 1567 as sometimes stated, - but the Lordship passed into the hands of the Montgomeries of Lainshaw shortly afterwards, and became their manor-place.

Lainshaw existed as a separate estate for a long period before this amalgamation took place. In the exercise of his inherited right to the lands of Stewartoun, James II granted that portion then called Langschaw to Sir Alexander Home of Holme in 1450. His son, afterwards first Lord Home, came into possession of the estate at his decease, and bestowed it upon the eldest son of his second marriage, who was called Thomas Home of Langschaw. The mother of the latter - Lord Home's second wife - was a daughter of the Master of Montgomerie; and as Thomas Home died without issue the lands of Langschaw came into the hands of the Eglintoun family. The first Earl of Eglintoun bestowed them upon his second son, Nigel (circa 1530), who became the first of the Montgomeries of Lainshaw.

The latter family held the estate by direct succession from father to son until 1654, when John Montgomerie died without issue, and was succeeded by his uncle, David Montgomerie of Cockilbie. As the Laird of Langschaw was concerned in the affair of Bothwell Brig, extreme measures were taken against him; but he managed to bequeath the estate to his son James, who became Lord Lyle of Session. On the death of Lord Justice-Clerk Lyle in 1726, the succession fell upon his nephew, David Laing, who assumed the name of Montgomerie, married a sister of Lord Auchinleck, and became the father of the wife of James Boswell the biographer. With his eldest son and daughter the family of Montgomerie of Lainshaw terminated; and the lands were sold by Sir Walter Montgomerie, Bart., in 1779, to William Cuninghame, third son of Alexander Cuninghame of Bridgehouse, whose representative is now proprietor. The first Cuninghame of Lainshaw, who was a collateral descendant of the Caprington Cuninghames, made his fortune in America, and established a lucrative trade with that country in Glasgow, which enabled him to retire to his new estate with security. He was thrice married, but devised Lainshaw to William, the only son of his second marriage, who entered into possession on his father's death in 1799. William Cuninghame was well known throughout Scotland for his voluminous writings upon the prophecies of Scripture, as well as for his latitudinarian views upon the Atonement. He died unmarried in 1849, and was succeeded by his half-brother John, the son of the first laird's third marriage. John Cuninghame of Lainshaw (1794-1864) was succeeded by his eldest son, the present proprietor, John William Herbert Cuninghame, Esq., late Captain 2d Life-Guards. One large square tower only of the original building of Stewartoun now remains; and in the course of so many changes in the proprietorship it is not easy to tell the dates of the various parts which form the imposing mansion of Lainshaw. The greater portion, probably, was erected about a century ago by the first William Cuninghame of Lainshaw.

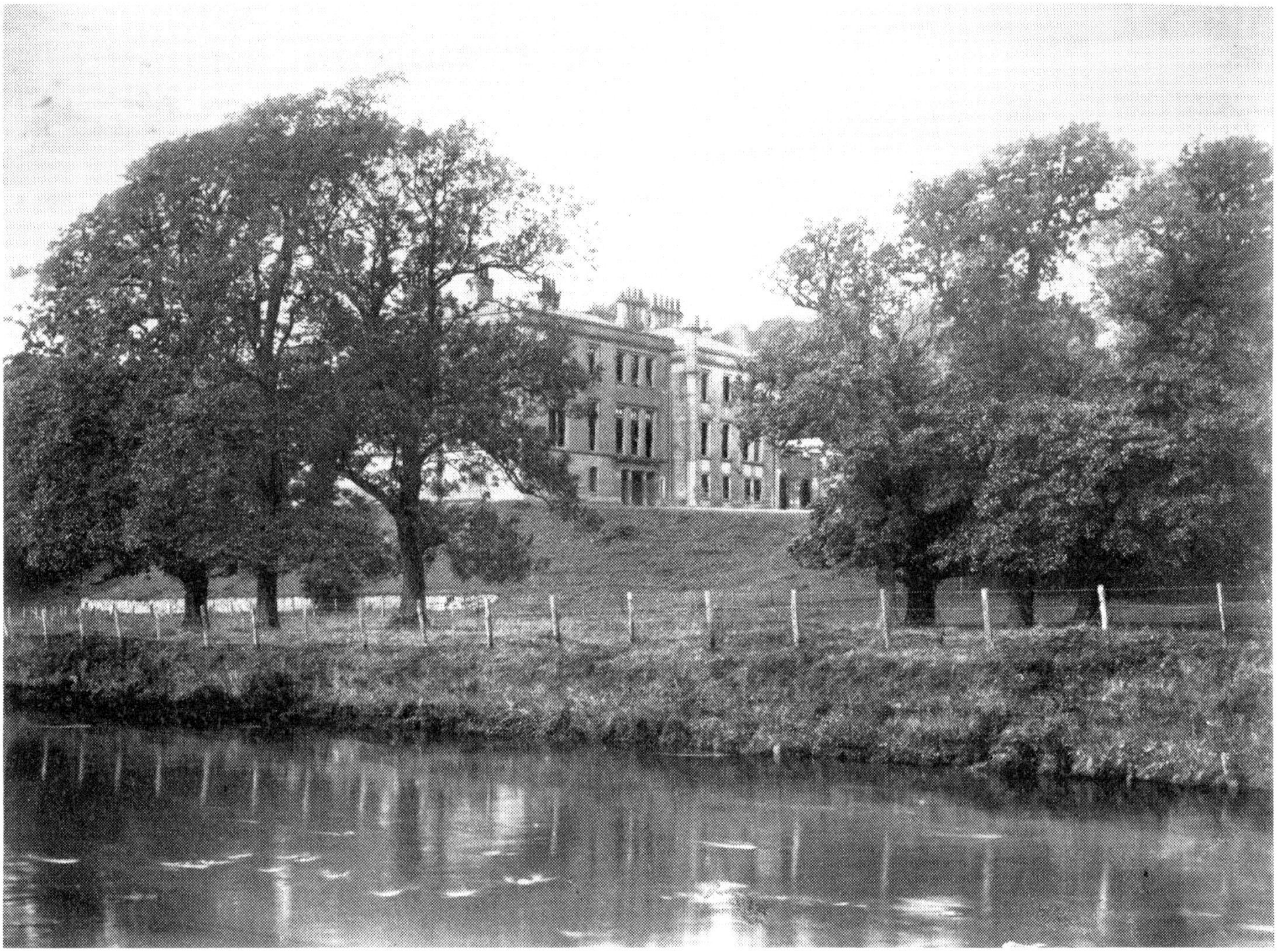

LANFINE HOUSE.

THE estate and house of Lanfine are in the parish of Galston, and the immediate neighbourhood of the town of that name. The original designation of the estate was Lenfene but it hopeless to attempt to discover its derivation. That the lands were of considerable value is indirectly made evident by the fact that they were in the possession of the Church at an early date. The precise period when the church at Galston was established is not known, though Chalmers states that it was granted to the Convent of Faile in 1252. "The church," he says, "was served by a vicar, who had a stipend of five chalders of victual yearly, with a manse and a glebe, and the brothers of Faile enjoyed the remainder of the revenues." That these revenues included Lanfine is probable, since the ecclesiastic appointed to the charge of the chapel founded at Galston in 1471 had "the lands of Lenfene" settled upon him for life. This endowment was confirmed in 1489 to Mr. John Charteris; and his successor, Alexander Arbukill, probably enjoyed the same privilege when appointed in 1551. He was the last chaplain, however, who held these lands in peace, for after the Reformation we find the patronage of the chapel in the hands of Campbell of Cessnock.

In 1573 Lanfine belonged to John Lockhart of Barr, and was acquired in 1769 by John Brown of Glasgow, one of the partners in the famous banking-house of Carrick, Brown, & Co. He also purchased Waterhough, which had previously belonged to the ancestors of his mother, the Campbells of Waterhough, a branch of the Loudoun family. The family of Waterhough is now represented by Miss Brown of Lanfine, the present proprietrix. It is to this lady that the inhabitants of Galston, Newmills, and Darvel are indebted for the erection of comfortable reading and recreation rooms. The library of Brown's Institute in Galston, which she founded in 1874, contains over 3000 volumes of well-selected literature.

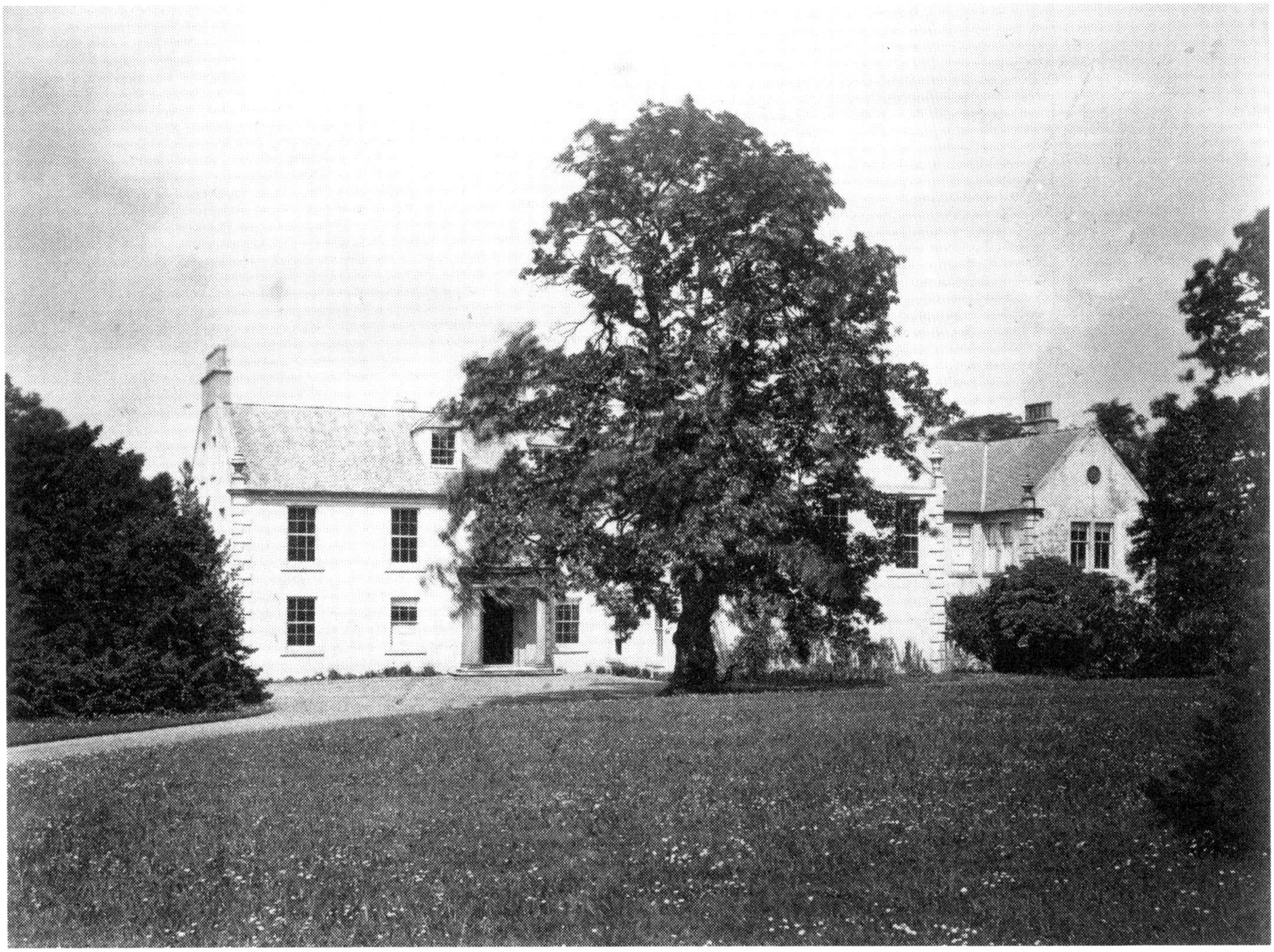

LOUDOUN CASTLE.

LOUDOUN CASTLE is linked with the annals of a house which gathers into itself the history of many families, each boasting a long line of historical ancestors going back to the Norman Conquest. The Lords of Loudoun can trace their lineage back as far as the year 1200; the hereditary Sheriffdom of Ayrshire, which came to them through a cousin of Sir William Wallace, was vested in the family for more than five hundred years. The House of Rawdon, whose head became the husband of the heiress of Loudoun in 1804, is heard of before Stephen's time, and amongst their titles was one, the Earl of Huntingdon, which had often been conferred on Scottish monarchs. Through Katherine Pole's marriage to Francis Hastings, the blood of the Plantagenets was in their veins; and her son Henry came within the shadow of the throne, being at one time thought of as the successor of Elizabeth. The Baroness Loudoun, the wife of the Earl of Moira, could match the proud traditions of her husband's family; her own name, Flora Mure, indicated the fact that she was the chief representative of the House of Rowallan, one of whose daughters was the wife of Robert II and a mother of kings. Loudoun Castle, both as to its site and aspect, can well sustain the dignity of all this rich accumulation of family renown. It is, indeed, not unworthy of the name of the Scottish Windsor.

Four hundred years ago the original seat of the Loudoun family was destroyed by fire in a raid of the Kennedies; and a fragment of that Mediaeval structure, now called the Old Place, with a portion of the moat, is still to be seen about a quarter of a mile to the north-east of the present Castle. In shape the latter is nearly a square, and it contains upwards of ninety apartments. Its principal builders were the great Chancellor, the first Earl of Loudoun, who died in 1652, and the Marquis of Hastings, who made additions in the first decade of the present century which cost not less than £100,000, even though the plans were not completed. The large tower is arched on the three lower stories; the three upper stories are all modern, and were built at the same time as the front. The arms of the Craufurds of Loudoun, with the motto "I bide my time," are to be seen on an old stone, taken, doubtless, from the ancient Castle and built into its successor. The plans of the Marquis of Hastings included a large banqueting-hall, which was never begun. He so impoverished himself that he could not afford to reside in the palace which he had erected; in less than two years after his return from India, where he had held sway as Governor-General for ten eventful years, he was compelled to seek a new appointment, and in a few months thereafter he died abroad while acting as Governor of Malta. Norman Macleod, who owed his first living to the Marquis's widow, tells us that his lordship's ample fortune "absolutely sank under the benevolence of his nature." A portrait of the Marquis, by Sir Joshua Reynolds, hangs in the billiard-room, along with portraits of his parents; his mother was a daughter of the pious Lady. Huntingdon.

In the dining-room is a portrait of Charles I, with marks (though it has been mended within the past seven years) of the ill-usage it received from Cromwell's soldiers when they seized the Castle; the Roundheads cut out the nose of the King with their swords. The same apartment contains a portrait by Lely of Lady Margaret Dalrymple, wife of Earl Hugh, the only daughter of the first and sister of the great Earl of Stair - a notable woman who died at Sorn Castle in 1777, in her hundredth year. Four years before her death, Dr Johnson was introduced to her at Loudoun Castle; she had all her faculties unimpaired, which, says Boswell, "was a very cheering sight to Dr Johnson, who had an extraordinary desire for long life." A melancholy interest attaches to the portrait of this centenarian lady's son, Earl John, who, being revoked from his position as Commander of the British forces during the American War, shot himself in the library at Loudoun in 1782. The exquisitely carved fire-place in the dining-room is of Irish marble from the quarries at Moira.

The entrance-hall, 70 feet long by 30, is open to the roof, from which it is lighted by a large circular window; the galleries surrounding it are supported by eight immense scagliola columns of great beauty. At the head of the first stair hangs the two-handed sword of Sir William Wallace, which has been in the possession of the family for centuries. When George IV visited Scotland, the sword was carried to Dalkeith Palace to be shown to the King. Since then it disappeared from view for thirty years; no one knew what had become of it, till it was accidentally discovered in the charter closet a few years ago. Another notable relic is an ancient clock from Rowallan Castle; the oaken case, less than a foot in width, is upwards of eight feet in height. On the panel are the initials of Sir William Mure, most likely the old Puritan poet of the seventeenth century. In the drawing-room there is a portrait of Gideon Loudoun, the Austrian Field-Marshal, who was one of Maria Theresa's most successful generals, and a special object of aversion to Frederick the Great. A portrait of Allan Ramsay, by his son, recalls the fact that the poet was a guest in the Castle of the fourth Earl, where, at his lordship's suggestion, he wrote his song of The Lass O' Patie's Mill. The latest additions to the artistic treasures are the portraits of Mr Charles Frederick Abney-Hastings (now Lord Donington) and of his late wife, the Countess of Loudoun, mother of the present Earl. In the library, a pillared room a hundred feet in length, whose walls belong to the ancient portion of the Castle, but the ceiling of which is new, is a portrait of the Earl of Huntingdon, who was spoken of as Queen Elizabeth's successor, and some other portraits of members of the same illustrious house. The books, which number about 8000, include many folios that belonged to the great Chancellor.

The Policies, which were laid out from plans of the Earl of Mar before 1715, include hundreds of acres of fine woodland that owes its existence mainly to John, the fourth Earl, who planted upwards of a million of trees, many of which were brought from America and the Continent by himself. He formed one of the most extensive collections of willows ever made in this country. The most remarkable of all the trees is a yew growing close to the south side of the Castle, which would have been made the front but for the sake of the venerable king of the forest; it is 13 feet 9 1/2 inches in girth, and of unknown antiquity. There is good reason to believe that it is at least eight centuries old. One of the family charters is said to have been signed under its branches in the reign of William the Lion; one of the Articles of Union was also subscribed in its shade by Earl Hugh; and in the Covenanting times, Lord James, while an exile in Holland, addressed the letters for his lady, "To the Gudewife at the Auldton at the Old Yew Tree of Loudoun, Scotland." In the garden may be seen the first "Ayrshire rose;" it was brought hither by Lord John from America, and is yet growing fresh and vigorous. The family vault at Loudoun Kirk, a quarter of a mile to the west of the Castle, is visited by many pilgrims, from respect to the memory of Lady Flora Hastings; in her mother's grave was interred the right hand of her husband, the. Governor-General.

Loudoun Castle, with the estates appertaining to it, was sold by the last Marquis of Hastings, the year before his death, to his cousin the Marquis of Bute. Two years afterwards the Castle and estates were purchased from the latter for the sum of £300,000 by the late Countess of Loudoun; and on her death, in 1874, these devolved on her husband, Mr Abney-Hastings (now Lord Donington), while their eldest son, the young Earl of Loudoun, succeeded to the family inheritance of Rowallan.

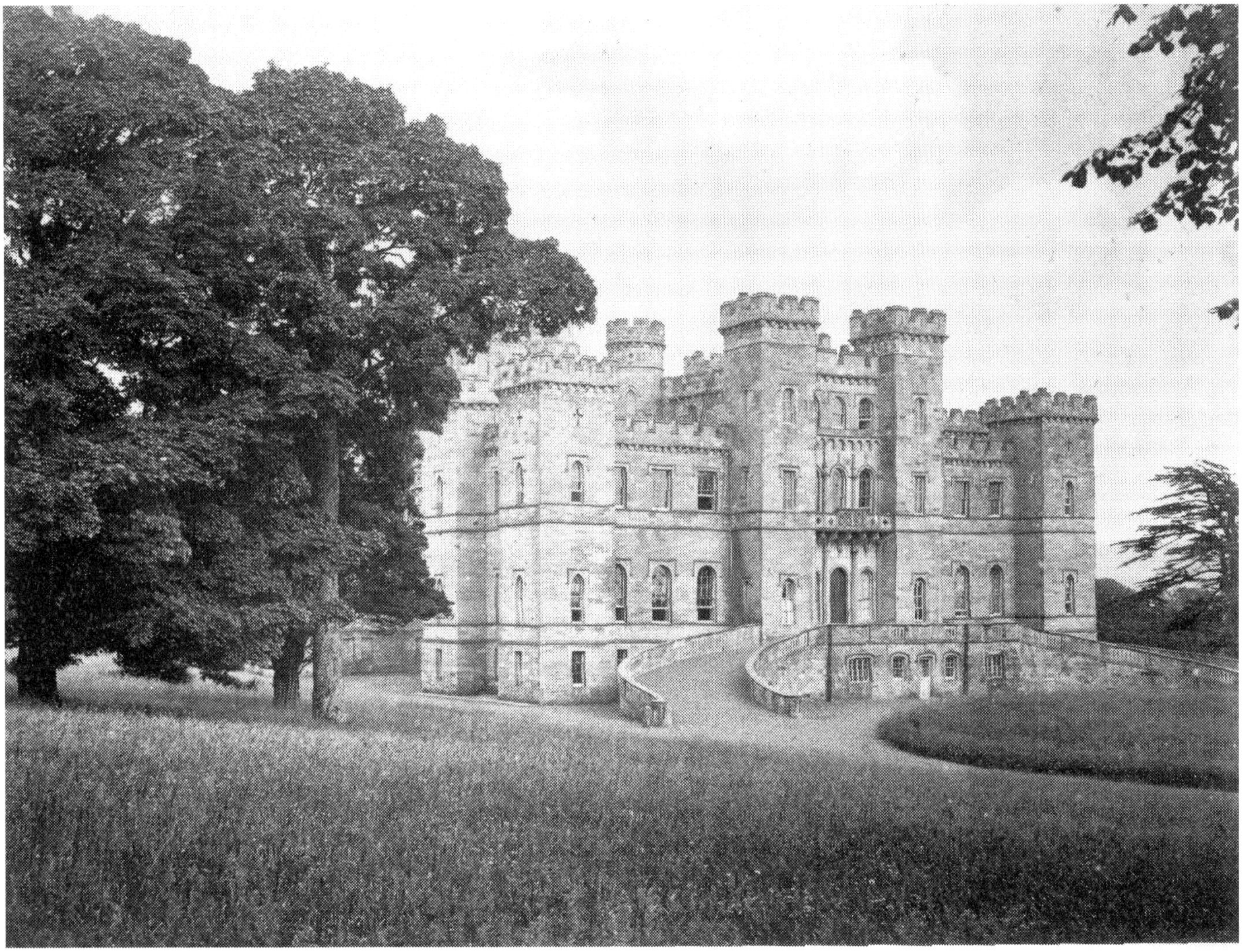

MOUNT CHARLES.

WHEN the Barony of Alloway was disposed of by the magistrates of Ayr in 1754, some of the finest estates in the neighbourhood of the county-town were originated. Amongst these may be mentioned Doonholm, Cambusdoon, Belleisle, and the property now known by the name of Mount Charles. At the time referred to, Charles Dalrymple, Esq. of Orangefield, purchased two lots, named respectively Dykehead Moss and Alloway Mill; and joining them together, he called the estate Mount Charles after his own forename, and built a residence for himself upon it. When he died in 1787, the place was purchased from his trustees by Captain Robert Gairdner of Ayr, who retained the portion formerly called Dykehead Moss, and disposed of Alloway Mill to the tenth Earl of Cassillis. Captain Gairdner's son, who was Commissioner to the Earl of Eglinton, sold Mount Charles, in 1819, to Major James Davidson of the East India Company's Service; and from the widow of the latter it was acquired by the late Lieutenant-General Hughes in 1827.

The family of the new proprietor belonged originally to Wales, but had settled in Surrey, and he won distinction in the army both in India and America. When he returned to this country he married Hamilla, sixth and youngest daughter of the late John Hamilton of Sundrum and Lilias, sister of the twelfth Earl of Eglintoun, and some time afterwards he purchased Mount Charles. He died in 1832 in his sixty-ninth year, and was buried in the kirkyard of Alloway, where a handsome mausoleum has been erected as a memorial of him. As he left no issue, his estates of Mount Charles and Balkissock fell to his nephew, Henry Hughes-Onslow, Esq., whose son, Arthur Hughes-Onslow, succeeded in 1870, and is the present proprietor. He resides principally at Balkissock, near Ballantrae.

The house which Mr Dalrymple erected was removed by General Hughes to make room for the modern mansion of Mount Charles, which was completed in 1829. It was the residence of his widow until the time of her death.

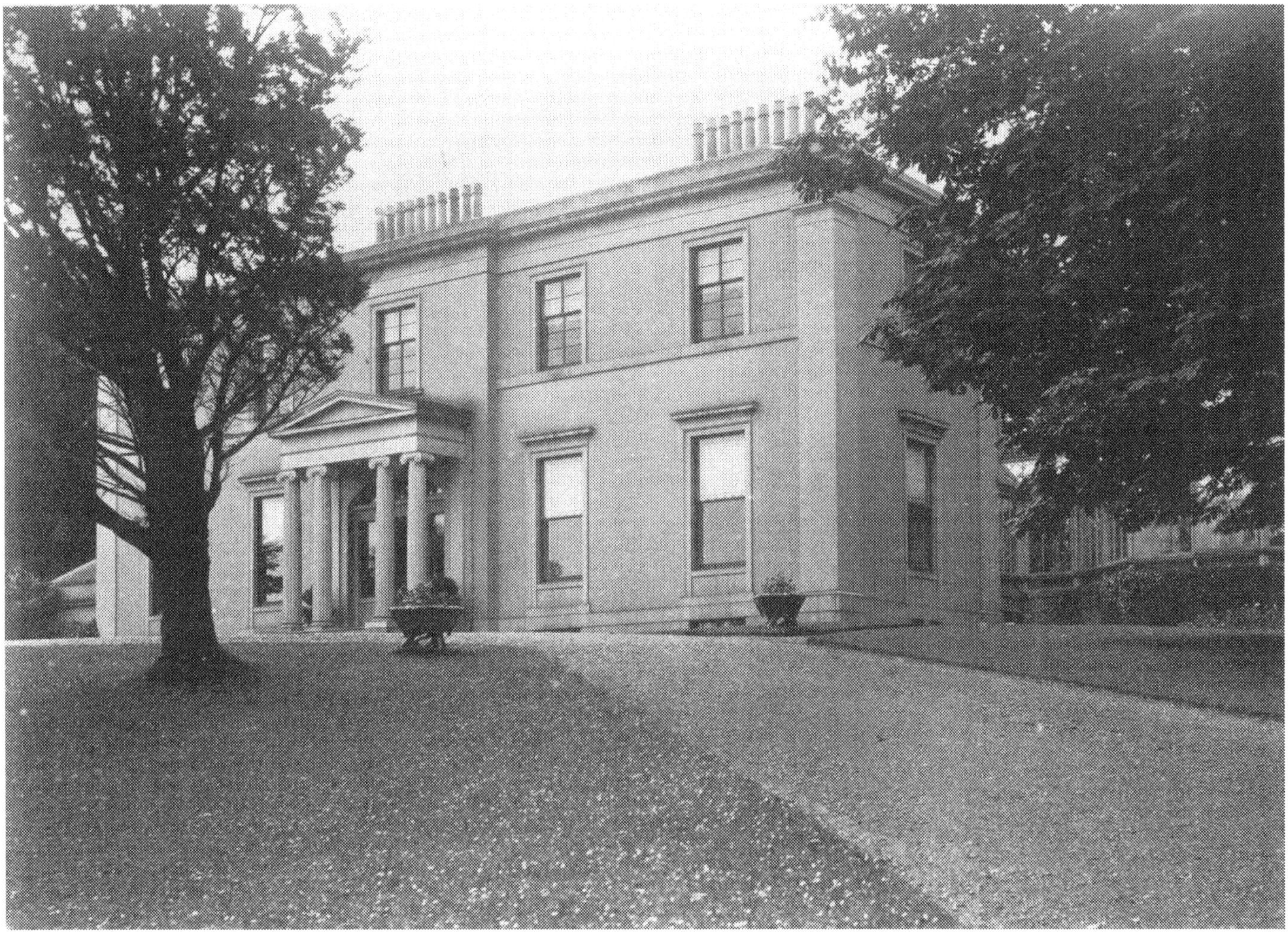

NEWARK CASTLE.

THE Castle of Newark, in the parish of Maybole, about three miles from Ayr, was one of the numerous seats of the Kennedy family, and still belongs to the Marquess of Ailsa, who is the chief titled representative of that race. The oldest portion of the fortalice was probably built about the beginning of the eleventh century, and it was used as a residence for some of the younger members of the Culzean family until the middle of last century, when it was abandoned under peculiar circumstances, and suffered to fall into a ruinous condition. The castle was reconstructed and repaired about thirty years ago, and is now inhabited.

The last Kennedy who bore the territorial title of Newark had a strange history. His grandfather, Sir Archibald Kennedy, was descended from the Knight of Culzean, who was assassinated by Mure of Auchendrane, and had been made a baronet of Nova Scotia in 1682. Sir Archibald died in 1710, and was succeeded by his son, Sir John Kennedy, who married Jean Douglas of Mains, Dumbartonshire, and had a family of twenty children by her. The eldest son became second baronet, and was followed by his brother, Sir Thomas Kennedy of Culzean, who ultimately succeeded as ninth Earl of Cassillis. The third son, David Kennedy of Newark, was raised to the title of tenth Earl of Cassillis on the death of his brother without issue in 1775. He was trained to the profession of the law, passed as advocate in 1752, and represented Ayrshire in Parliament from 1768 till 1774, but was defeated in the latter year by Sir Adam Fergusson of Kilkerran. Having attained the Earldom, he sat as one of the representative peers for Scotland continuously from 1776 till 1790; and as he died unmarried in, 1792, the title reverted to his remote kinsman, Captain Archibald Kennedy, R.N., who became eleventh Earl of Cassillis, and whose lineal descendant is the present Marquess of Ailsa. Newark Castle was little occupied after the elevation of David Kennedy to the Earldom, and thus became the prey of wind and weather; but it has now been restored to more than its original glory.

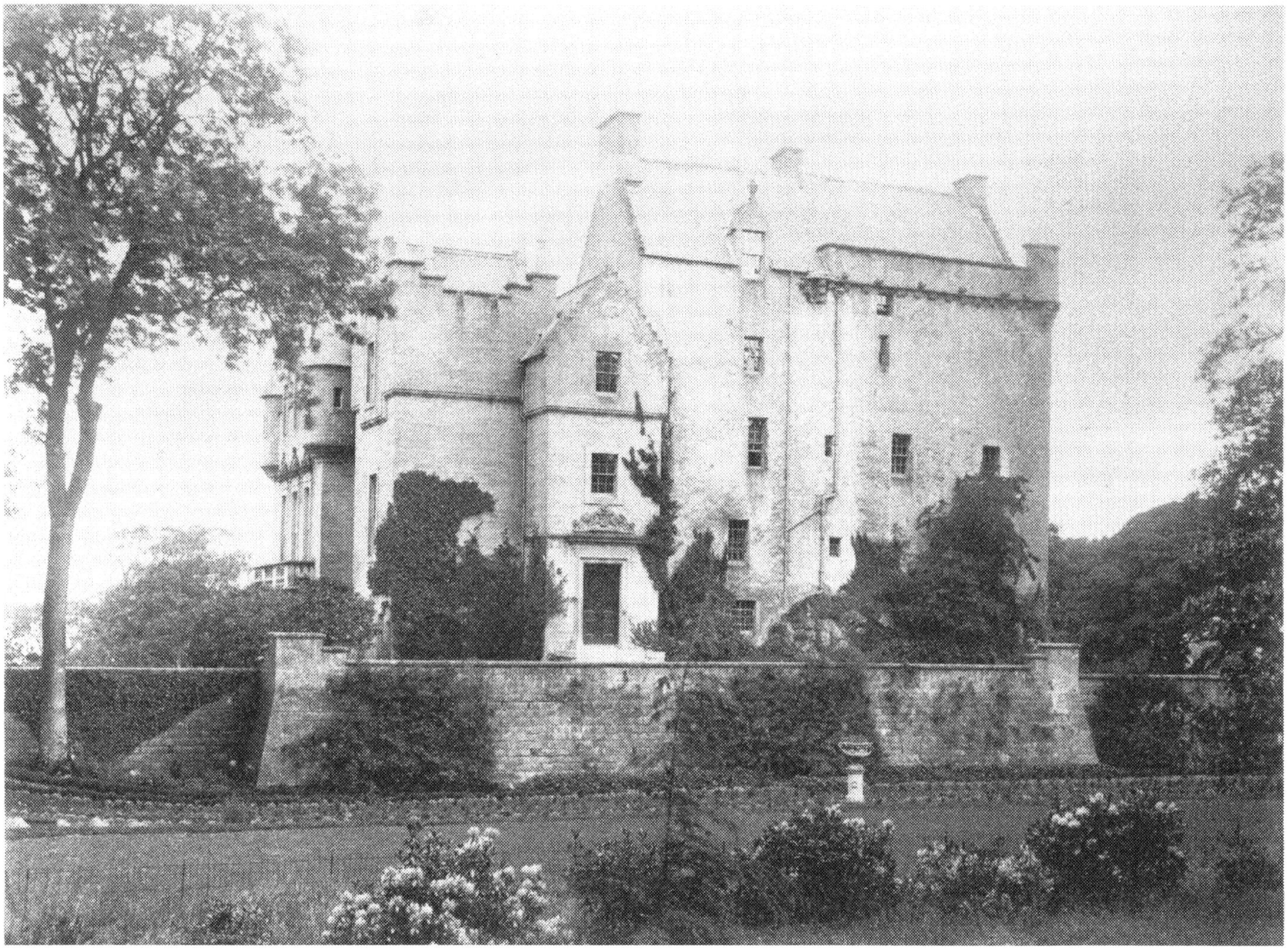

NEWFIELD.

THE ancient name of Newfield was *Galrigs*, which was spelled, under the lax rules of orthography that formerly prevailed, "Gariggis," "Galrix," and "Garrickis." The first family connected with the estate of which any trace has been found is that of Wallace of Gariggis, who held the lands in 1578. This branch of the Wallace family seems to have been of some standing in the locality, since its members married with the Fullartouns, Blairs, and Boyds - the most potent names in the neighbourhood. The exact succession to the estate cannot now be determined; but it is certain that the last of the family was William Wallace of Galrigs, who entered as heir, to his great-grandfather and grandfather in 1714, and was in possession of the property in 1720. For a short time afterwards the place was occupied by Captain Lawrence Nugent, whose name appears with the territorial affix "of Newfield," from 1725 till 1758. It is likely, therefore, that the change of name in the estate may be attributed to him.

In the records of the estate of Newfield a serious hiatus exists between the dates 1758 and 1783, and it is impossible to tell at this time whether the Nugent family continued in possession during this quarter of a century or not. At the latter date the lands came into the hands of a scion of one of the oldest Ayrshire families. Major Craufurd, who claimed to be chief of the name of Craufurd through his descent from Patrick Craufurd of Auchinames (circa 1580), returned from India, where he had won merited distinction, in 1783, and sought to obtain standing in his ancestral county by the purchase of Newfield. Shortly afterwards he married a daughter of the family of McKerrell of Hillhouse, and at his death, in 1794, he was succeeded by his eldest son, Robert, who claimed to represent the families of Craufurd and Crosbie. As the discussion upon the rights of the Auchinames and Newfield families rests upon points of recondite genealogy, we may safely leave to the decision of experts, noting only that so far as the Newfield Craufurds are concerned, the claim is practically abandoned. Major Craufurd died in 1794, and his son Robert, who was Colonel of the Ayrshire Yeomanry and a Deputy-Lieutenant, left the estate of Newfield to his eldest son, Robert, in 1843. It was sold in 1843 to James Finnie, Esq., an Ayrshire gentleman who had made his fortune in London; and it is now in the possession of his third son, William Finnie, Esq. of Newfield, appointed Deputy-Lieutenant of Ayrshire in 1871, and M.P. for the northern division of the county of Ayr from 1868 to 1874. The present mansion is in the Jacobean style, introduced to Scotland by the Duke of York (afterwards James VII), though the building is of a more recent date, and may have been erected by Captain Nugent, *circa* 1725.

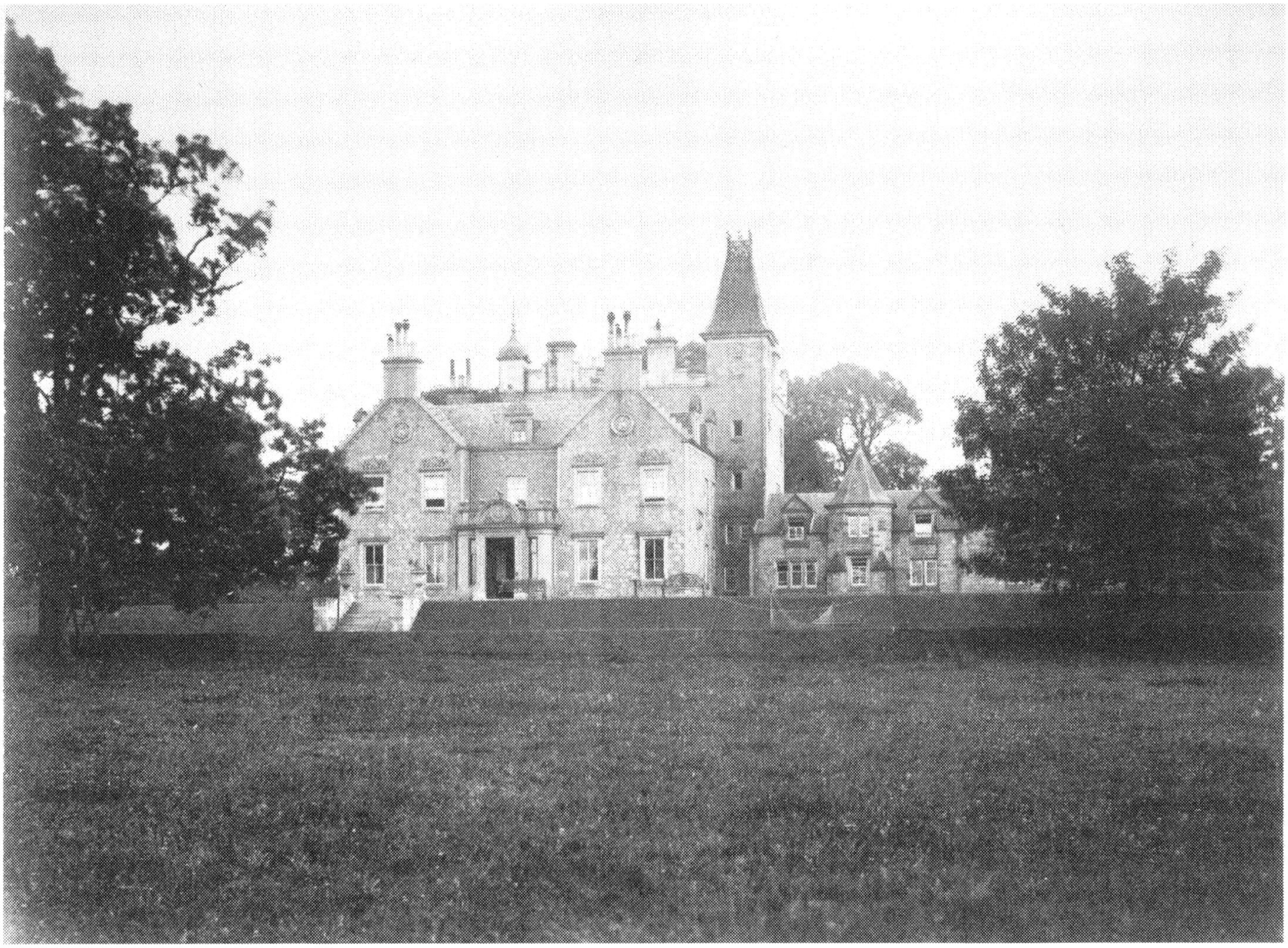

PENKILL.

THE Castle of Penkill was originally a square tower or *peel*, with corner turrets, probably built about 1500, although the late Mr George Street, the celebrated architect, considered that it belonged to an earlier period from the style of ornamentation on one of the existing dormer windows. A much larger building was added to this peel by Thomas Boyd in 1628, after his marriage with Marion Mure of Rowallan; and the new portion was connected with the old by a projecting circular staircase, over the doorway of which his coat of arms, the initials of himself and his wife, and the date of the erection were carved. This staircase had fallen into a ruinous condition during the minority of the late Spencer Boyd, and he replaced it by a much larger decorated staircase, of similar construction, after he came of age.

The estate of Penkill was acquired by Adam Boyd, grandson of Robert, Lord Kilmarnock, early in the sixteenth century, and has remained in the family since that time. The first Boyd of Penkill died circa 1530, and was succeeded by his son Adam. The grandson of the latter died in 1596, and his son Thomas added the larger building, to which allusion has been made. The estate descended from father to son, almost without interruption, till the death of Alexander Boyd of Penkill in 1750, when the succession fell to John Boyd of Trochrig, the head of the family from which Zachary Boyd and Principal Robert Boyd of Glasgow had sprung. When his daughter and heiress died without issue, the estate came to Spencer Boyd, a descendant of James Boyd, second son of John Boyd of Penkill and Trochrig, who had spent his early years as a physician in the United States of America. He died in 1782, and was succeeded first by his eldest son, James, and ten years afterwards by his second son, Spencer Boyd. The son and namesake of the latter became Laird of Penkill in 1820; and at his death in 1827, the succession fell to his infant son, Spencer, to whom reference has already been made as one of the principal improvers and reconstructors of the castle. Miss Alice Boyd, his sister, - the present proprietrix, - has recently added a large hall, with open timber ceiling, to the structure for a dining-room and picture-gallery.

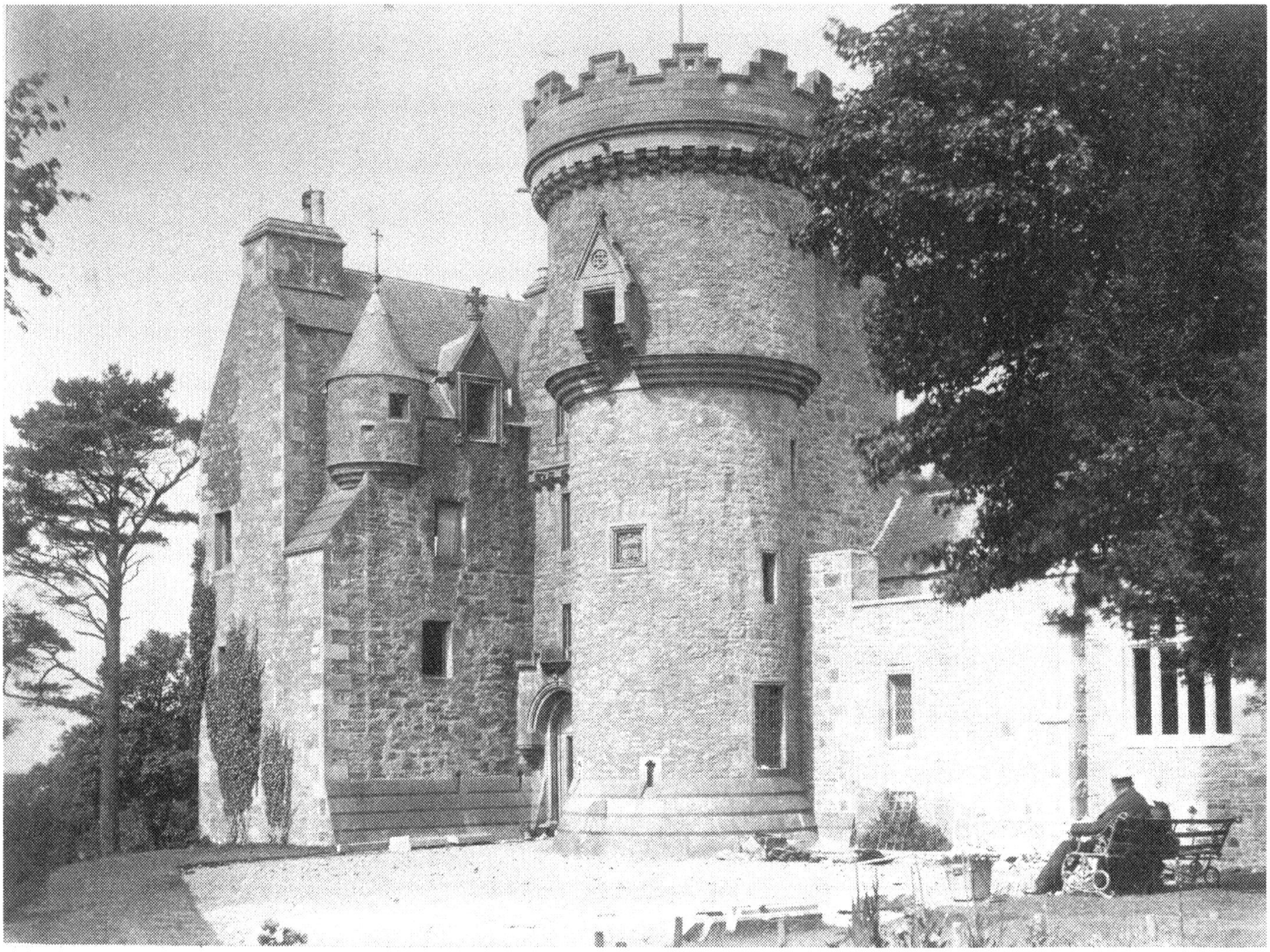

PERCETON.

PERCETON, or, as it was called of old, Peristoun or Pierstoune, has long been the residence of families of standing in the county of Ayr. Originally Crown lands, it passed by charter from King Robert I to James Stewart, son of Sir John Stewart of Bonhill, and grandson of Alexander, Lord High Steward of Scotland. The Stewarts of Peristoun ended in an heiress, who married into a branch of the great House of Douglas. "Jac de Douglas de Peristoune" is witness to a charter signed in the parish church of Perceton - "apud ecclesiam parochialem de Peristoune" - 5th March 1467; and soon afterwards, again it is said by marriage, the Barclays - possibly of the Ardrossan family - came into possession.

In 1668 Sir Robert Barclay, knight, was created a Baronet of Nova Scotia, and in 1720 his grandson, Sir James Barclay, the fourth Baronet, sold Perceton to Andrew Macredie. The Barclays have no longer any connection with Ayrshire, but the family still flourish, and are settled in the island of Mauritius.

Andrew Macredie, the new proprietor of Perceton, was a member of a Galloway family. His residence was in Stranraer, where he built what at that time was the best house in the place, and lived there in a style of great hospitality. He was the Provost of the burgh, and universally respected. Mr Macredie was succeeded in Perceton by his only son, Andrew, who married Jean Boyd, only daughter of Thomas Boyd of Pitoon, one of the best families in Ayrshire. He died in 1764, leaving issue, William, his only surviving son and successor, and three daughters, of whom the eldest, Christian, married Archibald Cunninghame of Caddel and Thornton; Helen, the second, married James Campbell of Treesbank; and Jane, the youngest, was drowned at Arran in 1795.

William Macredie, third of Perceton, had married, in 1762, Barbara Wilson, a most excellent and accomplished lady, and by her had a large family - John, his successor in Perceton; Andrew, captain of an East Indiaman, and who was lost at sea; Robert, who also commanded an East Indiaman, and afterwards retired and lived at Williamfield, near Irvine; William, Captain of Artillery, H.E.I.C.S., and who was killed at the siege of Seringapatam; Archibald, who was also in the H.E.I.C.S., and died when on the march to the same fortress; and Thomas, an Army Surgeon in H.M. service, and afterwards of Cromla in Arran. Mrs Reid of Adamton, a well-known Ayrshire lady, was one of William Macredie's daughters.

John Macredie, fourth of Perceton, was an officer in the Royal Navy when he succeeded his father, and had served his country in Rodney's great victory. On his marriage to Mary Rachel, daughter of Major David Morrison, H.E.I.C.S., he left the service, and lived at Perceton till his death in 1834. He had an only daughter, Rachel Ann, who married, in 1835, Patrick Boyle Mure, Advocate, second son of Thomas Mure of Warriston, Midlothian, a cadet of the ancient family of Mure of Caldwell.

Mr Mure-Macredie died in 1868, leaving two sons-Thomas Mure Mure, Advocate, whose untimely death in 1876 at the terrible railway accident at Abbots Ripton was universally deplored in the county and by his many friends; and John Macredie Mure, a Captain in the 34th Regiment, whose inventions in scientific musketry, and skill in applying them, gained him the appointment of Deputy-Assistant Adjutant General for that branch of the service; he died in India in 1879. Mr Thomas M. Mure was unmarried, and Captain Mure left no children.

Mrs Rachel Ann Mure-Macredie, fifth of Perceton, survives her husband, and, with her daughters, Mary Rachel and Helen Jane, resides at the old family place.

The old house of Perceton was taken down about 1770, and the present one was built at the same time a little to the south of the former site. It is pleasantly situated, among fine old timber, in the parish of Dreghorn and district of Cunninghame.

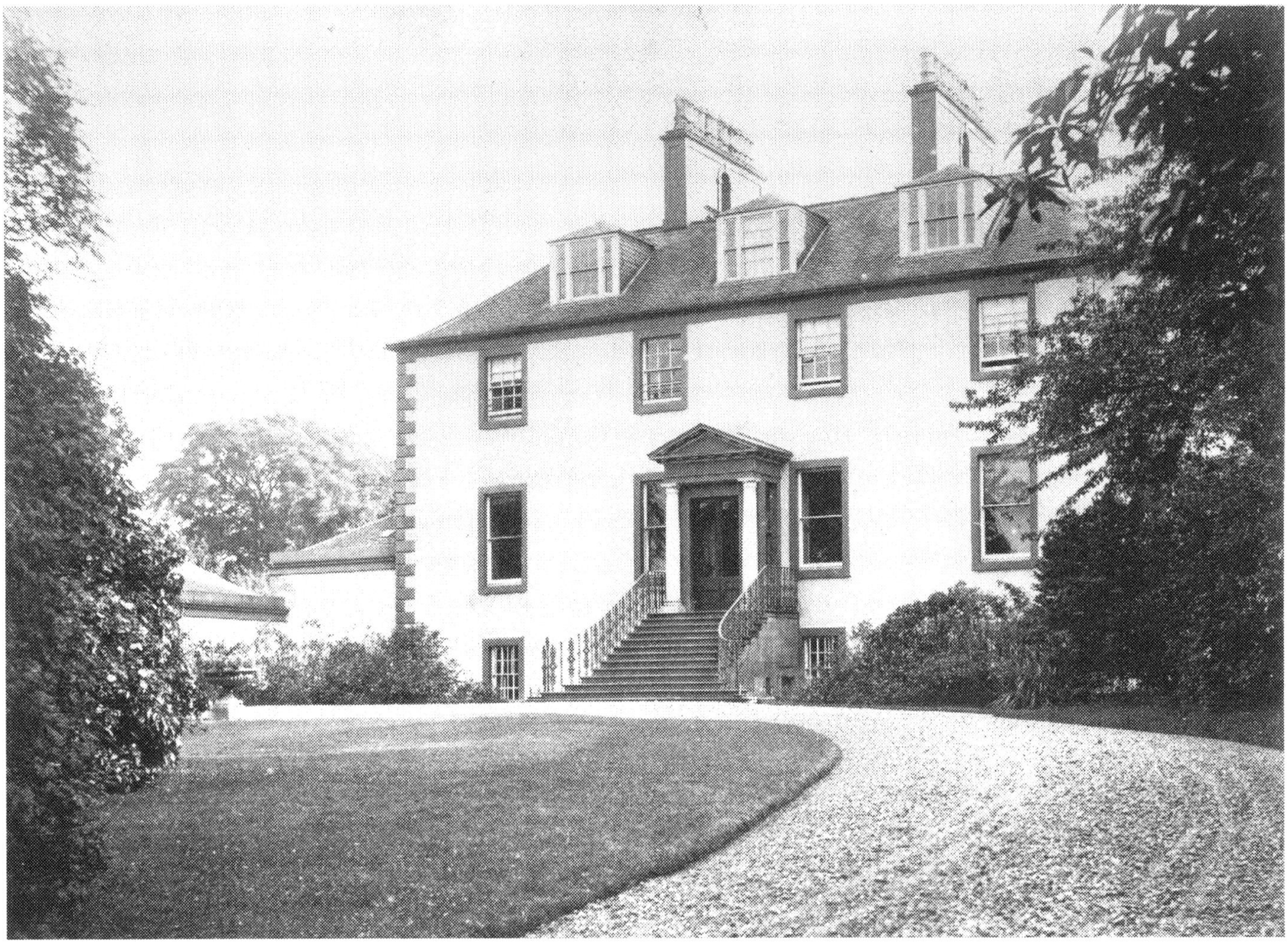

PINMORE.

THE Hamiltons of Pinmore are descended from Hugh Hamilton of Glengall, who was married to Jean Ferguson of Castlehill, and became the progenitors of the Hamiltons of Bourtreehill and of Sundrum. The third son of Hugh Hamilton was the Rev. Hugh Hamilton, minister of the Gospel at Girvan, who died in 1788 at the age of eighty-one. His son, Hugh Hamilton, acquired the estate of Pinmore, and at his death, without direct heirs, was succeeded by his cousin, Colonel Alexander West Hamilton, second son of the Laird of Sundrum. Colonel Hamilton married his cousin, Hamilla, daughter of Alexander Montgomerie of Annick Lodge, and cousin of the twelfth Earl of Eglintoun (he died in 1837), and by her had, with daughters, Hugh, the present Laird of Pinmore, who was formerly Captain in the King's Dragoon Guards, and is a Deputy-Lieutenant of Ayrshire.

Pinmore is situated in the parish of Colmonell, on the river Stinchar, and not far from Daljarrock, which belongs to the same proprietor. The original house was built in the sixteenth and seventeenth centuries, in the Scottish Baronial style of architecture. It was destroyed by fire in 1876, and has been restored in the same style. It stands on a rising ground on one of the most lovely bends of the Stinchar, and is surrounded by beautifully wooded hills.

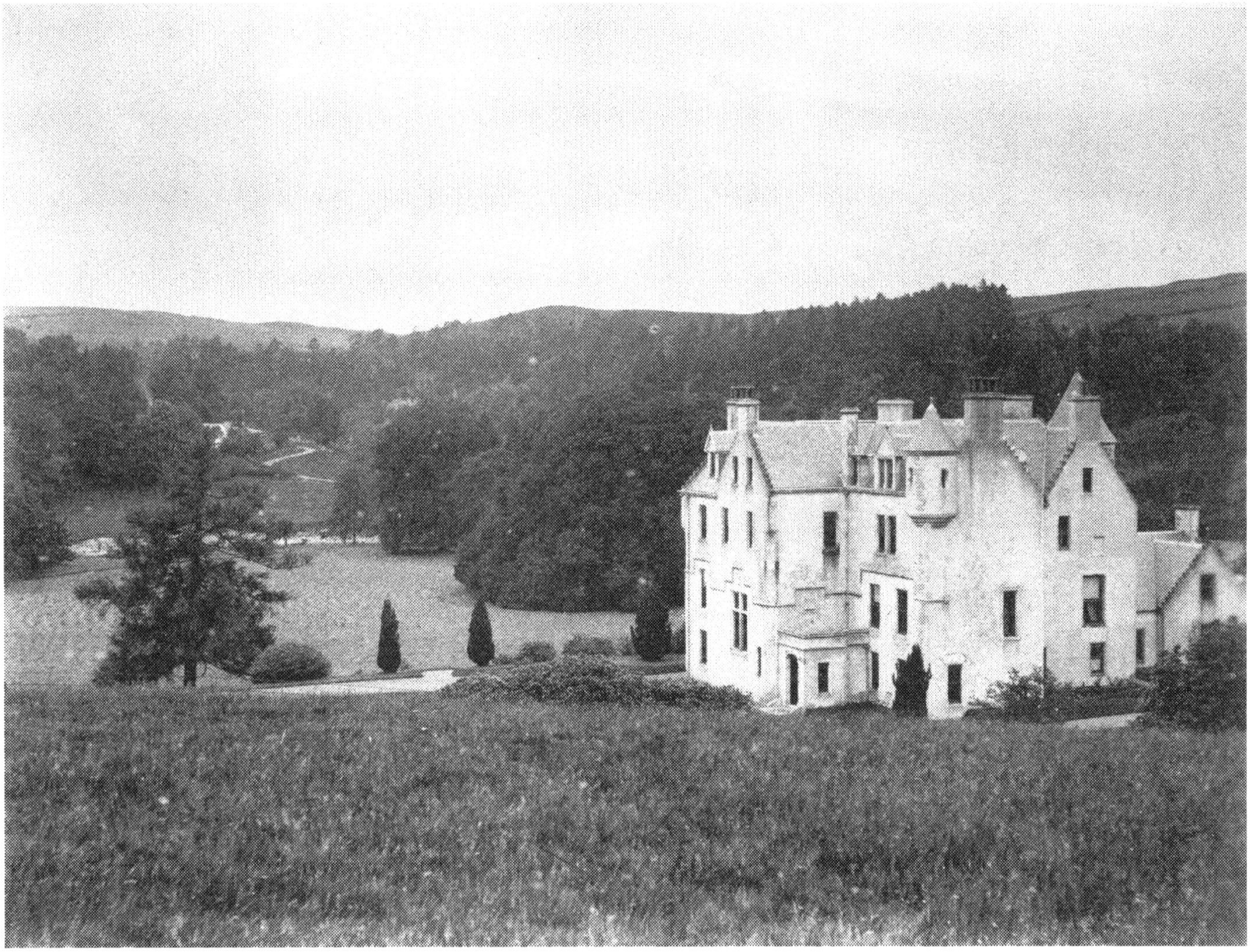

ROSEMOUNT.

THE mansion of Rosemount was rebuilt by Dr William Fullartoun about 1770, and has undergone few alterations since that time. The estate upon which it stands was formerly called Goldring; and under that title it can be traced back to 1549, when it belonged to the Schaws of Sornbeg. There are not many properties in Ayrshire that have passed through so many vicissitudes as this one. During the remainder of the sixteenth century it was in the hands of "George Jamesoun, burgess of Air," and afterwards of John Wallace of Craigie. It came back to the Schaws in the early part of the seventeenth century, but passed to the McKerrels of Hillhouse in 1636. William Cuninghame of Previck had the lands in 1647, but they were in the possession of the third Earl of Dundonald in 1690. From the sixth Earl they were acquired by Patrick Fullartoun, of the family of Fullartoun of that Ilk, who died in 1743, and was succeeded by his eldest son, that Dr Fullartoun to whom we have alluded. The latter had been a surgeon in India, and he did much to improve the estate by planting timber, and introducing methods of artificial manuring. He died without issue in 1805, in his sixty-eighth year. Rosemount was next occupied by Lord James Stuart (1794-1859), brother of the late Marquess of Bute, who took the territorial title, and represented first the Ayr Burghs, and then Ayrshire, in Parliament from 1834 till his death. The estate was in the possession of George Bogle, Esq., in 1839, and was purchased afterwards by the late William Baird, Esq. of Elie, whose son is now proprietor. Rosemount is in the parish of Symington, near the main road between Monkton and Kilmarnock.

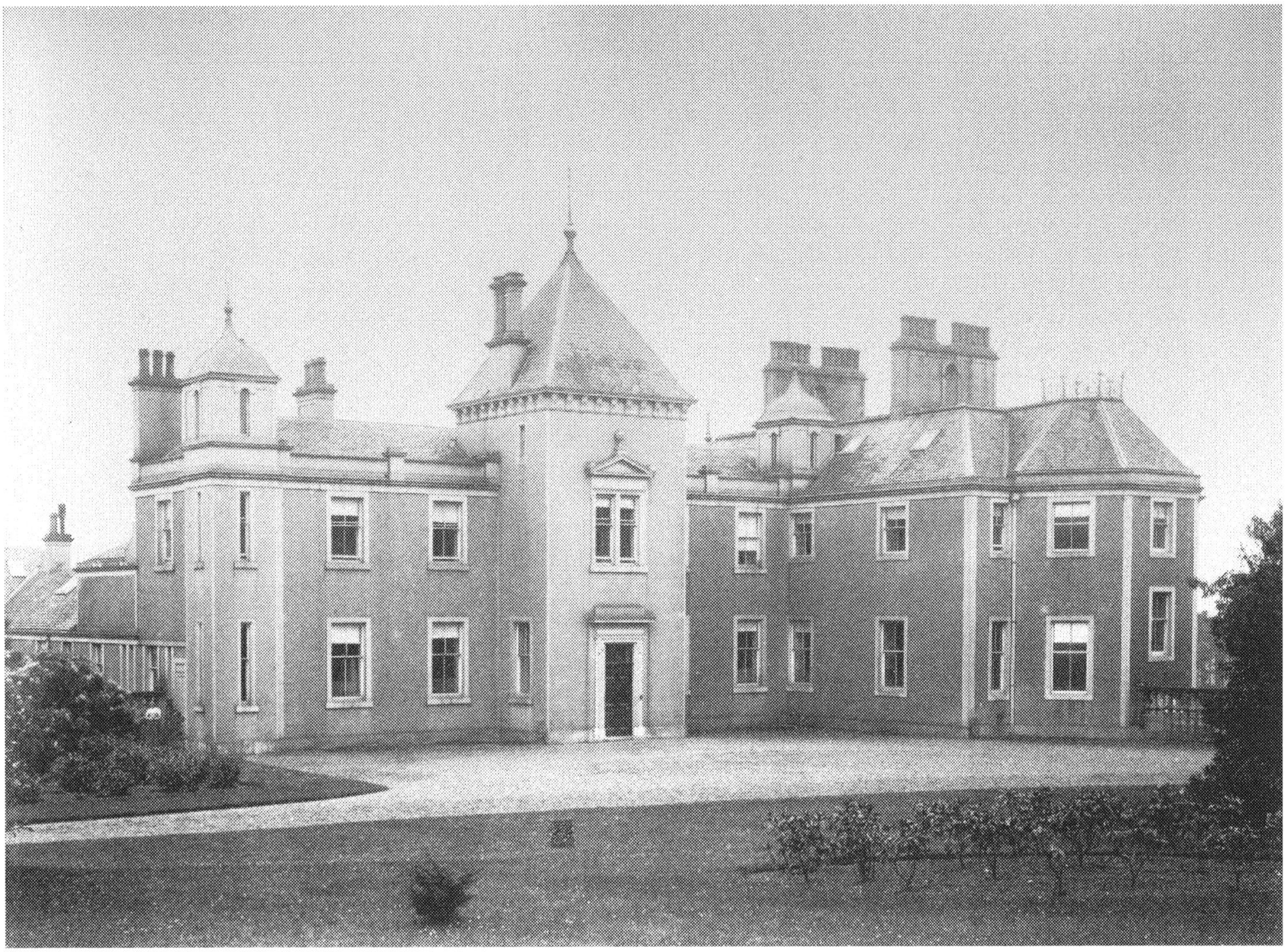

ROWALLAN.

ROWALLAN CASTLE is perhaps as picturesque as any of the numerous baronial mansions in Ayrshire, and though it is now deserted and fast falling to ruin, it still retains some portion of its former grandeur, and is hallowed by many memories of the olden times. For centuries it was associated with the ancient and honourable family of Mure, and numbered amongst its inhabitants not a few of the patriots of Scotland. The castle stands upon the banks of Carmel Water, about three miles north of Kilmarnock; and it is conjectured that at a remote period the river swept closely around the base of the gentle eminence upon which the original fort was erected, thus justifying the name of "the Craig of Rowallan," which it once bore.

The oldest portion of the building is a vaulted lower apartment, which probably dates from the thirteenth century, and may have been the birthplace of Elizabeth Mure, the first wife of Robert II of Scotland, and mother of the Duke of Albany, and the Earls of Carrick, Fife, and Buchan. This part of the castle has been surrounded by more recent erections of various dates. The main front, with the staircase and double turrets, was built circa 1562 by John Mure of Rowallan and his wife, Marion Cuninghame, and their names and armorial bearings may yet be found on the upper portion of the structure. Several other dates are carved on different parts of the castle, marking the times when alterations or repairs were executed. The Royal Arms of Scotland, fully blazoned, are carved over the main entrance, together with the shields of the Cumin family, from whom the Mures claimed descent, and the Moor's head, which forms the Rowallan crest. It has been suggested that the latter emblem may have been assumed to commemorate some feat of prowess against the Saracens during the Crusades; but it is more likely to be merely a term of canting heraldry - a *jeu-de-mot* on the name *Mure*.

From a genealogical account of the Mures of Rowallan, drawn up early in the eighteenth century, it appears that in the time of Alexander III (ascended 1245) the barony belonged to Sir Walter Cumin (Comyn or Cuming), whose only daughter and heiress, Isobel, was bestowed by the king upon Sir J. Gilchrist Mure as a reward for his valour at the memorable battle of Largs in 1263. The first Mure of Rowallan was either the builder or the repairer of the old castle, as the conjoint arms of himself and his wife were visible upon the oldest portion of it last century. He died in 1277, and was buried in Mure's Aisle at Kilmarnock. His grandson, Sir Robert, the third Baronet, had only one daughter, who married Sir Adam Mure, second son of Lord Abercorn, and whose daughter was that Elizabeth Mure, the Queen of Robert II, to whom allusion has been made. From Sir Adam's three younger brothers sprang the numerous branches of the Mure family afterwards settled in Caldwell, Thornton, Glanderstoun, Treescraig, Auchendrane, Cloncaird, Aucheneil, Craighead, Park, Middleton, Spittleside, and Brownhill. The succession descended from father to son, without interruption, from the time of Sir Adam, the fourth Baronet (*circa* 1350), till the death of Sir William, sixteenth Laird of Rowallan, in 1700. During this long period many noble matrimonial alliances were made, and several of the members of the family distinguished themselves both in literature and in arms. Sir William Mure, twelfth Laird, was knighted by James VI, "who had value for him, and never mentioned the House of Rowallan but with great respect as one of the families he was come of." He died in 1606, and was succeeded by his son, Sir William, who was knighted by Charles I in 1633. * He was thrice married, and left a numerous family at his death in 1639. His son, Sir William, is perhaps best known to the nation as one of the poets to whom the General Assembly committed the task of preparing a metrical version of the Psalms of David, which received the approbation of Robert Baillie, but was rejected for the version by Francis Rous still used in Scotland. He wrote a history of his own family, and was Member for Ayrshire in the Convention of 1643-44. Thought an ardent Covenanter, he was opposed to the execution of the king, and composed an elegy on his death. A curious fact regarding his connection with Glasgow University has not been recorded by his biographers. His kinsman, Zachary Boyd, Rector of the University and author of Zion's Flowers, had lent considerable sums of money to Rowallan, the Earl of Loudoun, the Earl of Glencairn, Maxwell of Nether Pollok, and others, holding their bonds for repayment; and when Boyd died he left this money by will to the Senate, "to be imployed for building of newe buildings in the said College" The bonds were not immediately redeemed, and for several years the estate of Rowallan contributed towards the erection of the High Street frontage of 'the old Glasgow College buildings. Sir William Mure died in 1667. His grandson, who bore the same name, was the sixteenth and last Mure of Rowallan. He represented Ayrshire in Parliament from 1690 till his death in 1700, and gave his hearty support to William of Orange. His daughter was married to the first Earl of Glasgow, and her elder daughter married Sir James Campbell of Lawers, third son of the Earl of Loudoun, who thus became Laird of Rowallan. He was Member for Ayrshire from 1727 till 1741, and died on the field of Fontenoy in 1745. His son, Major-General James Mure Campbell of Rowallan (1726-86), became fifth Earl of Loudoun in 1782. His only daughter, Flora, Countess of Loudoun in her own right, married the first Marquess of Hastings in 1804, and died in 1826; and her great-grandson, Charles Edward Hastings Abney-Hastings, eleventh Earl of Loudon (born 1855, succeeded 1874), is the present proprietor of Rowallan Castle, and the representative the ancient Scottish families of Mure and Campbell of Loudoun.

* The compiler of the *Lineage of the Muirs of Rowallan* is evidently wrong in his chronology at this point, as he makes the first Sir William attain an incredible age, and almost outlive two of his successors. The dates should run thus: John Mure, born 1515, *died* 1581, aetat. 66. Sir William, b. 1546, d 1606 = 60. Sir William, b. 1576, d. 1639 = 63. Sir William, b. 1604, d. 1667 = 63

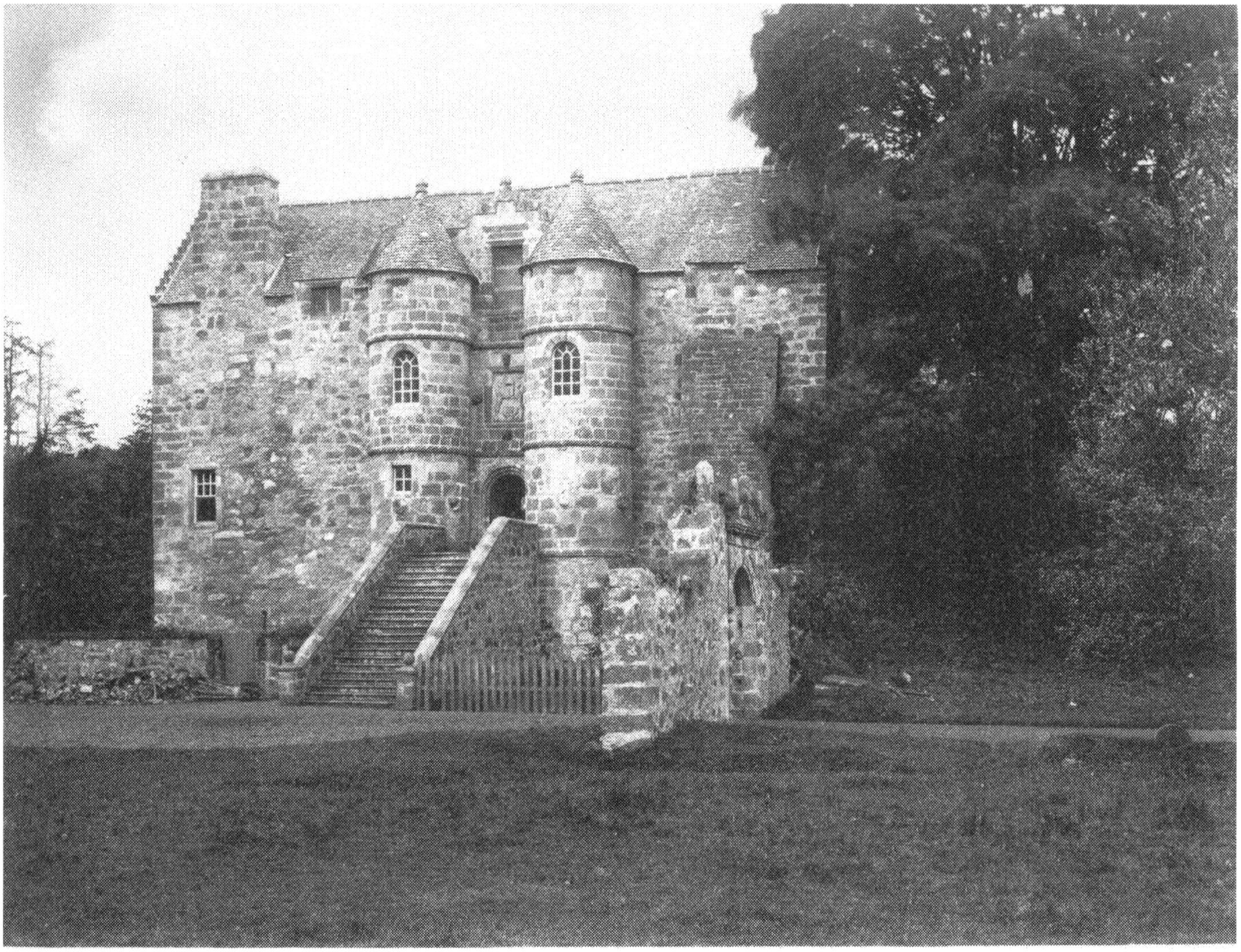

SEAFIELD.

SEAFIELD, near Ardrossan, is a modern building, in which the architectural peculiarities of the Scottish Baronial, Jacobean, and Italian styles are blended so as to make a very pleasing combination. When seen from the avenue by which it is approached, it presents the appearance of a French chateau. The sloping terrace upon which it is erected, and the staircase leading to it, seem to favour this illusion. The original mansion was built by Mrs Bartlemore, great-aunt of the present proprietor, in 1820, and consisted of a substantial, roomy house, with ornamental portico, in the prevailing style of that period. In 1858 it was acquired by W. G. Borron, Esq., of Glasgow, who made extensive additions to the old house, and erected the tower and turrets which form the most striking feature in the building. It was purchased by the present proprietor, A. D. Bryce-Douglas, Esq., in 1880, and he has also made considerable and judicious alterations and extensions of the structure.

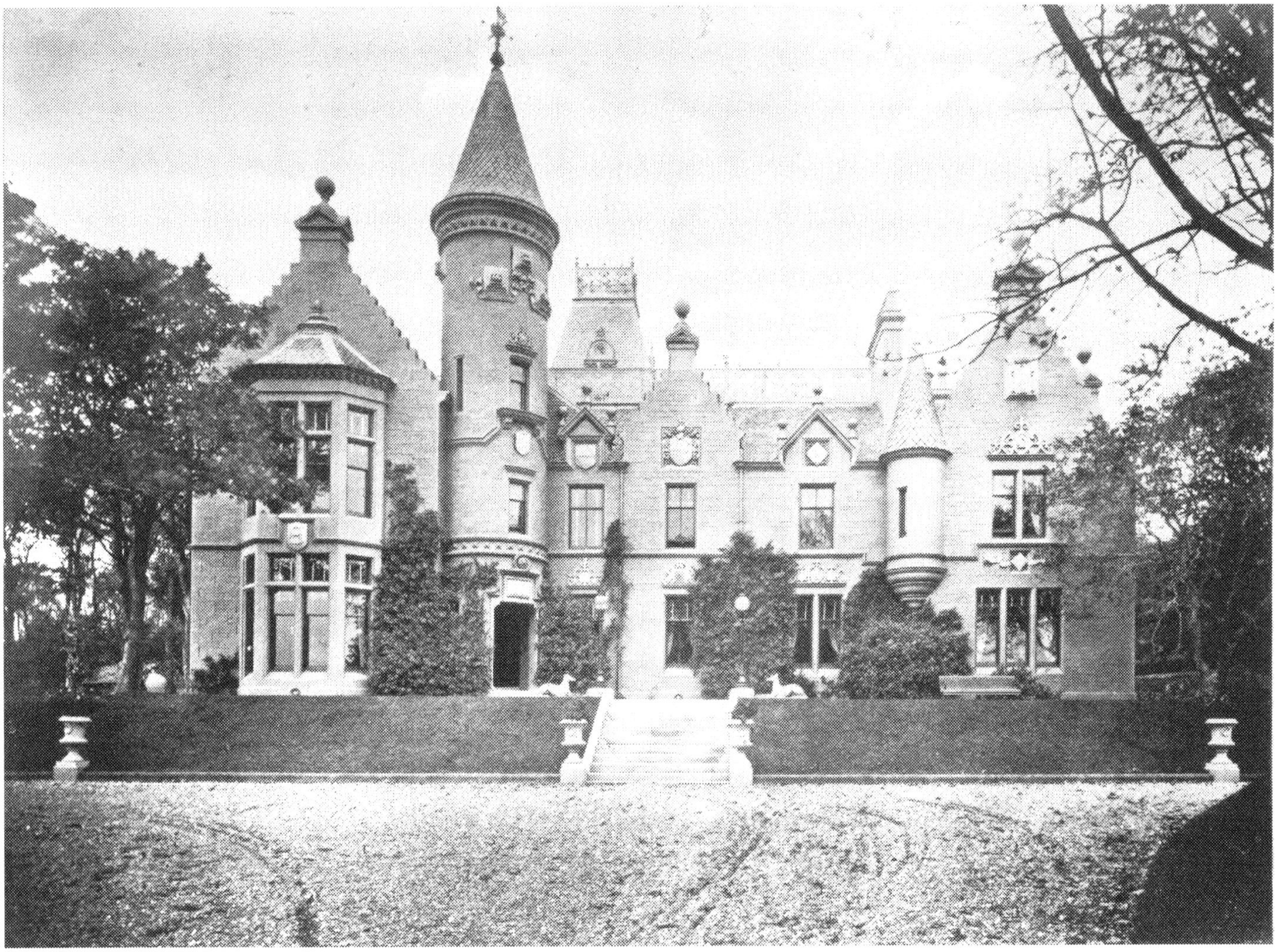

SHEWALTON HOUSE.

SHEWALTON HOUSE, the seat of Captain David Boyle, R.N., is in the parish of Dundonald, on the left bank of the river Irvine, and about two miles from Irvine town. The estate can be traced back till the fifteenth century; and the manor-place "was one of those square towers of former times, adapted more for security than convenience, which latterly became ruinous and uninhabitable." It stood until the present mansion was erected in the year 1806 by the Colonel Boyle of Shewalton mentioned below.

The first Laird of Shewalton that can be traced is Lambert Wallace, who held the lands under Fullartoun of that Ilk in 1473. Though the exact succession of this family cannot be made out, from stray notices we find that the Wallaces were in possession of the estate down till 1715. At that time the three estates of Shewalton, Waxford, and Maress were sold by Edward Wallace to William Boyle, Esq., brother of David, first Earl of Glasgow. Patrick Boyle, son of the latter was raised to the Bench in 1746 by the title of Lord Shewalton, and died in 1761. The Hon Patrick Boyle, second son of the second Earl of Glasgow, was Laird of Shewalton at his death in 1798. He was succeeded by his eldest son, John, who was Colonel of the Ayrshire Militia, and died unmarried in 1837. His only surviving brother, the Right Hon. David Boyle, Lord-Justice-General and President of the Court of Session (1772-1853) came into the estate, and adopted the designation of "Shewalton" instead of "Maress," which he had formerly held. His long and brilliant career is too well known to need recapitulation. He represented Ayrshire in Parliament from 1807, when he was Solicitor-General, until he was raised to the Bench in 1811. He was twice married, and left a numerous family. The eldest son, Patrick Boyle, M.A., Advocate, succeeded him at his death in 1853; and when the latter died in 1874, the present proprietor Captain David Boyle, R.N., his son, became Laird of Shewalton. He was appointed a Lieutenant of Ayrshire in 1871, and became Convener of the county in 1882.

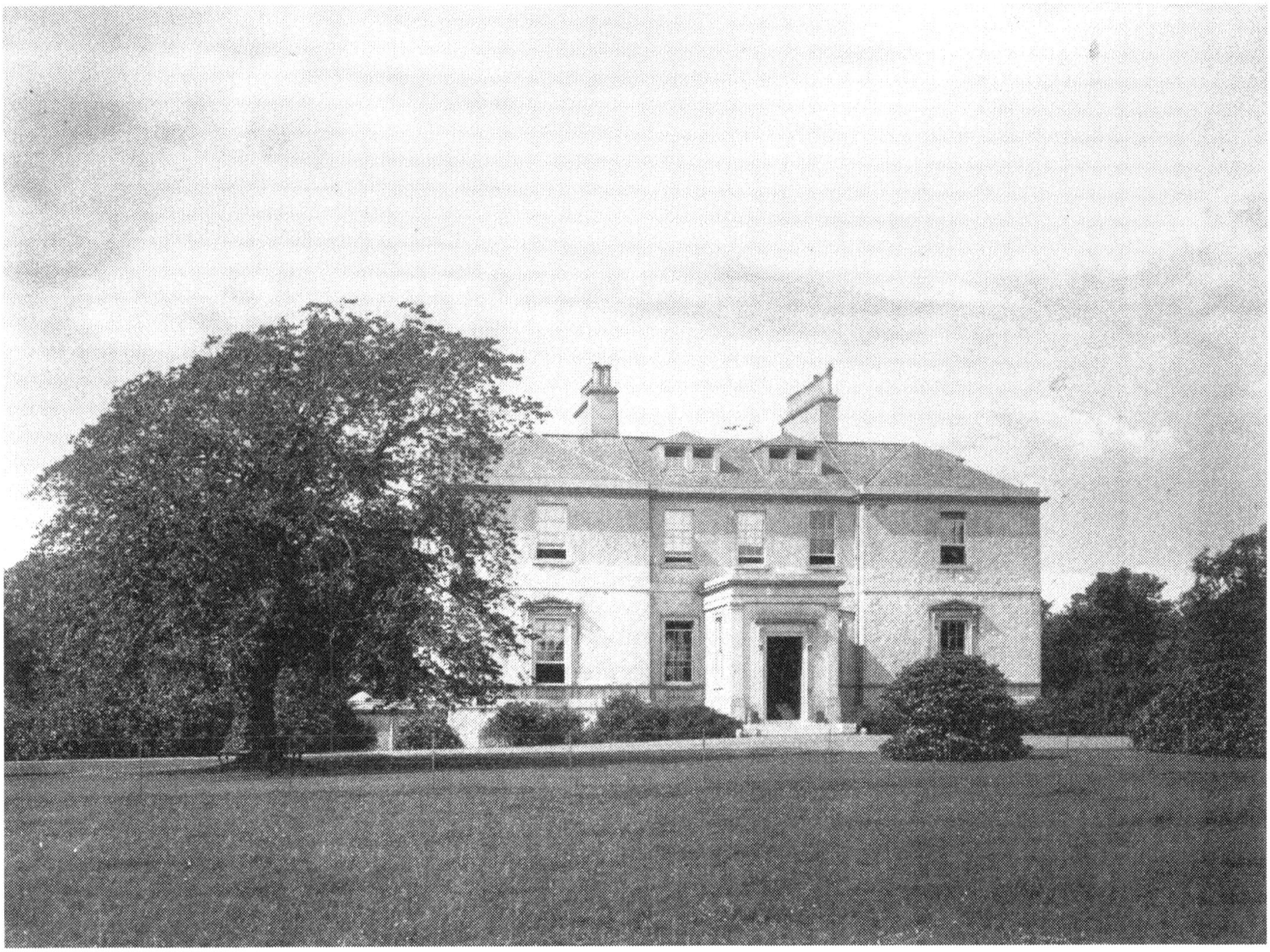

SKELMORLIE CASTLE.

THE old baronial Castle of Skelmorlie, near Largs, belongs to the present Earl of Eglintoun and Wintoun, and the earliest portion of it was erected by his ancestor, the second Montgomerie of Skelmorlie in 1502. Many additions have been made to it since that time, but its extension has been by means of accretion rather than renovation, and the appearance of the first castle may still be distinguished. It is one of the oldest inhabited houses in Ayrshire, and Pont's description of it in 1608, as "fair weill bult housse and plesantly seatted, decorred with orchards and voodes," is applicable to it in our own times. The castle has long been tenanted by James N. Graham, Esq., of Glasgow, who is well known as one of the most munificent patrons of art in the West of Scotland.

The estate of Skelmorlie belonged to the Cuninghames of Kilmaurs during the reign of Robert III (1390-1406); but about 1460 it was divided, the northern portion falling to the Montgomeries, and the southern part remaining with the Cuninghames, each division being distinguished by the addition of the name of its possessor - i.e., Skelmorlie-Montgomerie. and Skelmorlie-Cuninghame. It is usually asserted that in "1461 Sir Alexander de Montgomerie of Ardrossan, *first* Lord Montgomerie, granted a charter of the lands of Skelmorlie to his second son, George Montgomerie, who thus became the progenitor of the Montgomeries of Skelmorlie;" but this is manifestly wrong, as both the first lord and his son were dead before this time, Lord Alexander dying in 1451, and his son and namesake in the following year without having assumed the title (Burke's Peerage," *sub* Eglintoun). The Castle of Skelmorlie was probably built, therefore, by a brother of Hugh, first Earl of Eglintoun, whose father was Alexander, second Lord Montgomerie, and grandson of the first Lord.

A title was first brought into the Skelmorlie family by Robert Montgomerie, son of Robert Montgomerie of Skelmorlie and Dorothy, daughter of Lord Sempill, who was knighted by James VI., and created a Baronet by Charles I. on December 23, 1628. He was married to Margaret, daughter of Sir William Douglas of Drumlanrig, who died in 1624, and to whose memory he erected the eccentric structure known as the Skelmorlie Aisle in the old burying-ground of Largs. He was Member for Buteshite in the Convention of 1644, and died in November 1651, leaving the succession to his grandson and namesake. The latter died on 7th February 1684, and was followed by his son, Sir James, who represented Ayrshire in the Convention and Parliament of 1689, and was one of those deputed to administer the oath to King William and Queen Mary in that year. He adhered to the Jacobite faction, however, and was unseated in 1693, not having signed the Assurance. He was married to a daughter of the Earl of Annandale, and died in September 1694, being succeeded by his son, Sir Robert, fourth Baronet of Skelmorlie. As the latter had no male heirs, he sold the estate to his uncle, Hugh Montgomerie of Busbie, Lord Provost of Glasgow, to whom the title reverted, and who had sat as Member of Parliament for Glasgow from 1702 till 1708. Sir Hugh entered upon his acquisition in 1731, but he also died in 1735 without issue, and the baronetcy thus became extinct. The estate fell to Lilias, daughter of the fourth Baronet, who married her kinsman, Alexander Montgomerie of Coilsfield, and became progenitrix of the families of Eglintoun and Annick Lodge. Her son, Hugh, succeeded as twelfth Earl of Eglintoun in 1796 (see article *Coilsfield*), and his great-grandson, Archibald William Montgomerie, is the fourteenth and present Earl of Eglintoun and. Wintoun.

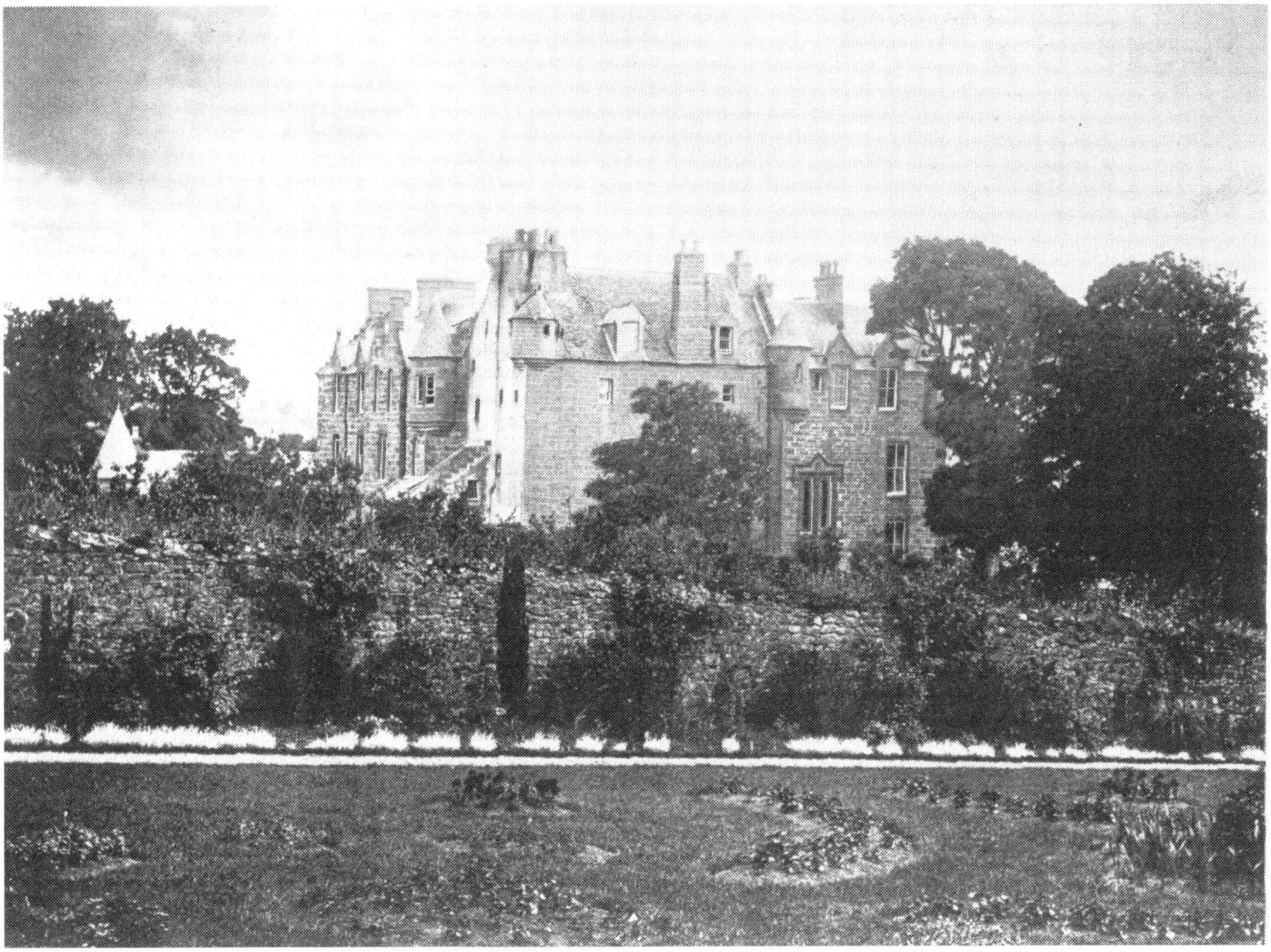

SORN CASTLE.

THE date of the erection of the first castle at Sorn cannot be determined, though authorities are agreed that such a stronghold did exist from very early times. The first family that we find associated with the territory is Keith of Galston, which was a branch from the Keiths, afterwards Earls Marischal. Jonetta Keith, heiress of Galston, was married to Sir David Hamilton, third Lord Cadzow (*ob.* 1392), the progenitor of the ducal house of Hamilton; and in 1406 she bestowed the estate of Sorn upon her fourth son, Andrew, who became ancestor of the Hamiltons of Udston and of Barncluith. In 1533 Sorn was acquired by a descendant of the second Lord Cadzow, *viz.*, Sir William Hamilton of the Cambuskeith Hamiltons, and afterwards Lord High Treasurer to James V. He is usually termed Sir William Hamilton of Sanquhar, having purchased that estate in 1539; and was Captain of Edinburgh Castle, and one of the Senators of the College of Justice. His daughter Isabel was married to George, fifth Lord Seton-the "truest friend " of Mary, Queen of Scots - and the wedding is said to have been the occasion of special rejoicings at Sorn Castle. There is a romancing story told by the Rev. George Gordon, the author of the article on "Sorn" in the old Statistical Account, and repeated by later writers, to the effect that "King James V honoured his Treasurer with a visit at Sorn Castle on occasion of the marriage of his daughter to Lord Seton. The King's visit at Sorn Castle took place in winter, and being heartily tired of his journey through so long a track of moor, moss, and miry clay, where there was neither road nor bridge, he is reported to have said, with that good-humoured pleasantry which was a characteristic of so many of his family, that 'were he to play the Deil a trick, he would send him from Glasgow to Sorn in the middle of winter.' However humorous the story may be, it is absolutely without foundation, since King James was dead years before the marriage took place; and it is expressly stated by Sir Richard Maitland, in his *Historie of the House of Seytoune*, that the union was devised to bring about an alliance betwixt the Setons and the Governor Arran, to whose house Sir William Hamilton belonged. Yet this marriage was considered to be of such political importance that a medal commemorating it was struck, bearing the initials of the bride and bridegroom: I. H.- G. S., and the motto *Ung Dieu, ung loy, ung foy, ung roy*. The children of this marriage all rose to distinction, and amongst the family were Robert Seton, first Earl of Wintoun; Sir John Seton of Barns; Alexander, first Earl of Dunfermline; and Margaret, mother of the first Earl of Abercorn. Lady Seton died in 1604, at the age of seventy-five.

Robert Seton, first Earl of Wintoun (*ob.* 1603), succeeded to the estate on the death of his father in 1585; and his second brother, the third Earl, sold both the lands and Castle of Sorn to the Loudoun family, with whom they remained for over a century and a half. They were purchased in 1782 by Mr William Tennent of Poole, and sold by him shortly afterwards to Mr Graham of Limekilns and Mr Stevenson of Dalgain. Mr Somervell of Hamilton Farm acquired the Castle and estate in 1795, and it came into the possession successively of his son and his two daughters. On the death of the youngest of this family, the estates fell to Mr Graham Russell, fifth son of the late Colonel James Russell of Woodside, Stirlingshire, who assumed the name of Somervell. He was married to his cousin, a daughter of the family of Stirling of Kippendavie, and was Deputy-Lieutenant and Convener of the county of Ayr from 1860 till his death. His son, James Somervell, Esq. of Sorn, Captain of Ayrshire Yeomanry, is the present possessor of the estate, and resides at the Castle.

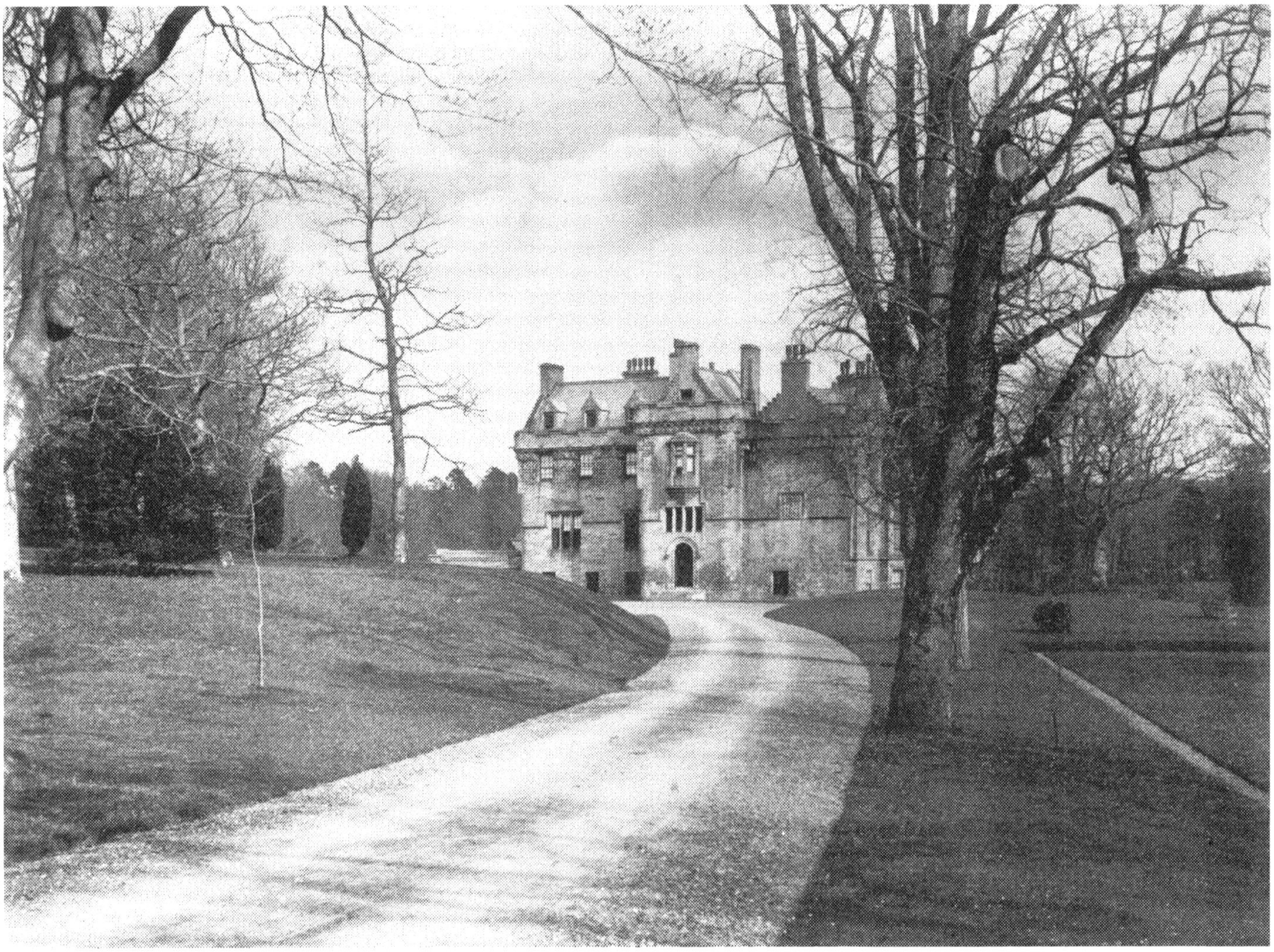

SUNDRUM.

THE mansion of Sundrum is situated on an eminence, around the base of which the Water of Coyle flows, and is one of the most ancient houses in the county. Though it has undergone frequent alteration, the earliest portion of the structure is still distinguishable. The style in which the old tower has been built shows that it was erected during a lawless period, and long before the time when the feudal fortalice had gone out of fashion. The greater portion of the existing mansion was constructed by the first Hamilton of Sundrum in 1792; and as the older parts are skilfully wrought into the newer building, there is an undeniable air of antiquity thus imparted to the whole. The walls of the old tower are ten feet in thickness, and this part was probably built' at a very early period. The arms of Alan, seventh Baron Cathcart, quartered with those of his wife, Elizabeth, daughter of the first Viscount Stair, were recently found by the present Laird carved on a stone in Sundrum, and were fixed by him in the wall of the old church of Coylton, near the family vault of the Cathcarts and Hamiltons of Sundrum.

The actual builder of this old tower cannot be accurately identified, though there can be no question as to the fact of its being an important baronial residence in the beginning of the fourteenth century. Tradition asserts that the tower was of Pictish origin, but this legend rests upon no reasonable foundation. The first historical name associated with it is that of Sir Duncan Wallace, who had a charter of the baronies of "Sondrom and Dalmelyntoun" in 1373. At his death Sundrum and Auchencruive became the property of his nephew, Alan de Cathkert, the son of Sir Duncan's sister, arid the great-grandfather of the first Baron Cathcart (*ob.* 1499); and these two estates were united into the barony of Cathcart in 1713 by Alan, seventh Baron Cathcart (1647-1732). Sundrum came into the possession of the Hamilton family in 1750, and still remains with a member of that race.

John Hamilton, second son of Hugh Hamilton of Clongall, served in the Royal Navy, and afterwards settled in Jamaica. He was drowned when returning from the West Indies, and left an only son, John, then an infant, under the charge of trustees. The estate of Sundrum was purchased for this son by his guardians in 1750, when he was eleven years old, and he remained Laird of Sundrum until 1821. He was married to his cousin, a sister of Hugh, twelfth Earl of Eglintoun, and became progenitor of the Hamiltons of Pinmore and of Rozelle. For a long period he was a Vice-Lieutenant of Ayrshire, and was Convener of the county for thirty-six years. He was succeeded by his eldest son, John (1764-1837), who was a Commander in the naval service of the East India Company; was married in 1804 to Christian, eldest daughter of George Dundas of Dundas; and left six sons and eight daughters. His eldest son, John, who is now proprietor of Sundrum, has been a Deputy-Lieutenant for Ayrshire since 1838.

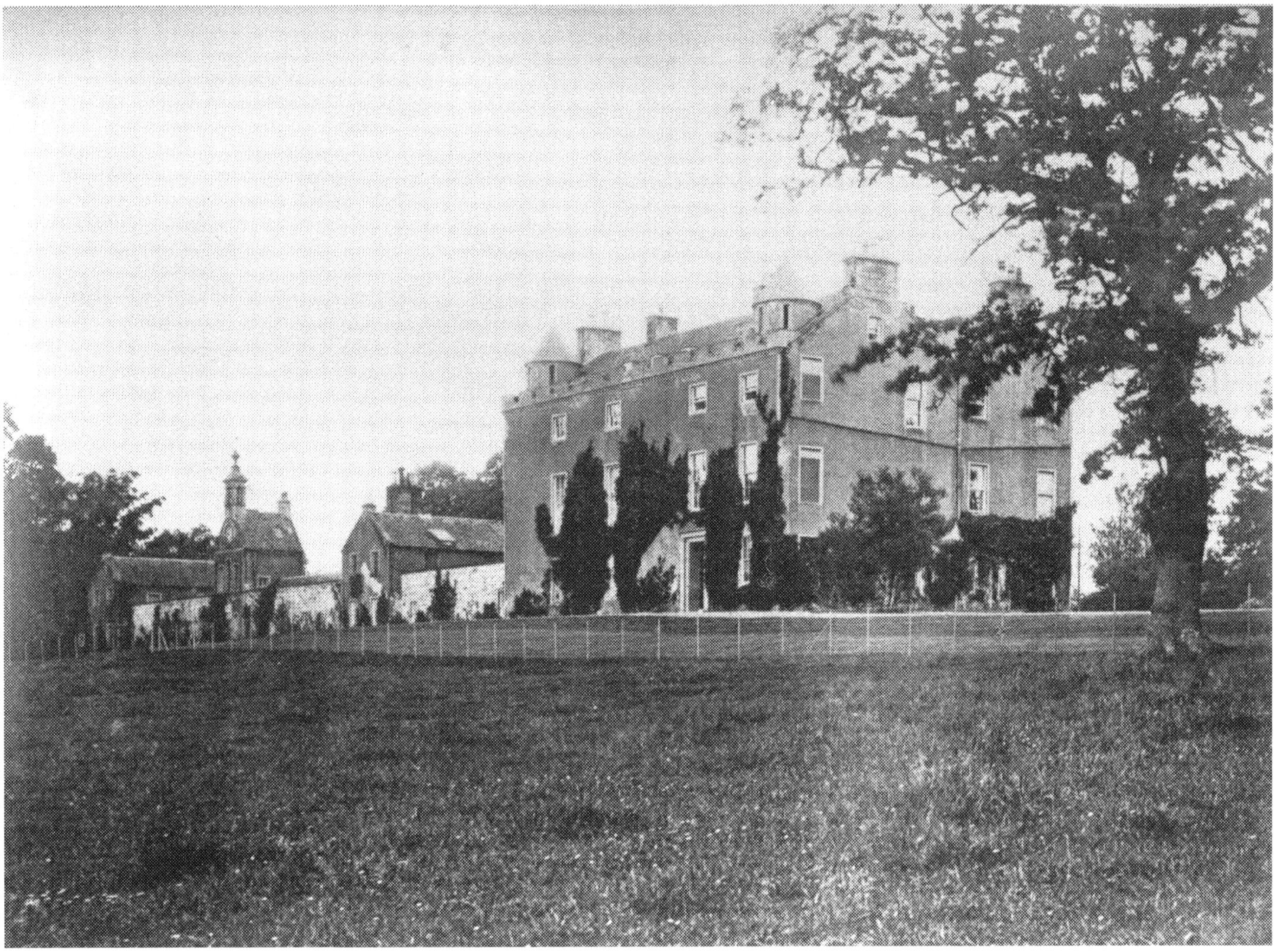

SWINDRIDGEMUIR.

THE present mansion-house of Swindridgemuir, near Dalry, was erected by the then proprietor, John Smith, about 1830. The estate formed a portion of the old Barony of Kersland, but had been acquired absolutely by Andrew Smith, great-grandfather of John, about 1700, and descended to the latter without interruption. The builder of Swindridgemuir was born in 1754, and passed his early years in the army, but retired after the conclusion of the American War, and turned his attention to agriculture. He increased the estate considerably by purchasing various properties in the neighbourhood; and at his death, without issue, in 1838, it fell into the possession of his nephew, William Neill of Barnweill, in the parish of Craigie. The latter was descended from a branch of the MacNeills of Barra, which had settled in Ayrshire about 1550. His grandfather was a successful merchant in Ayr, and purchased the lands of Schaw in Ochiltree parish in 1738. The father of William Neill was a solicitor in Ayr, and acquired the estate of Barnweill in 1784, having married Margaret, sister of John Smith of Swindridgemuir, in 1799. William Neill, who was born in 1784, assumed the additional name of Smith on succeeding to his uncle's estate. He was a Captain in the Army, Lieutenant-Colonel of the Ayrshire Militia, and a Deputy-Lieutenant for the county for over thirty years. He died in 1850, leaving three sons and three daughters; all of the former having won distinction in the army. The second son, John Martin Bladen Smith-Neill, was Colonel of the 40th Regiment, and served through the second Afghan Campaign under General Nott in 1842, and was appointed Deputy-Adjutant-General of Victoria. He was killed at Melbourne by a fall from his horse in 1859. The eldest son rose to even higher honours, and will ever be remembered as one of the heroes and victims of the Indian Mutiny of 1857. James George Smith-Neill was born in 1810, and entered the East India Company's service whilst a mere youth, spending his early years in India. He led the Turkish Contingent through the Crimean War; and on the outbreak of the Sepoy Rebellion he was placed in the very midst of the disaffected troops at Cawnpore, Benares, and Allahabad. A brigade under his command was led from Cawnpore to the relief of Lucknow, and while carrying the batteries at the point of the bayonet, he fell at the head of his victorious column. The brilliant exploits which he had performed and the military renown he had achieved were fittingly acknowledged; and his widow was raised to the rank which she would have held had her husband survived to receive the Knight-Commandership of the Bath, which would have been his reward. A full-length colossal statue in bronze, mounted upon a granite pedestal, has been raised to his memory in Wellington Square, Ayr, and bears this inscription: "James George Smith-Neill, C.B., Aide-de-Camp to the Queen, Lieutenant-Colonel of the Madras Army, Brigadier-General in India, a brave, resolute, and self-reliant soldier, universally acknowledged as the first who stemmed the torrent of rebellion in Bengal. He fell gloriously at the Relief of Lucknow, 25th September 1857, aged 47." There is also a memorial-bust of this valiant soldier erected in the vestibule of the parish church of Dalry. General Neill was succeeded by his eldest son, William James Smith-Neill, Esq. of Barnweill and Swindridgemuir, who was formerly a Captain in the Royal Artillery, and is the present possessor of the conjoined estates.

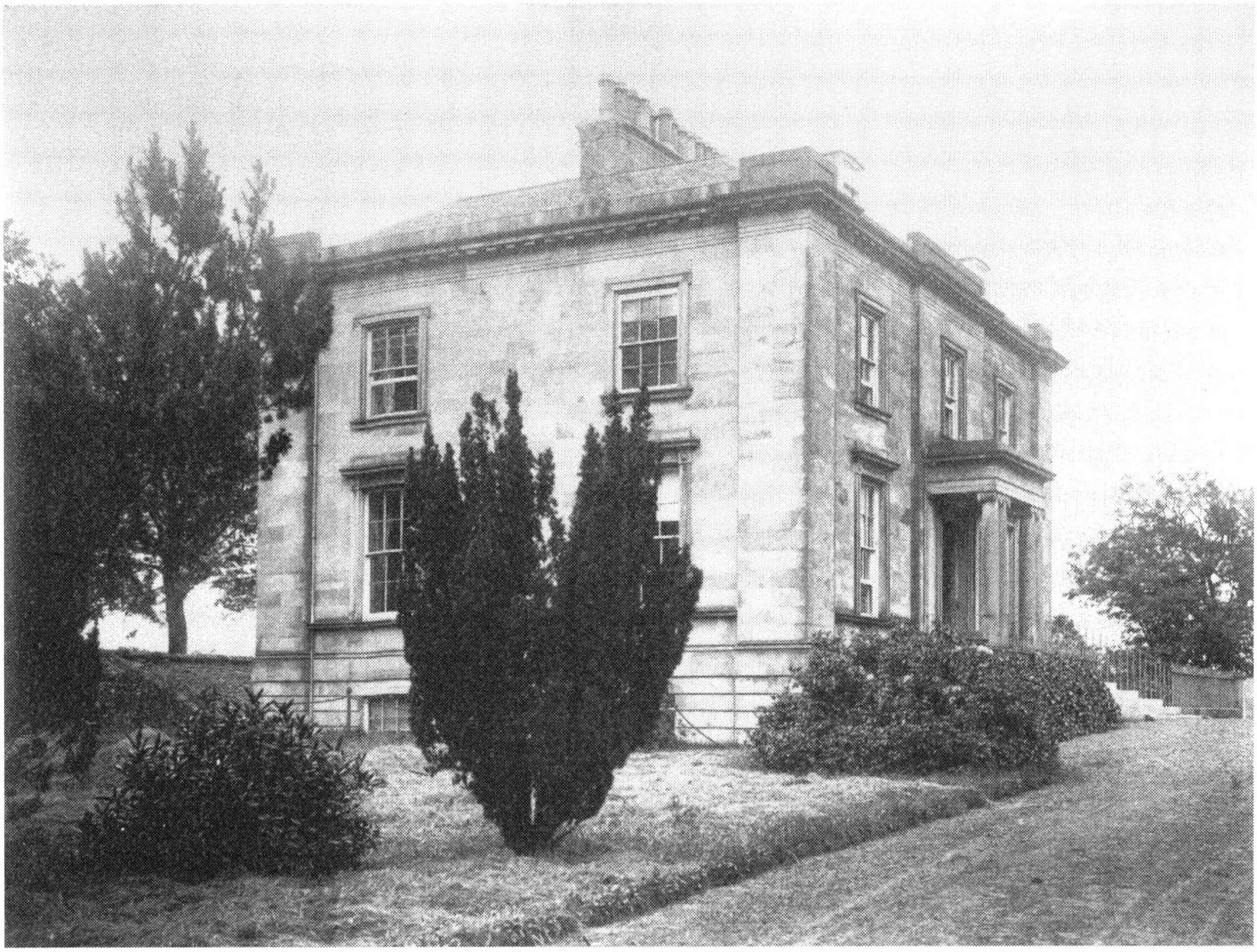

TREESBANK HOUSE.

THE mansion of Treesbank is in the parish of Riccarton, at a short distance from Kilmarnock, and about a mile from Caprington Castle. The building, which was merely a plain manor-house before 1838, was considerably enlarged at that time; and it now forms one of the most attractive mansions in the district. The original structure was erected about 1672 by the first of the Campbells of Treesbank, part of an old tower then standing having been incorporated in the building; and the property has descended from father to son, without intermission, till this date.

James Campbell of Treesbank (circa 1650-1740), second son of Sir Hugh Campbell of Cessnock, obtained the lands from his father probably at the time of his marriage with Jean, daughter of Sir William Mure of Rowallan, in 1672, and became male representative of the House of Cessnock on the death of his brother, Sir George, without male issue. He was succeeded by his eldest son, George, about 1742, who was married to a daughter of David Boswell of Auchinleck, and whose eldest son, James, became third Laird of Treesbank. The latter died in 1776, and his son by a second marriage - then in infancy - succeeded to the estate. George James Campbell of Treesbank died in 1815, and his eldest son and namesake succeeded him. The second George James Campbell of Treesbank was born in 1800, and was Lieutenant-Colonel, Ayrshire Yeomanry, and Deputy-Lieutenant of Ayrshire from 1828 till his death in 1880. He was twice married - first, to Elizabeth McKerrel Reid, daughter of Colonel John Reid, by whom (who died in 1826) he had a son, George James, died 1829, and two daughters - Elizabeth, married Count Einsiedel -Wolkenbourg (Saxony), and succeeded her grand-uncle in the estate of Adamton, Ayrshire; and Mary, married to James Campbell, Esq. of Jura. Mr Campbell married, secondly, Catharine Indiana, daughter of the late Major Jones, 25th Light Dragoons, and by her (who died 1879) he left surviving issue two sons - George James, his successor, and William Hugh, Captain 4th Regiment Scots Fusiliers; and a daughter, Jemima, married to Baron de Schaeffer, Colonel of Dragoons in the service of Prussia.

The present Laird, George James Campbell, served in the 4th Light Dragoons and in the army of Wurtemberg, when he attained the rank of Captain, and married, 1870, Pauline, daughter of Baron Nesselrode-Hugenpoeth, and has issue a son, George James. Mr Campbell is Chief of the House of Cessnock, and as such claims to be male representative of the Campbells of Loudoun.

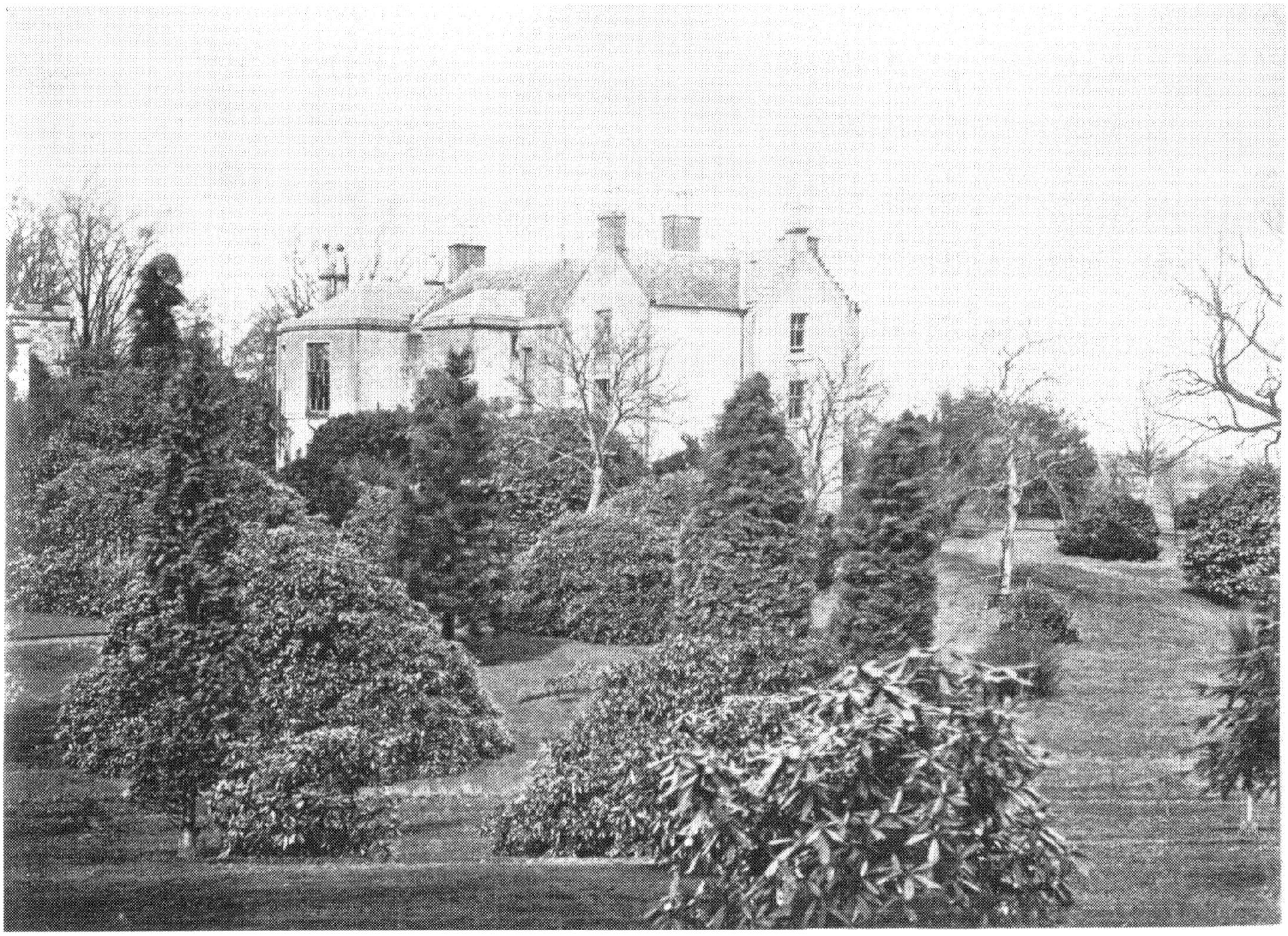

WELLWOOD.

THE estate now known as Muirkirk, in the parish of that name, is composed of several smaller properties, which have been gradually amalgamated. The lands of Under, Middle, and Over Wellwood, which were long in the possession of a branch of the Campbells of Glaisnock, are all included in the estate of Muirkirk; and the modern mansion of Wellwood is the residence of John G. A. Baird, Esq., the present proprietor of Muirkirk. The Campbells held the three Wellwoods continuously for over two hundred years, but the property was sold after the death of the last Campbell of Wellwood in 1787. The Duke of Portland purchased these lands and formed them into the estate of Muirkirk, reserving the place for the younger children of his family. Lord George Cavendish-Bentinck and his brother, Lord Henry, were successively proprietors, but in 1863 it was acquired by the late James Baird, Esq. of Knoydart and Cambusdoon, at the price of £135,000. The estate contains 17,566 acres. The present proprietor succeeded his uncle in 1876, and erected the mansion-house shortly afterwards. He has also made various improvements on the farm-steadings, and has planted extensively. Mr Baird is the third son of the late William Baird, Esq. of Elie, and was married in 1881 to Susan Georgina, daughter of Sir James Fergusson of Kilkerran. All the locality near Wellwood is rich in historical associations connected with the Covenanters. Airsmoss, the scene of Richard Cameron's final struggle, is in the vicinity; and there are many memories still preserved of the troubled period

*"When in Wellwood's dark valley the standard of Zion
All bloody and torn 'mong the heather was lying."*

Priesthill, the place of John Brown's martyrdom, is also near Muirkirk, and monuments have been erected to mark these interesting spots.

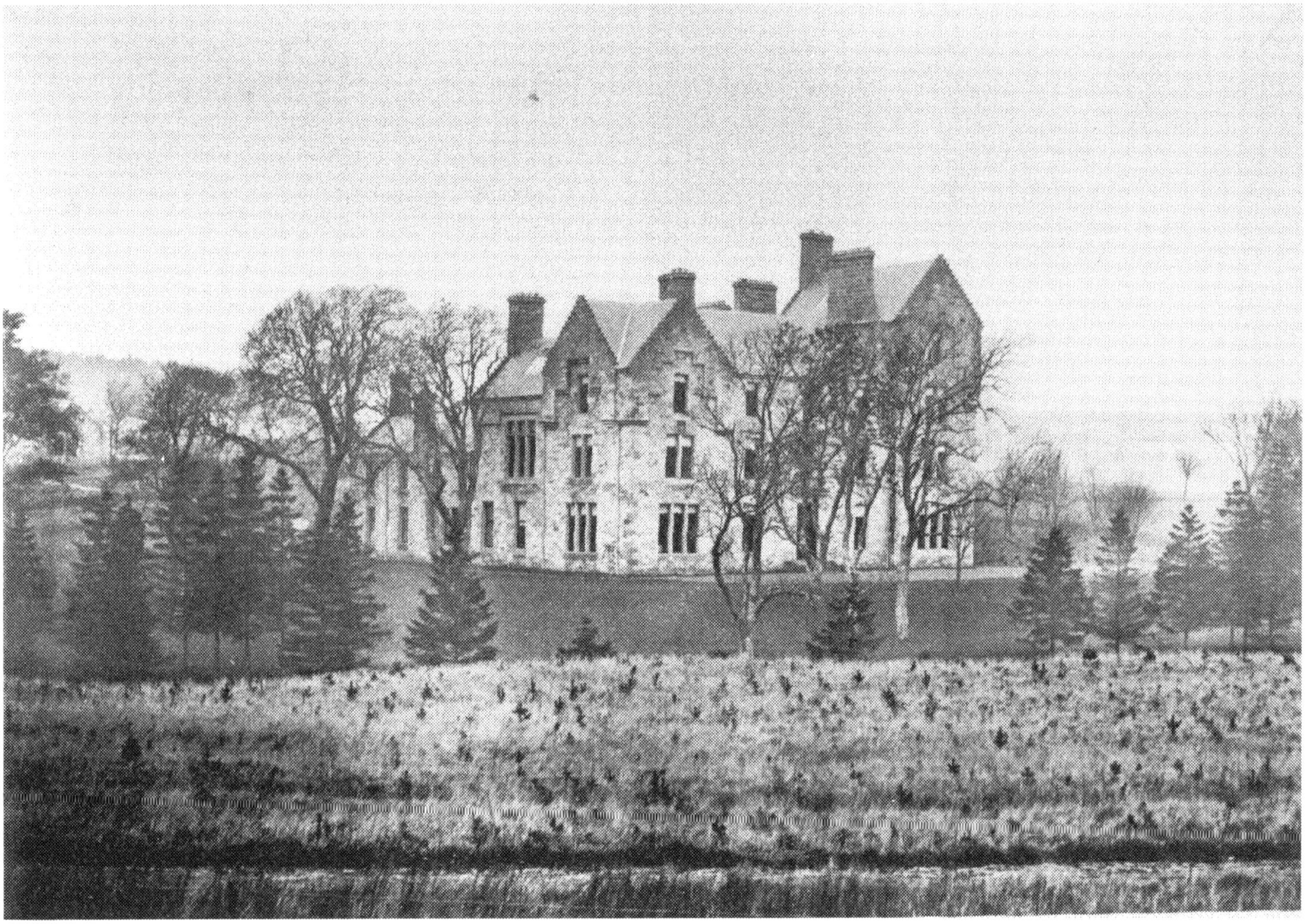

WOODSIDE.

WOODSIDE, near the town of Beith, is the seat of Robert William Cochran-Patrick, Esq. of Ladyland and Woodside; who has been Member of Parliament for North Ayrshlre since 1880. For a long period it was the residence of the Ralstouns of that Ilk, an ancient family which was settled in Renfrewshire early in the thirteenth century. Several of the members of this family rose to eminence in the political and military service of their country; and they were related by marriage to some of the most prominent families in Scotland. Hew Ralstoun of that Ilk, whose father was slain at the' battle of Pinkie (1547), acquired the estate of Woodside and Turnerland, in 1551, from Gavin Hamilton, Commendator of Kilwinning, and built the square tower which still forms a portion of the present mansion, intending to make it the chief seat of his family. When Timothy Pont visited the place in 1608 the original builder was alive, and the topographer's description of it is in these words: "Wood-syde is a proper duelling, and belonges to ye Laird of Raalstoune." Hew Ralstoun died at Woodside in 1613, and was succeeded by his grandson. William Ralstoun, only son of the latter, came into the estate in 1625, and increased it by the purchase of several adjoining properties. During the unsettled times of Charles I and the Commonwealth he took an active part with the Royalists, and held a commission from the King as Lieutenant-Colonel. Latterly he joined himself to the Covenanting party, but only to share in their misfortunes; and he was finally compelled to flee for safety to Argyllshire, where he died at an advanced age in 1691. He probably made several alterations upon the mansion of Woodside- Ralstoun, as a carved stone still exists bearing the arms and initials of himself and his first wife, Ursula Mure of Glanderstoun, who died some time before 1674. Gavin Ralstoun succeeded his grandfather in 1691, and severed the connection of the family with Renfrewshire by the sale of the ancient estate of Ralstoun to the Earl of Dundonald in 1704. His grandson and namesake (born 1735, died 1819) was the last of this ancient family. He spent his early years in Virginia, and on his return in 1758 he married Annabella, daughter of James Pollok of Arthurlee, and settled at Woodside. He made extensive additions to the mansion-house, removing the old turrets, erecting a new roof, and transforming it into a modern dwelling. Two stones are inserted in the corners of the gables, near the eaves, which bear his initials and those of his wife, with the date 1759. Having been overtaken by misfortune and involved in pecuniary difficulties, principally, it is said, through cautionary obligations, Gavin Ralstoun was compelled to part with the estate of Woodside in 1771; and it was then purchased by Dame Jean Stirling of Auchyle, wife of James Erskine of Alva, Lord Barjarg of Session, and afterwards Lord Alva. When Lady Alva died the estate fell to her heir, Alexander Graham-Stirling of Duchree - gazetted General in 1837 - who disposed of it in 1833 to William Patrick of Roughwood, W.S., a descendant of the Ralstouns by the female side. The latter proprietor made still further additions to the mansion in 1848, leaving it nearly in the condition, structurally, in which it is now. The house became the residence of his nephew, William Charles Richard Cochran-Patrick, and his wife, Agnes Cochran, heiress of Ladyland; and their son, Robert William Cochran-Patrick, M.P., succeeded to the estate on the death of his grand-uncle, William Patrick, in 1861.

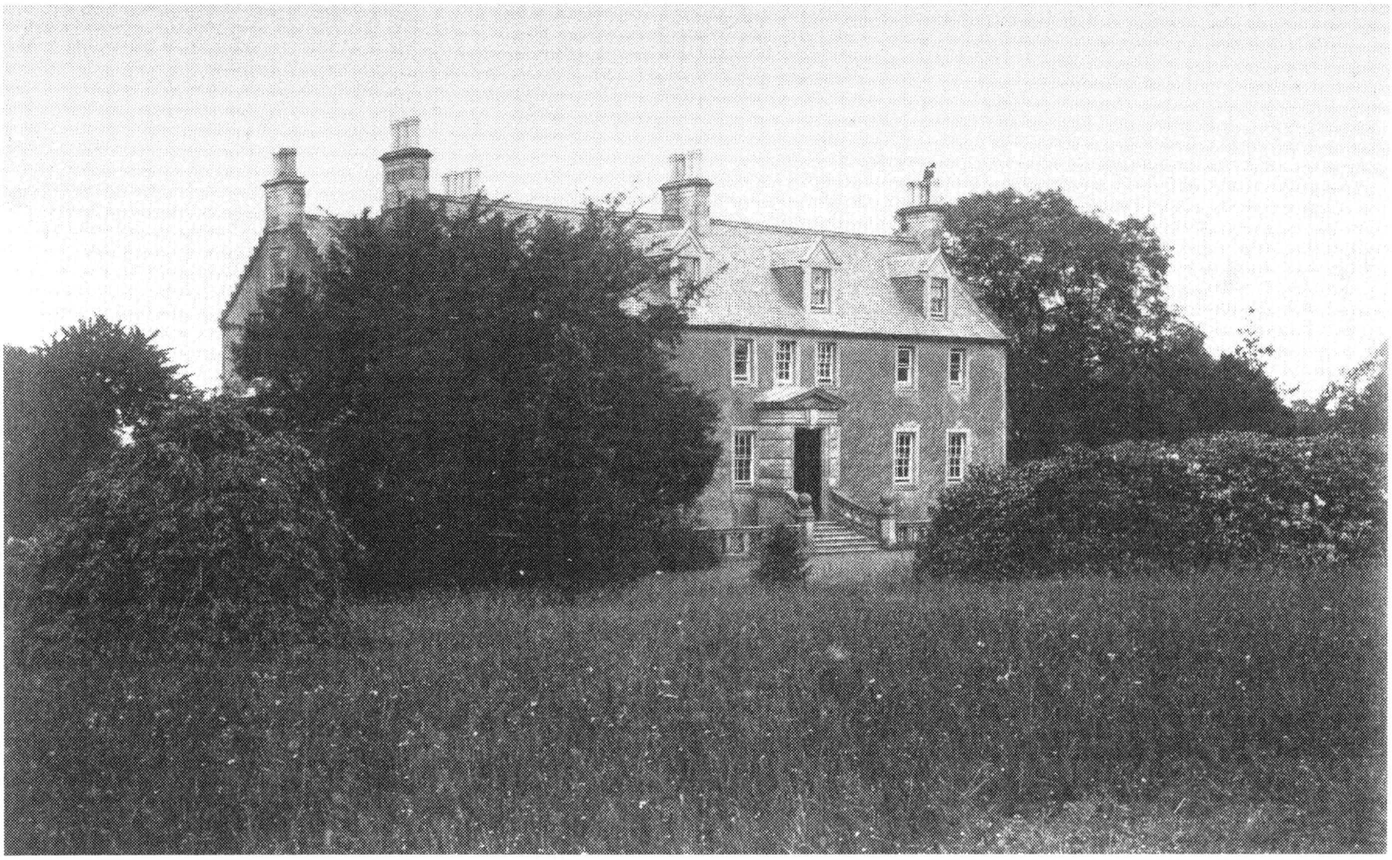

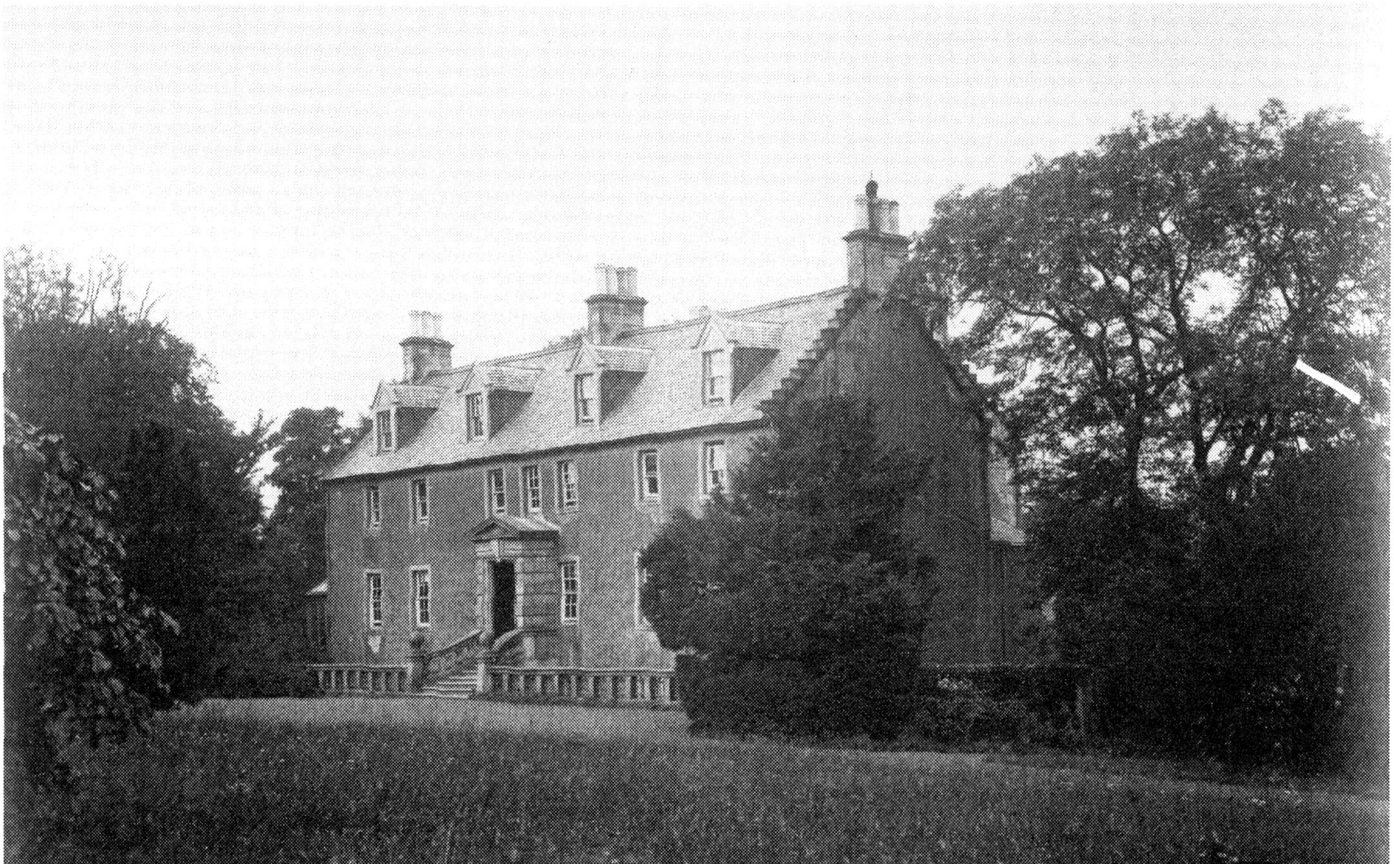

Milton Keynes UK
Ingram Content Group UK Ltd.
UKHW052201141223
434416UK00004B/111